chocolate AMERICAN STYLE

chocolate AMERICAN STYLE

LORA BRODY

Photographs by Webb Chappell

Clarkson Potter/Publishers
New York

Also by Lora Brody

Growing Up on the Chocolate Diet
Indulgences
Cooking with Memories
The Kitchen Survival Guide
The Entertaining Survival Guide
Chocolate (Williams Sonoma Kitchen Library)
Fruit Desserts (Williams Sonoma Kitchen Library)
Stews (Williams Sonoma Kitchen Library)
Bread Machine Baking Perfect Every Time
Desserts from Your Bread Machine Perfect Every Time
Pizza, Focaccia, Flat, and Filled Breads from Your Bread Machine—
    Perfect Every Time
Stuff It! (with Max Brody)
Plugged In
Basic Baking
The Cape Cod Table
Slow Cooker Cooking

Copyright © 2004 by Lora Brody
Photographs copyright © 2004 by Webb Chappell

Published by Clarkson Potter/Publishers, New York, New York.
Member of the Crown Publishing Group, a division of
Random House, Inc.
www.crownpublishing.com

CLARKSON N. POTTER is a trademark and POTTER and colophon are registered trademarks of Random House, Inc.

Printed in China

Design by Caitlin Daniels Israel

Library of Congress Cataloging-in-Publication Data
Brody, Lora, 1945–
        Chocolate American style / Lora Brody.
1. Cookery (Chocolate)   2. Cookery, American.   3. Desserts.   I. Title.
        TX767.C5.B755   2004
641.6'374—dc21   2003008925

ISBN 1-4000-4597-5

10   9   8   7   6   5   4   3   2   1

First Edition

For Carrie Arnold, who blessed our lives and made this world a better place.

Acknowledgments

Grateful thanks to all the people who made this book such a joy to write. When it came to researching, testing, and fine-tuning recipes, Emmy Clausing and Susan Schwartz were my dream team. Their generosity, creativity, good humor, and unending willingness to "try it one more time" gave this book its soul. I gave Emmy note-filled, chocolate-smeared scraps of paper and she turned them into coherent, cohesive recipes. Susan, who never seems to sleep, would answer my desperate e-mails 24/7. Yes, she could figure out how to make that frosting less runny; yes, she could increase the serving size of those brownies; yes, she could help with food styling for the photographs. And yes, she could do this while teaching cooking classes and being a full-time mom to four children under the age of eleven.

I am indebted to the supremely talented writer–editor Arthur Boehm for many things: for his support, guidance, and enthusiasm for this project and his invaluable help with the proposal, for his friendship, and for his conviction that this book belonged at Clarkson Potter.

Chocolate is among the most difficult foods to photograph, but Webb Chappell was more than up to the challenge. Working with chef–food stylist Stan

Frankenthaler, who made everything look just as scrumptious on film as it did in real life, Webb did a masterful job of capturing the essence of each dish he photographed.

Thanks as always to my friend and chocolate diva P. J. Hamel, who took time from writing her own baking book to offer help at every stage of this project. I am grateful for the support of the King Arthur Flour Company, as well as Chris Tracy and Calphalon Cookware. Both Lesley Abrams-Schwartz and Jennie Pakradooni were terrific recipe testers.

The following people generously allowed me to use one of their recipes: Bill and Cheryl Jamison, Adrienne Schwartz, Bruce Weinstein, and Diane Phillips. Alan Starr at Boston Showcase Company lent perfect props for the photo shoot.

I have spent many happy hours eating chocolate with my agent, Susan Ginsburg. Her friendship, expertise, and ability to (oh-so-gently but firmly) make me see the light are priceless gifts. Every author should be so lucky.

Heaven is a place where a cookbook author has an editor like Pam Krauss. Her wisdom, patience, unbridled enthusiasm, and years of experience make her truly wonderful at her job. That she's a great cook who loves chocolate makes her a perfect friend.

The fact that this beautiful book looks good enough to eat is a result of the talents and efforts of two very special people. My undying gratitude goes to Caitlin Daniels Israel, who designed it, and to Marysarah Quinn, creative director, who knew just how to put it together.

Contents

Introduction

Somewhere right this very minute in Chicago, El Paso, Cleveland, or Miami there's a mom wiping a chocolate ice cream mustache from her son's upper lip. In Madison or Mattawan a grandmother is sliding a tray of chocolate chip cookies into the oven in expectation of young visitors; Girls Scouts in Little Rock and Albuquerque sit around a campfire, roasting marshmallows to make s'mores; and a commuter on the IRT is nibbling a brownie behind the business section of the *New York Times.* In Indianapolis or Bar Harbor or Portland, Oregon, someone is writing HAPPY BIRTHDAY or CONGRATULATIONS! or I LOVE YOU on top of a triple-decker chocolate cake, and in a candy store in Boston a young man is thoughtfully choosing a selection of chocolate truffles for his wife. Americans love chocolate, and we love it in a very special way.

While the rest of the world has a subdued fondness for the Food of the Gods, politely nibbling a diminutive cookie or petit four, we want our cookies giant-size and packed with chocolate chips, and make that a hearty slice of chocolate cake crowned with a generous amount of fudge frosting. America's appetite for chocolate is celebrated with the same enthusiasm we lavish on professional sports, going for the gusto with every bite. Chances are you wouldn't see a bumper sticker that reads HONK IF YOU LOVE CHOCOLATE on the rue de Rivoli.

What exactly is chocolate American style? It's a Best Birthday Cake, a Tunnel of Fudge Cake, and a towering chocolate-dipped Dairy Queen ice cream cone. It's velvety smooth, Rockefeller-rich hot-fudge sauce melting a scoop of Chocolate Malt Ice Cream or a thick wedge of Black Bottom Pie. It's breakfasts of chocolate-glazed pancakes and chocolate-dipped doughnuts. It's the sort of desserts we grew up on, the ones that elicit comments like "Lemme at it" instead of "It's much too pretty to cut."

America's take on food, and specifically on chocolate, is refreshingly different from that of the rest of the world. When it comes to cooking and eating, we possess a sense of limitless possibility energized by fearless creativity. This, combined with our business acumen and sense of humor, has shaped a unique relationship with chocolate. Constantly reinventing ourselves, we boldly weave what we learn from the world's greatest cooks with our own dining experiences to produce singular expressions of our chocolate love. What other country has given the world not only fudge, but chocolate body paint, truffles the size of cannonballs, and the opportunity to have your face (or any other part of you) reproduced in chocolate?

This book represents what I consider to be the best of the best American chocolate recipes. Most are "down-home" and others are a little showier, but the thing that unites them is that the star of the show is chocolate—long may we rave.

My team and I had a huge amount of fun working on this book, creating and testing recipes and of course eating our fill. We hope that you will have just as much fun when you get out the chocolate and start cooking.

1. A Primer for the Home Cook

Weighing and Measuring

Know Your Ingredients

Equipment

Other Helpful Information

I understand and can absolutely relate to the fact that you want to jump right in and start cooking so you can get down to the more important business of eating. However, just to make sure we're both cooking from the same recipe (as it were), I offer the following information, which will, I hope, prevent you from e-mailing me with an angry or frustrated message that begins, "Hey, your recipe didn't work."

Editors tend to groan when they see the length of my recipes, but the more you know about what I did to get the results I got, the better the chances that you'll be smiling and saying nice things about me when you serve up your handiwork instead of scraping the burned bottoms off of chocolate chip cookies and wishing that you'd never picked up this book. As always, my goal is that each of my readers, no matter how much or how little kitchen expertise he or she has, be able to make any dish in the book by following clear directions. Obviously, your level of experience and the complexity of the recipe will affect the length of time a given recipe requires. My wish is that you end up with a dessert that tastes as wonderful as it looks, fulfills your desire for a serious chocolate hit, and delivers exactly what the headnote promises.

What follows is an overview of ingredients, techniques, and equipment that I use in my kitchen and that I used in formulating the recipes in this book. I have tried to avoid esoteric ingredients and hard-to-find equipment. In the few instances where I have called for something I thought might be hard to find in a local supermarket or cookware shop, I've included a source. You'll also find a Sources list on page 271. If you have any questions or need help with a recipe, I'm just an e-mail away at blanche007@aol.com. I'm always delighted to hear about your successes, and I'm available to help with recipes that didn't turn out the way you thought they should.

weighing and measuring

Chances are that if five people were handed a sack of flour and a one-cup measure and asked to measure one cup of flour, each cup would contain a different weight. Measuring dry ingredients using measuring cups is an inexact way to cook and impacts the finished product. Weighing dry ingredients, on the other hand, is extremely accurate. A digital kitchen scale is an affordable and essential cooking tool. If you get into the habit of weighing dry ingredients rather than using a measuring cup, you will have more consistent success in baking. Knowing that there are those who resist weighing, I've given volume and weight measurements for all dry ingredients in these recipes. If you do use measuring cups for dry ingredients, it's important to know that I use the scoop and level method for things like flour and cocoa powder. This means I get five ounces per cup of flour.

All the recipes in this book, unless otherwise indicated, were tested with extra-large eggs. Several recipes call for uncooked eggs. To avoid salmonella it is essential to use eggs from a reputable source, making sure the shells are clean and intact. Infants and elderly people should avoid eating raw eggs altogether.

Use a glass (Pyrex, for example) spouted measure for liquids, and standardized measuring spoons for small amounts of both liquid and dry ingredients.

Butter amounts are expressed in both volume and weight.

Bulk chocolate amounts are expressed in weight only; chocolate chip amounts are expressed in both volume and weight.

know your ingredients

CHOCOLATE

The recipes in this book were tested with a variety of very high quality American-made chocolate. We used Peters, Merckens, Ghirardelli, and Scharffen Berger (bars, nibs, and cocoa powder), both Hershey's and Nestlé chocolate chips and cocoa powder, and Ghirardelli ground chocolate. We also used Tropical Source organic chocolate. You can tell a lot about the quality of a chocolate from its ingredient label. It should indicate that the chocolate is made from cocoa or chocolate solids, cocoa butter, and vanilla (or vanillin, a synthetic product). It should contain at least 60 percent cocoa solids (for bittersweet, semisweet, or sweet chocolates), and should not contain any substitute fats such as coconut or palm kernel oils. I tell the students in my classes that there is no miracle that takes place in a 350-degree oven that turns a dessert made with inferior ingredients into something you want to eat. If the chocolate tastes good enough to eat on its own, then chances are excellent that you will be delighted with the way it makes the recipe taste.

Unsweetened baking chocolate (also called chocolate liquor) is made of roasted, ground cocoa nibs, which are the insides of the cocoa beans. This product yields the biggest chocolate impact in cooking. A product made by Nestlé called Choco Bake is pre-melted, unsweetened baking chocolate mixed with hydrogenated vegetable fats (along with a bunch of other stuff not found in nature), which keep the mixture in liquid form. I find it delivers the biggest chocolate impact of all. It's an acceptable substitute for unsweetened baking chocolate, if you don't mind the rather long list of chemical-sounding ingredients.

The next step up from unsweetened baking chocolate is a big one. *Dark chocolates*—bittersweet, semisweet, and sweet—contain more cocoa butter (the fat in chocolate) than unsweetened chocolate, along with a modest amount of sugar. These chocolates undergo a process called "conching," in which the ground chocolate mixture, combined with sugar and vanilla (or vanillin), is moved through a series of rollers that refine and smooth the particles. The amount of time given to conching generally determines the ultimate smoothness of the finished chocolate. Some manufacturers use lecithin, which makes chocolate smooth but sometimes means one of the processing steps has been abbreviated.

The amount of sugar added to chocolate determines whether the end product is labeled bittersweet, semisweet, or sweet. There don't seem to be any industry standards for exactly how much sugar individual manufacturers add to make their chocolate bittersweet, semisweet, or sweet; you'll find that one manufacturer's bittersweet is as sweet as another's semisweet or sweet chocolate. These three dark chocolates can be used interchangeably as long as you remember that the more sugar in the product, the less chocolate impact it has. The key is to taste the chocolate before you use it in a recipe. When I call for bittersweet chocolate in a recipe, it's perfectly fine to substitute semisweet or sweet chocolate, or vice versa. You cannot, however, substitute milk or white chocolate for dark chocolate.

The three above-mentioned dark chocolates should be stored well wrapped (I use freezer-strength resealable plastic bags) in a cool, dark place, but not in the refrigerator or freezer, where they may acquire moisture on their surfaces. Stored properly, away from sunlight, heat, and foods or products with strong smells, dark chocolate will keep for years.

Milk chocolate contains the same ingredients as dark chocolate, with the addition of milk solids. The solids render milk chocolate milder in flavor and lighter in color than dark chocolate. Because of the milk solids, milk chocolate has a shorter shelf life, and should be used within three months of purchase. It should be stored the same way as dark chocolate; take particular care to keep it away from strong-smelling foods, as it very readily absorbs odors.

White chocolate, which has the mildest (least chocolate) taste of all, is simply cocoa butter, milk solids, and sugar. Since it's the cocoa butter that delivers what chocolate taste there is in this product, it's important to read the label to make sure that what you're buying doesn't contain palm kernel or coconut oil, which some manufacturers add in place of the more expensive and less stable cocoa butter.

In fact, when buying any chocolate it's important to read the label to make sure it contains cocoa butter. This magic fat

melts at body temperature, which is why when you hold a piece of real chocolate in your hand for a few seconds too long, it begins to melt.

As important as cocoa butter is to the chocolates we cook with, it is an unstable fat. This presents a challenge to the home cook who tries to melt it, mold it, and have it return to the glossy, hard state so desirable when making candy or chocolate decorations. Melting chocolate so that it forms a smooth, hard coating is called "tempering," a time-consuming process that is definitely a learned skill (see page 11). To avoid having to temper chocolate, some people use a product called *compound coating,* which contains no cocoa butter at all, giving it the taste, texture, and personality of a candle stub. It is not recommended.

Finally, you can find chocolate flavored with everything from raspberries to green tea. While they can be delicious to eat out of hand, for the recipes in this book I suggest you stick to unflavored chocolate.

I buy chocolate in 10-pound blocks, since this is economical and I have the space to store it. I use a clean chisel and a hammer to chop portions for use in cooking. Of course, chocolate in smaller quantities is fine, although it does take a lot of time to unwrap all those 3- or 4-ounce bars. If you have a Trader Joe's in your area you might want to check out the store-brand chocolate that they sell. The price is right and the quality is superb. Another option for buying in bulk is chocolate wafers, which are uniformly small pieces of bar-quality chocolate. They melt evenly and do not require chopping. You can buy these from the King Arthur Flour Company through their Baker's Catalogue, as well as from most bakery suppliers. Make sure you are buying wafers that are made with cocoa butter, not a substitute fat. Wafers are different from chocolate chips, which contain less cocoa butter than the high-quality blocks, bars, and wafers; chips maintain their shape in baking precisely because they have less cocoa butter. Chips should be used only in recipes that specifically call for them.

You can buy bulk chocolate from candy and bakery supply houses or by mail order (see the Sources section on page 271). I store large quantities of chocolate in big food-service-grade plastic containers with snap-on lids. It's a good idea to label unsweetened and dark chocolates, as they look too much alike to trust anything but taste to tell the difference.

working with chocolate
MELTING

While there's no "foolproof" method for melting chocolate, there are several ways that work very well, if you are careful. Once you burn chocolate or bring it in contact with even a small amount of water, it becomes impossible to use, so throw it away.

MICROWAVE METHOD
This is best for melting 1 pound or less. Chop the chocolate in small pieces and place them in a microwaveable container large enough to let you stir the contents easily. I use a 2- or

4-cup Pyrex liquid measure, depending on how much chocolate I need to melt. Microwave the chopped chocolate on high for 40 seconds, stir with a rubber spatula, microwave for another 15 seconds, stir again, and continue to microwave and stir at 15-second intervals until the chocolate is almost completely melted. It's better to remove the chocolate before it's completely melted than to take the chance of burning it. Vestigial lumps will melt if you continue to stir the chocolate after it's removed from the microwave.

DOUBLE BOILER METHOD

The ideal amount is 2½ pounds or less. You don't see a lot of "regulation" double boilers anymore. These are two pots that fit snugly, one inside the other, with water in the lower one and whatever you're heating or melting in the upper one. I find it much more practical to set a fairly large (1½-quart) metal mixing bowl over a 3-quart saucepan of gently simmering water. If you are melting a large amount of chocolate you'll require a larger bowl and a large pan to rest it on. The bottom of the bowl should not touch the water. I choose a bowl large enough that it sits over, not in, the saucepan, and that fits snugly enough that steam from the water below can't get into the melting chocolate; if that happens, the steam reacts with the cocoa butter and the chocolate "seizes," or becomes stiff, grainy, and unusable. The finer the chocolate is chopped, the faster it will melt. Stir once or twice until it is smooth. Do not let the water in the lower pan boil. Keep it at a very low simmer.

OVEN METHOD

When I need to melt a large quantity of chocolate (more than 2 pounds), I chop it into medium-size (1½- to 2-inch) chunks and place them in a heavy roasting pan in a very low (125°F.) oven, stirring every 10 minutes until the chocolate is melted and smooth. This can take up to 30 minutes or longer depending on the amount of chocolate to be melted, and you must monitor the chocolate carefully to make sure it doesn't burn.

TEMPERING

For making some candy and coating things like cookies, you may want a pure chocolate finish that dries with a glossy sheen and snaps when you break it. To achieve this, you need to temper the chocolate, or melt it under carefully controlled conditions. Chocolate that is melted at too high a temperature or not allowed to cool correctly before it is used (or chocolate that has been stored in a warm place) becomes streaked and grainy because the cocoa butter separates out from the solids. Tempering avoids that separation. Bloomed chocolate, as this is called, is still fine to cook with if you are going to melt it first.

There are several methods for tempering chocolate. The simplest is to melt the chocolate at such a low temperature that it never goes "out of temper," but this takes a very long time and isn't terribly reliable. There are home tempering machines that do the job perfectly, but they are pricey, and, unless you are going to temper chocolate on a regular basis, it might be hard to justify the purchase. The method that has worked best for me (until I caved in and

actually bought a home tempering machine) takes some patience and practice, so my advice is to practice a bit before you offer to bring five pounds of chocolate-dipped fruit to the next office party.

A tool that will make tempering much easier is an accurate digital thermometer with a probe at the end of a flexible, heat-proof metal cable. The one made by Polder is terrific. Temper at least a pound* of chocolate at a time, as the temperature of smaller amounts is more difficult to control. Choose a large, heavy-duty saucepan (the larger the pan, the longer the water will stay warm) and a larger metal bowl that will rest over, but not in, the saucepan. Fill the pan halfway with water, then check to make sure that the bottom of the bowl does not touch the water when it sits on the saucepan. Chop the chocolate as fine as possible. Place the bowl on a work surface and place in it two-thirds of the chopped chocolate. Heat the water to a gentle simmer, then turn off the heat. Place the bowl of chocolate over the saucepan. Place the probe of the instant-read thermometer in the bowl of chocolate and stir gently with a rubber spatula until the chocolate is completely smooth. You want the chocolate to reach a temperature between 113°F. and 118°F., so you may have to heat the water beneath it a little more. The temperature of the melted chocolate must not exceed 122°F. When the chocolate has melted, remove the bowl from over the saucepan and wipe the bottom dry to prevent any water or steam from getting into the melted chocolate. Add the remaining chocolate, one-third at a time. Stir slowly at each addition, and wait for it to melt before adding another. Continue stirring until the chocolate reaches a temperature of 80°F. It is now ready to use.

Another tempering method that is less foolproof is the microwave. Chop up to 1 pound of chocolate as fine as possible. Place three-quarters of the chocolate in a microwave-safe bowl (I like to use plastic, as it doesn't retain heat the way glass does). Microwave on high for 40 seconds, stir, then microwave again for 30 seconds, stir, and continue to microwave and stir at 30-second intervals until about three-quarters of the

*While there aren't any recipes in this book that call for a full pound of tempered chocolate, it's still advisable to work with this amount. You can allow leftover tempered chocolate to harden and then reuse it for baking, or make several recipes that call for tempered chocolate.

chocolate is melted. Remove the chocolate from the microwave and add half the remaining chopped chocolate and stir gently until it melts. Add the rest of the chocolate and stir until that melts as well. Dip a finger into the melted chocolate and smear a little on your upper lip. When the chocolate feels exactly body temperature, it is ready to use.

Tempering is not a technique you'll master on the first or even second or third try, but stick with it, because when you do achieve the Zen of Tempering and watch your chocolate dry smooth and hard with a satin luster, you'll be glad you did.

UNSWEETENED COCOA POWDER

The recipes in this book use two kinds of cocoa powder: "Natural" cocoa powder is made by grinding cocoa nibs, pressing out most of the cocoa butter, and pulverizing the remaining "press cake." "Dutch-processed" cocoa powder is made by treating natural cocoa powder with an alkali to neutralize its acidity. Dutch-processed cocoa is darker, has a more intense flavor, and burns more easily than "natural" cocoa. Some recipes call for one or the other. If neither is specified, then either is acceptable. Both kinds have a long shelf life, but don't store them in flimsy containers on your spice shelf, unless you want paprika-flavored cocoa powder. Store them in plastic or glass containers in a cool, dark place, but not in the refrigerator.

BUTTER (AND MARGARINE)

Next to chocolate, unsalted (sweet) butter is my favorite ingredient. Superior both in taste and texture to salted butter, unsalted butter has a lower water content and doesn't get as greasy when it is softened. These days there are lots of sexy, imported unsalted butters in both supermarkets and specialty grocery stores. It's fun to experiment with different brands if your wallet can justify the indulgence. You cannot substitute whipped butter for stick butter in these recipes. Make sure to store butter in the refrigerator or freezer away from strong-smelling foods, as it absorbs odors readily.

Trying to make a chocolate dessert heart-healthy by using margarine instead of butter is like putting Astroturf on a golf course to save money on mowing. Unless you leave out the eggs and chocolate, the ends simply don't justify the means. On the other hand, my friends who keep kosher make my recipes with margarine and don't seem to have any complaints.

VEGETABLE OILS

I like the neutral taste of corn and canola oils in recipes that call for vegetable oil. Make sure to store oils in a cool, dark place, and check (by smelling or tasting) before you use them to make sure they have not turned rancid.

SOLID VEGETABLE SHORTENING

Solid vegetable shortening such as Crisco is called for in a few recipes in this book. It should be stored in the refrigerator. Cakes made with solid vegetable shortening have a lighter texture than those made with butter, but what you gain in texture you lose in taste. I can usually tell when a cake is made with shortening, because it leaves a film in my mouth. Because shortening melts at a higher temperature than butter, it's sometimes a better fat to use when the dough is going to be manipulated more than usual, as when you make pie crust. Using a combination of solid vegetable shortening and butter often creates that happy medium that makes for great texture and good taste.

FLOUR

My favorite flour, the one that performs consistently well, is made by the King Arthur Flour Company. Their all-purpose flour is unbleached and unbromated (not treated with chemicals). It's available nationwide, so if you see it on the supermarket shelf, give it a try. All-purpose flour, made from hard wheat, has about 12 grams of protein per cup (check the ingredient label, remembering that the values given are for 1/4 cup of flour). It's used in the majority of recipes in this book. A few call for cake flour, which contains about 8 grams of protein per cup and is made from soft wheat and usually bleached. Do not substitute self-rising cake flour for cake flour, as the former has a leavening agent in it.

Flour, like chocolate, should be stored in a tightly closed container in a cool, dry place, away from direct sunlight. As I mentioned earlier, in the recipes in this book it is assumed that you are using five ounces of all-purpose flour per cup.

SALT

Salt brings out nuances and gives depth to the other flavors in a dish. Things taste dull without it. Use regular table salt unless otherwise directed in these recipes.

EGGS

All these recipes were tested with extra-large eggs. A few recipes call for uncooked eggs. Cooked or raw, it's vital to use clean, fresh eggs from a reliable source to avoid contracting salmonella or other food poisoning. Store eggs in their carton in the refrigerator. You can bring eggs up to room temperature quickly by placing them in a bowl of warm—not hot—water.

SUGARS

Unless stated, all recipes that call for sugar use granulated sugar. Confectioners' sugar should be sifted before use, even if it looks lump-free. Both dark and light brown sugars should be packed solidly into the measuring cup. Superfine sugar, or "bar" sugar, is usually available in the baking aisle of the supermarket. You can make your own by placing granulated sugar in the work bowl of a food processor and using the pulse option to process it on and off for 30 to 40 seconds, or until the granules become very fine and almost powdery.

Other sweeteners, such as light and dark corn syrup, molasses, and honey, should not be substituted for each other or for granulated sugar. A good measuring tip is to pour a little vegetable oil into a measuring cup to coat the bottom and sides, then pour out any excess before pouring in the corn syrup, honey, or molasses. The ingredient being measured will pour right out without leaving any trace behind, effecting an accurate measurement and easier cleanup.

CHEMICAL LEAVENERS

Creaming butter and sugar together or folding beaten egg whites into a batter helps cakes and other baked goods rise. Chemical leaveners such as baking powder and baking soda also accomplish this task, sometimes by themselves, or, more often, in concert with beaten egg whites or creamed butter and sugar. Baking soda needs an acid and a liquid to make it

work. Since chocolate and cocoa powder are both acidic, you will very often find baking soda in recipes that call for these ingredients. In fact, the leavening ability of baking soda is increased by about four times that of baking powder when it is used with chocolate. Since baking soda begins to work as soon as it comes in contact with moisture, you must not waste time in getting your cake or cookies into the oven when they contain baking soda. Double-acting baking powder (the kind used in these recipes) contains both sodium bicarbonate (baking soda) and cream of tartar and/or sodium aluminum sulfate. This means it works once when it comes in contact with moisture and then again when it is heated, so you don't have to rush quite as much to get things into the oven to bake.

Yeast is an organic leavener that converts sugars into carbon dioxide and alcohol. The gasses released during this process cause air bubbles that become trapped in the web of gluten (protein) created when yeasted doughs are kneaded. As the dough bakes, the bubbles are stabilized. I use active dry yeast, which can be added right to the flour without being "proofed" (activated by mixing with water and a little sugar) ahead of time. I strongly recommend against rapid-rise yeast, which never gives the dough enough time to fully develop flavor and texture.

DAIRY PRODUCTS

Milk, cream, sour cream, cream cheese, butter, and yogurt all add fat and flavor to baked goods. Cakes, cookies, and breads made with dairy products will have a finer texture and a more delicate crust and crumb than those made without them. I emphatically recommend against substituting reduced-fat or fat-free dairy products for the full-fat varieties in these recipes. Condensed and evaporated milks are not interchangeable.

I've started using organic heavy cream. I find it tastes fresher. You can whip cream ahead of time, spoon it into a fine-mesh sieve set over a small bowl, cover with plastic wrap, and store it in the refrigerator for up to four hours before you plan to use it. The volume will diminish a bit as the buttermilk drains out, but it's perfect for serving in spite of this.

Buttermilk, which is low-fat milk that has been cultured with a lactic acid bacteria, can be used fresh in liquid form or reconstituted from powder. If you do use the powder, store the opened can or envelope in the refrigerator.

Recipes calling for cream cheese require the solid block form, not whipped. Do not substitute low-fat or reduced-fat for full-fat cream cheese. You can soften cream cheese quickly by taking the inner foil package from the box and placing the unopened foil-wrapped block in a bowl of warm water for a few minutes.

NUTS

Nuts provide texture and taste as well as fat. Unless otherwise indicated, they should be toasted whole before using. Preheat an oven to 325°F. with the rack in the upper third—but not the very highest position—of the oven. Scatter the nuts in one layer on a heavy-duty, shallow, rimmed pan and bake for 15 minutes. Remove the pan from the oven and use a wide metal spatula to flip the nuts over. Return them to the oven and bake for another 10 minutes, or until they are lightly colored and fragrant. Cool the nuts completely before chopping, grinding, or adding them whole to a recipe. If you are using hazelnuts that still have the papery skin on them, roast them as above and while they are still hot, rub the skin off with a towel. Not every bit will come off, but this is fine.

The food processor is a great tool for grinding nuts. Use the metal blade and pulse a half cup of nuts at a time. The pulsing action tosses the nuts up in the air and keeps them from turning into paste. Store nuts (whole and ground) in the freezer in heavy-duty resealable plastic bags. There is no need to defrost them before using. Nuts, by the way, are a perfect example of how weighing an ingredient is more accurate than measuring. Depending on how you fill a measuring cup, and depending on whether you measure before or after you grind, the weight of a cup of nuts can differ by many ounces.

EXTRACTS AND FLAVORINGS

When a recipe calls for finely grated citrus zest, you have the option of using citrus oils instead. An excellent line of products made by Boyajian (www.boyajianinc.com) is available nationally and can be found in most gourmet food stores and supermarkets. These oils must be used very sparingly, as their flavor is intense. I find that for most recipes, 1/8 to 1/4 teaspoon is plenty. If you do grate your own zest, an invaluable tool is an all-purpose kitchen rasp-type grater, now available in every cook shop.

Using pure vanilla extract makes an enormous difference in terms of taste, as does using freshly opened jars of spices.

DRIED FRUIT

Dried fruits add a counterpoint of flavor to baked goods, along with texture and sweetness. They should be stored at room temperature in tightly sealed containers or in heavy-duty resealable plastic bags to help them retain moisture. The easiest way to cut dried apricots, apples, pears, and other fruits is with a pair of kitchen scissors. Dried fruits can be briefly simmered in orange juice or spirits to plump them and enhance their flavor. Make sure to remove excess liquid before using by placing the soaked fruit in a fine-mesh strainer and pressing gently with a wooden spoon or rubber spatula.

OTHER INGREDIENTS

Espresso powder or granules (or instant espresso) can be found next to the instant coffee in the supermarket.

Nutella is a chocolate–hazelnut spread that can be found in many supermarkets (near the peanut butter), as well as in Italian food shops.

Peanut butter: As much as I love organic peanut butter, I've found that good old Skippy seems to work best in recipes. Make sure to keep opened jars in the refrigerator where peanut butter has less chance of going rancid.

Almond paste is available in the baking aisle of the super-market. It is made from ground almonds, sugar, and glycerin (to make it easy to roll out). It is not the same as marzipan, which is also available in the baking aisle, as marzipan contains more sugar. In a pinch you can substitute one for the other.

Spirits: Small amounts ($1/4$ cup or less) of alcoholic beverages can usually simply be omitted or replaced with orange juice.

Shredded coconut is available sweetened and unsweetened (the latter is also called dessicated coconut, and is sold in whole-food stores). The two should not be interchanged in recipes. To toast either kind of coconut in the oven, spread it on a shallow, rimmed baking sheet and place it in a preheated 350°F. oven for 10 minutes. Use a metal spatula to stir the shreds, then bake for another 5 minutes, or until the coconut is a very light golden brown. To toast coconut on the stove top, place it in a large nonstick skillet and cook over medium heat, shaking the pan or stirring continuously with a wooden spoon until the shreds turn light golden brown. This will take 10 to 15 minutes, depending on how much coconut you are toasting.

equipment

When creating and writing these recipes I tried to stick to regulation-size pans that you might already have in your

kitchen, or pans in sizes you'd end up using often if you had to buy them. I use Calphalon nonstick bakeware. I like it for several reasons: the price is right, its quality is consistently good, and it's available nationwide. The company makes bakeware in every size and shape you could ever want in your kitchen. No matter what brand you use, heavy-duty pans are essential to success in any sort of cooking. Baking in particular should be done in pans that distribute heat evenly and that will not warp in the oven. Darker pans absorb heat faster and hold it longer, which means you need to be especially vigilant when using them; set your timer to ring 5 to 7 minutes before the end of the recipe's suggested baking time. Use a cake tester to check the interior of cakes, and use a metal spatula to lift cookies to check their undersides for doneness. Even if you do use nonstick pans, it's still essential to prepare them according to the recipe. I don't put my bakeware in the dishwasher, as the abrasive detergent causes scratches on the surfaces.

THE FOLLOWING IS A LIST OF PANS THAT ARE USED IN THIS BOOK:

Two 9 × 2-inch round cake pans

10 × 2-inch round cake pan

9-, 9$1/2$-, and 10-inch springform pans with 3-inch sides

9$1/2$- or 10-inch (12-cup) Bundt pan (nonstick)

10 × 4-inch flat-bottom angel food cake pan (with a removable bottom)

8-inch square pan

9-inch square pan

9 × 13-inch baking pan

10 × 15-inch baking pan

9-inch pie pan

12-inch tart pan with removable bottom

Two 11 × 17 × 1-inch half-sheet pans (These pans can be used as cookie sheets. If you do use cookie sheets and they are not insulated, try doubling them up to avoid burning the bottoms of the cookies.)

Muffin tins: two standard tins (with twelve $1/2$-cup muffin cups); one jumbo tin (with six $3/4$-cup muffin cups); one mini-muffin tin (with twenty-four $1/4$-cup muffin cups)

OTHER EQUIPMENT

It's fine to use ovenproof glass bakeware, such as Pyrex. Cooking times tend to be longer, as the glass doesn't absorb and retain heat the way metal does. Be sure not to place a hot-from-the-oven glass pan on a cold surface, as it will shatter. You can cut bars and squares directly in a glass pan without worrying about scratching the surface, as you would with metal.

Individual brioche pans (approximately $1^3/4$ inches high and $3^1/2$ inches across the top)

Loaf pans (6- and 8-cup capacity)

Ovenproof ramekins or small soufflé dishes ($1/2$-cup capacity)

$2^1/2$-quart ovenproof baking dish

OTHER ESSENTIAL STUFF YOU WILL NEED

Two wire cake racks

Assorted heavy-bottomed saucepans

Liquid (glass) and dry (metal or plastic) measuring cups and spoons

Rubber spatulas

Wooden and metal spoons

Wire whisk

Flexible metal spatula, for frosting cakes

Large chef's knife and/or chisel and hammer, for chopping chocolate

Paring knife

Dishwasher-safe cutting board

Rolling pin

Assorted mixing bowls, both metal and glass (for the microwave)

Cake tester or toothpicks

Pot holders and dish towels

Timer (I like the kind I can wear around my neck in case I need to leave the kitchen.)

Parchment paper

Plastic wrap

Sifter (I use a medium-mesh metal strainer set over a bowl to sift dry ingredients.)

NONESSENTIAL, BUT GREAT STUFF TO HAVE IF POSSIBLE

Kitchen scale (digital, if possible)

Offset metal spatula, for lifting bars and squares out of pans

Long serrated knife for splitting cake layers

Marble slab, for rolling out pastry

Oven thermometer

Instant-read thermometer

Candy thermometer

Ovenproof silicone pan liners, such as Silpat

Deli wrap (comes in sheets and is available in kitchen supply stores)

Heavy-weight aluminum foil

Turntable, for decorating cakes

Disposable or reusable pastry bags, and a few metal piping tips

Pastry brush

Fluted foil or paper muffin cup liners

Kitchen string

Citrus zester (Microplane brand)

Bench knife (a straight-edge blade for manipulating dough and scraping counters)

Kitchen scissors

ABOUT YOUR OVEN

Now that almost everyone owns a self-cleaning oven, there is hardly any excuse for baking in anything but a spotlessly clean oven. The smell of burned-on food will be absorbed by anything you bake, especially when it has chocolate in it. Use an accurate oven thermometer to make sure your oven is correctly calibrated, so that when the dial is turned to 350°F., that's what the oven temperature really is. Make sure your racks are even—not tilted to one side—or you'll have cakes that are thin on one side and thick on the other, and unevenly baked cookies. Also be sure to use the proper size baking sheets for your oven. Sheets that are too big block the flow of air, trapping hot air below and resulting in burned bottoms on whatever you bake. If you find that things cook faster in the back of your oven, make sure to rotate the pan 180 degrees halfway through the baking time. If you use two cookie sheets at once, it's a good idea to reverse them (rack to rack) and rotate them 180 degrees halfway through the baking time, to ensure even cooking.

Many of you have the option of baking by convection, or hot air circulated through the oven during the baking time. Since not everyone has this ability, these recipes were tested without it, in conventional ovens. If you do wish to use a convection oven, make sure to lower the baking temperature by 25 degrees and watch for things drying out, especially delicate layer cakes. Don't use convection when baking meringues, soufflés, or other very fragile desserts, as the force of the air circulating can actually deform the surface.

With the exception of one recipe in this book, it's essential to remember to preheat the oven before baking, and to make sure the rack is in the specified position. Oven temperature and rack position are the first things you'll see in the recipe instructions, unless the oven is not used until later in the recipe preparation, as in recipes using yeasted dough.

MIXERS AND FOOD PROCESSORS

Using a heavy-duty stand mixer such as a KitchenAid or Kenwood will save you time and effort. A handheld (portable) electric mixer will also perform well in the majority of these recipes. Of course, hand mixing works, if you have the stamina.

There are several recipes here that I find work best in a food processor, a kitchen tool that in its relatively short lifetime has become all but indispensable.

For yeasted recipes, I've tried, when possible, to include directions for preparing the dough with a stand mixer, food processor, and bread machine (on the manual or dough cycle). All these doughs can be made by hand as well.

other helpful information

The suggested serving size is simply that: suggested. If you know that the people standing by to eat your dessert are chocolate-crazed maniacs who think a dozen cookies per person is starvation rations, then perhaps you will look at a cake that I say serves eight and see six servings as a more realistic number.

Checking for doneness is absolutely necessary; even with carefully tested recipes cooking times should be considered just a ballpark number, as ovens vary wildly. I usually set a timer to ring an average of 1 to 2 minutes early for every 10 minutes of cooking time: a cake that should take an hour gets a check in 50 minutes, and cookies that should take 12 minutes get eyeballed at 10. Besides observing the visual cues contained in the recipe (the top should be dry and golden brown in color, for example), use a cake tester or toothpick to check that the interior of a cake is no longer wet (the tester will come out clean and dry). Check cookies by flipping one over in the middle of the pan (where they cook less quickly) to make sure the bottom is brown and crisp. Check yeasted desserts by inserting an instant-read thermometer in the center to make sure that the internal temperature is between 190 and 200°F.

The cooling process is an important one, and it varies from recipe to recipe. These recipes specify which things should be unmolded onto cooling racks as soon as they come out of the oven, and which things need a longer rest in the pan in which they were baked. If you delay the unmolding, the dessert can become overly moist, or even soggy, from steam trapped in the pan; if you rush the rest period, you run the risk of having things fall apart on you.

Decorating, garnishing, and frosting all improve the appearance and taste of a recipe. Something as simple as placing a doily on a serving plate can dress up the plainest cake; sifting some confectioners' sugar or unsweetened cocoa powder on top adds something as well. A swirl or spoonful of freshly whipped cream and a few berries can transform a simple sliver of cake into a classy dessert, and adding some raspberry sauce catapults it into a whole other realm. Some people like to decorate with fresh flowers, and, while I really like to be able to eat everything on my plate, flowers are fine unless they are poisonous (stay away from, among others, lily of the valley, yew, and poinsettia). You don't have to be an expert at using a pastry bag to make something look pretty. A layer cake with a swirl of frosting on top is a beautiful thing to behold, but if you are determined to pipe a decoration or a message on a cake, practice first on wax paper. Another option is to simply grate some chocolate on top. You're not doing a photo shoot for *Gourmet*; less is more, and simpler is better.

Lastly, remember that no matter what your dessert looks like, the fact that you took the time and energy to make it instantly puts it ten pegs above anything you could buy in a store.

2. The Candy Store

Cranberry Pecan Cups à la Serenade

Chocolate Truffles

Chocolate-Covered Almond Butter Crunch

Sand Dollars

Viennese Truffles

Chocolate-Dipped Coconut Macaroons

Chocolate-Dipped Figs

Chocolate-Dipped Orange Slices

IN BROOKLINE VILLAGE, Massachusetts, there is a chocolate shop unlike any other. When you step into Serenade Chocolatier the delicious aromas of butter, caramelized sugar, roasted nuts, and melted chocolate make you believe you've found the place that Burl Ives sings about in the song "Big Rock Candy Mountain." "Welcome" is called out in Russian, Chinese, Yiddish, Turkish, or Arabic, depending on who is sitting at the tempering machines, packing gems into gold foil gift boxes, or filling trays with sugarplums, almond bark, and chocolate-covered nut clusters. Spending time at Serenade both in front of and behind the counter with my friend, owner and proprietress Nur Kilic, has given me countless hours of pleasure as well as a chance to see firsthand how the best-quality candy is made.

I would imagine that it is every chocolate lover's dream to watch caramel centers, marshmallows, and nuggets of crystallized ginger or thin strips of candied orange and grapefruit peel be lowered efficiently into a slowly moving vat of chocolate, under a chocolate waterfall, then almost immediately scooped up with a wire dipping fork, gently tapped to remove any drips, and laid to harden to a rich gleam on a pan full of similarly coated confections. The urge to stick your finger in the chocolate bath is strong enough to make even the most disciplined soul stand with her hands clasped tightly behind her back.

I love watching the faces of the shoppers who come through the lace-curtain-lined door. The harried "all-business" look of someone with way too many errands and not nearly enough time is transformed almost instantly into a look of sublime happiness. Those who came to buy a gift for someone else more often than not leave the shop with a second box for themselves. Who said you can't package happiness?

If you ever have the opportunity to watch someone hand-dip chocolates, don't pass it up. You will be inspired. Candy-making is a craft that takes years to learn and even longer to perfect, but you're not looking for perfection—you're looking for delicious. Start with fudge and move right along to truffles. With practice and patience you can delight your friends and family with a dazzling assortment of exquisite confections—and don't forget to save a box for yourself.

Cranberry Pecan Cups à la Serenade

Makes about 24 candies

Here is a gem of a confection from my friend Nur Kilic, whose chocolate shop is famous for its creative combinations of scrumptious ingredients. The flavors of orange and chocolate mingle deliciously in these two-bite-size candies, which hold a surprise of pecans at the bottom and are crowned with lots of tangy dried cranberries. Cooking with pure citrus oils has become much easier, thanks exclusively to my friend John Boyajian, whose company makes a vast rainbow of all-natural specialty oils. (Visit his website at www.boyajianinc.com to get an idea of what adventures await you.) Once you taste lemon, tangerine, or lime, you may find you like the unusual flavors better than the traditional orange. It's essential not to go overboard on these oils, so measure them carefully. A little goes a very long way and too much will completely ruin the flavor of the candy.

1 pound bittersweet chocolate, finely chopped

1 tablespoon corn oil

$1/8$ teaspoon orange, lemon, tangerine, or similar oil (see headnote)

1 cup (4 ounces) pecan halves, toasted

$1/2$ cup (2 ounces) dried cranberries

Temper the chocolate according to the directions on page 11. Stir occasionally with a rubber spatula until completely smooth. Add the corn oil and the orange oil and stir to blend well.

Set 24 fluted paper candy cups with a 2-fluid-tablespoon capacity on a tray. Place 2 pecan halves in each cup. Transfer the melted chocolate mixture to a disposable piping bag. Snip a very small piece off the end of the bag and pipe chocolate into each cup, filling it about three-quarters full. Gently rap the tray on the work surface to settle the chocolate, then press 4 dried cranberries onto the surface of each candy. Refrigerate for 10 to 15 minutes, just until the chocolate has hardened.

The candies may be stored at cool room temperature (under 75°F.) for several weeks.

Chocolate Truffles

Makes 40 to 50 truffles

Before some genius thought of rolling a mixture of chocolate and heavy cream into rough-hewn balls and coating them with cocoa, the only truffles we knew about were a delicacy hunted by specially trained pigs (or dogs) and then, because they are more costly than diamonds, shaved sparingly onto pasta or risotto (among other things). With the advent of chocolate truffles, "sparingly" is no longer an issue; your only limit is how many you can eat at a sitting.

These truffles, without the cocoa and confectioners' sugar coating, may be used as the center component in Molten Chocolate Cakes (page 238) or the Tunnel of Fudge Cake (page 82).

1 cup (8 ounces) heavy cream

16 ounces (1 pound) chocolate (bittersweet, semisweet, milk, or white), coarsely chopped

2 tablespoons (1 ounce) unsalted butter

1 tablespoon instant espresso powder or granules (optional)

2 tablespoons grated orange zest (optional)

2 to 3 tablespoons Grand Marnier, Chambord, or Bailey's Irish Cream (optional)

¼ cup (.75 ounce) unsweetened cocoa powder

¼ cup (1 ounce) confectioners' sugar

Line a rimmed baking sheet with wax paper or parchment paper.

Place the cream in a medium, heavy saucepan. Set the pan over medium-low heat and bring the cream almost to a boil. Remove the pan from the heat. Stir in the chocolate, butter, and the instant espresso powder, orange zest, and liqueur, if using. Stir the mixture with a wooden spoon until the chocolate is melted and the mixture is smooth. Scrape the truffle mixture into a medium metal bowl and place it in the freezer for about 20 minutes, or until it is firm.

When you are ready to roll the truffles, sift the cocoa powder with the confectioners' sugar onto a plate or into a small, shallow bowl. Use a teaspoon to scoop up a full teaspoon of the truffle mixture. Roll the truffle quickly in your hands to make a ball about 1 inch in diameter. (The truffles will melt on your hands, but just work quickly and wipe your hands frequently.) Roll the truffle in the cocoa mixture and place it on the baking sheet. Continue forming and rolling truffles with the remaining truffle mix. Refrigerate the truffles for about 20 minutes, or until the truffles are firm.

Truffles can be stored in an airtight container in the refrigerator for up to 2 weeks, or frozen for up to 3 months.

Chocolate-Covered Almond Butter Crunch

Makes about 4 cups of candy (about 2 pounds)

Making almond or peanut brittle is a little like making magic. Watching the sugar caramelize and turn deep honey-gold, seeing the mixture froth and fizz when the baking soda is added, and finally seeing the glistening sheet of nut-filled amber solidify is to bear witness to the best sort of alchemy. Of course, coating each piece with dark chocolate is the ultimate Cinderella story. With a good recipe on your side, you could certainly serve this confection at the ball.

An important tip: You'll have better luck making brittle that isn't sticky if you wait for cool, dry weather.

4¹/₂ cups (18 ounces) whole almonds, toasted

1¹/₂ cups (12 ounces) sugar

¹/₂ cup (4 ounces) light corn syrup

1¹/₂ teaspoons unsalted butter

1 teaspoon baking soda

¹/₂ teaspoon salt

12 ounces bittersweet chocolate, coarsely chopped

Line a baking sheet with parchment paper or a silicone liner.

Set aside 1¹/₂ cups of the toasted almonds and place the remaining 3 cups in the work bowl of a food processor. Pulse 4 or 5 times until the nuts are coarsely chopped. Scrape onto a large, flat plate and set aside.

Place the sugar, corn syrup, and ¹/₄ cup (2 ounces) of water in a 3-quart saucepan. Attach a candy thermometer to the side of the pan, making sure that the end doesn't touch the bottom of the pan. Have the butter, baking soda, and salt measured and ready. Set the pan on medium-high heat. Cook the mixture and occasionally wash down the sides with a pastry brush dipped in water to prevent sugar crystals from forming. Cook until the mixture reaches 320°F. Use a wooden spoon to stir in the reserved 1¹/₂ cups of whole almonds, then remove the pan from the heat. Add the butter, baking soda, and salt, and stir to combine. The baking soda will make the mixture bubble. Pour and scrape the mixture onto the lined baking sheet and spread it quickly so the brittle is about ¹/₄ inch thick, or slightly thicker. Allow it to cool completely. When cool, break the brittle into small pieces with your hands.

While the brittle is cooling, prepare the chocolate coating. Melt the chocolate in a metal bowl set over, but not touching, a pan of gently simmering water, or in a microwave-safe bowl in a microwave oven. Stir the chocolate with a wooden spoon as it melts. When it is melted and smooth, remove the pan from the heat. Use the lining material to lift the broken brittle pieces from the baking sheet and reline the sheet. Use a wooden spoon or a kitchen fork to toss the brittle, several pieces at a time, in the chocolate. As the pieces of brittle are coated, use a wooden spoon to transfer them to the plate with the chopped almonds. Coat both sides of the brittle with nuts, then set them aside on the freshly lined baking sheet to allow the chocolate to set.

Store the brittle in an airtight container at room temperature for up to 2 weeks.

VARIATION

Make Chocolate-Covered Peanut Brittle by substituting $4\frac{1}{2}$ cups (18 ounces) of dry roasted peanuts for the almonds in the above recipe. You do not need to toast the peanuts, as they are already roasted.

Sand Dollars

Makes 24 to 30 candies

Flat puddles of chocolate make a platform for all sorts of lovely bits of flavor and textures. I created this recipe in my head one day while my young children were playing in a tide pool on a Cape Cod beach. They pulled flat, round sand dollars from the warm, shallow water, putting them in pails along with sea horses and hermit crabs. Later that evening, faced with a bowl of melted chocolate left over from another recipe, and a jar of assorted nuts and dried fruits, I spooned some chocolate onto a parchment-covered tray, then plopped on the crunchy topping. The result was an instant hit. One of the kids said, "These look like chocolate sand dollars!" and the name stuck.

1½ to 2 cups (6 to 8 ounces) total of a mixture of any of the following:

- **Toasted slivered almonds**
- **Coarsely chopped toasted pecans**
- **Coarsely chopped toasted hazelnuts**
- **Coarsely chopped toasted walnuts**
- **Candied ginger, cut into ¼-inch dice**
- **Dried cherries (sweet or sour or a combination of both)**
- **Dried cranberries**
- **Dried mango, cut into ¼-inch dice**
- **Dried apple slices, cut into ¼-inch dice**

10 ounces best-quality bittersweet or semisweet chocolate, finely chopped

Place the toppings you have selected in a medium bowl and toss to combine. Set aside.

Line several baking sheets with aluminum foil or parchment paper. Temper the chocolate according to the directions on page 11. Pour and scrape the tempered chocolate into a heavy-duty 1-quart resealable plastic bag. Force the air out of the bag, seal it, then use a pair of scissors to snip off a very small piece of one of the bottom corners. Make sure to cut a very small hole—you can always make it larger if you have to. Hold the bag over a prepared baking sheet and pipe out a 1½- to 2-tablespoon circle of chocolate measuring 3 to 4 inches in diameter, depending how big you want the sand dollars to be. Leave enough room between disks so that you can use an off-set spatula or kitchen knife to flatten them to the same thickness. While the chocolate is still soft, sprinkle a generous measure of the topping on each disk, and press gently with your fingers or a rubber spatula to push the pieces into the chocolate.

Allow the sand dollars to harden at room temperature, then carefully peel them off the pan covering. If your kitchen is particularly warm you may want to refrigerate the candies for 15 to 20 minutes, or until the chocolate has set. Store them at room temperature in a covered container, with wax paper between the layers, for up to 1 month.

Viennese Truffles

Makes 3³/₄ pounds

There was a time when these three-layer confections were a staple in every high-class box of assorted chocolates. When my amazingly generous and wildly talented friend Nur Kilic offered to teach me how to make these, I was thrilled.

Hazelnut butter can be found in most health-food stores and many supermarkets. Superfine sugar can be found in the baking section of most supermarkets, or by mail order from the King Arthur Flour Company's Baker's Catalogue (see Sources, page 271).

You'll need a kitchen scale for this recipe.

24 ounces (1.5 pounds) hazelnut butter

12 ounces (1²/₃ cups) superfine or bar sugar (see page 16)

24 ounces (1.5 pounds) bittersweet chocolate, finely chopped

12 ounces (.75 pound) milk chocolate, chopped

Line the bottom of an 8 × 11-inch pan (or one close in size) with parchment paper. Set aside.

Place the hazelnut butter (well mixed to incorporate any oil that might have risen to the surface) in a large mixing bowl. Add the sugar and stir to combine. Set aside.

Place the bittersweet chocolate in a large metal bowl. Place the milk chocolate in another large metal bowl. Choose two pans that the large bowls can be set over. Temper the chocolates according to the instructions on page 11. When the chocolates are melted, smooth, and tempered, turn off the heat under the pans and leave the chocolates where they are.

Stir the hazelnut mixture. Weigh out 12 ounces and stir it into the milk chocolate. Stir the remaining 24 ounces of the hazelnut mixture into the bittersweet chocolate. Pour and scrape half the bittersweet chocolate mixture into the prepared pan.

Smooth it evenly with a rubber spatula. Tap the pan gently on the work surface to remove any air bubbles. Place the pan in the refrigerator for 10 minutes, or until the chocolate is firm. Pour and scrape all the milk chocolate mixture over the chilled bittersweet mixture, smooth it with a rubber spatula, and refrigerate it until firm, 15 to 20 minutes. (If the remaining bittersweet chocolate starts to harden, carefully reheat the water under it.) Pour and scrape the remaining bittersweet chocolate over the milk chocolate layer. Smooth it with a rubber spatula and tap the pan on the work surface. Refrigerate for 20 minutes, or until the surface is hard.

Place a cutting board on top of the pan and invert it. Remove the pan and the parchment from the candy. Use a long, thin, sharp knife to trim the edges so they are even, then cut the hardened chocolate into 1-inch squares. Place each square in a little fluted candy cup, if desired.

Store the candy in a covered container in a cool place (under 75°F.) for several weeks. These are best if not refrigerated.

Chocolate-Dipped Coconut Macaroons

Makes about 24 macaroons

I'm sure I'm not the only one who learned to make these cookies in Girl Scouts (or was it Brownies?). I remember thinking how strange it was to earn a merit badge to sew on my sash by stirring a few ingredients around in a bowl and then using my fingers to form them into balls. I also remember wondering why anyone would eat anything with coconut in it. Having since developed a fondness for piña coladas, I know better. In fact, it was my fondness for piña coladas that inspired at least one of the variations on page 41.

²/₃ cup (5 ounces) sweetened condensed milk

1 extra-large egg white

1¹/₂ teaspoons vanilla extract

¹/₈ teaspoon salt

3¹/₂ cups (14 ounces) sweetened shredded coconut

10 ounces bittersweet chocolate, coarsely chopped

Preheat the oven to 325°F. with the rack in the center position. Line a baking sheet with parchment paper or a silicone pan liner.

In a large mixing bowl, whisk the sweetened condensed milk and the egg white together. Whisk in the vanilla and salt. Use a wooden spoon to stir in the coconut, mixing well to coat the coconut thoroughly with the milk mixture. Press portions of the dough firmly into a 1-tablespoon measure, loosen them from the measure, and round them with your fingers, then place the portions on the prepared baking sheet, leaving 1 inch of space between portions.

Bake for 20 minutes, or until the somewhat irregular surfaces of the cookies have browned lightly and the bottoms are golden brown. Let the cookies rest on the pan for 10 minutes, then transfer them to a baking sheet lined with wax paper.

Melt the chocolate in a medium metal bowl set over, but not touching, a pan of simmering water, or in a microwave-safe bowl in a microwave oven. When the cookies are cool and the chocolate is smooth and warm, hold a macaroon by the top and dip the bottom in the melted chocolate so that the chocolate comes about ¹/₄ inch up the base of the cookie. Let the excess chocolate drip back into the bowl, or use a kitchen knife to smooth off the excess chocolate. As they are dipped, return the macaroons to the lined baking sheet. When the chocolate has set, store the macaroons in an airtight container at room temperature for up to 1 week.

VARIATIONS

Almond Macaroons:

Substitute 1½ teaspoons almond extract for the vanilla in the recipe for Chocolate-Dipped Coconut Macaroons, and fold 1 cup slivered toasted almonds into the batter with the coconut. Shape, bake, and dip the almond macaroons as directed for Chocolate-Dipped Coconut Macaroons.

Orange Macaroons:

Add 1 tablespoon grated orange zest to the recipe for Chocolate-Dipped Coconut Macaroons, and eliminate the vanilla extract. Shape, bake, and dip the orange macaroons as directed for Chocolate-Dipped Coconut Macaroons.

Lime Macaroons:

Add 1 tablespoon grated lime zest to the recipe for Chocolate-Dipped Coconut Macaroons, and eliminate the vanilla extract. Shape, bake, and dip the lime macaroons as directed for Chocolate-Dipped Coconut Macaroons.

Piña Colada Macaroons:

Substitute 1 tablespoon rum extract for the vanilla in the recipe for Chocolate-Dipped Coconut Macaroons. Shape, bake, and dip the piña colada macaroons as directed for Chocolate-Dipped Coconut Macaroons.

Chocolate-Dipped Figs

Makes 12 figs

It used to be that fresh figs appeared in the market for a few weeks in the fall and then disappeared, leaving those of us who love the tiny gems of exotic sweetness reflecting on the ephemeral nature of seasonal produce. All that has changed and now fresh figs from all corners of the world can be had in almost any season if you are willing to pay the price. As autumn approaches and the prices become relatively palatable, buy a flat, eat as many as you can right out of the box, and then save the rest to dip in chocolate—the result is beautiful to behold and the combination of textures and flavors is extraordinary. If you can find them, the bright green Calimyrna variety offers the best visual contrast with the chocolate.

10 ounces bittersweet chocolate, melted and tempered (see page 11)

12 fresh, firm figs (very slightly underripe)

Wipe the figs gently with a damp paper towel and allow them to dry completely. Set a sheet of wax paper, deli paper, or silicone liner on a flat baking sheet.

Pour and scrape the melted chocolate into a small bowl or measuring cup so that you have a depth of at least 3 inches. Grasp a fig by the stem and lower it into the chocolate to cover three-quarters of the surface, leaving a small area and the stem uncovered. Place the covered fig stem-side up on the prepared surface and continue until all the figs have been dipped. Depending on the size of the figs, you may have chocolate left over. Allow it to harden and use for future baking.

Place the dipped figs in a cool place or in the refrigerator for about 20 minutes, or just until the chocolate sets. When the chocolate is completely hard, transfer the figs to a serving plate. These are better left unrefrigerated and should be consumed within 2 days.

Chocolate-Dipped Orange Slices

Makes about 48 slices

In New York City in the 1970s there was a chocolate genius named Tom Kron who made confections that until then had existed only in the minds of people who dream in bittersweet. At the very top of the long list of the things for which I would have traded my soul to the devil were his chocolate-covered orange slices. Pretty, they were not—long, slightly lumpy, uneven crescents of chocolate that looked like a more careful chocolatier's mistakes, the beauty was in the biting. First your teeth sunk through a shell of intensely bittersweet chocolate and then into a startlingly bright shock of citrus. It was hard to smile while you had a mouthful of chocolate and fresh orange juice was running down your chin, but no one—and I do mean no one—who stood in the shop and ate one could resist.

This is a time when the quality of the orange is key—you want the most flavorful, juiciest, seedless oranges that you can find, the ones that can easily be pulled apart into segments.

1 pound (16 ounces) bittersweet chocolate, tempered (see page 11)

4 navel oranges, divided into segments, white membrane pulled off

Line 2 baking sheets with wax paper, deli paper, or silicone liner. Pour and scrape the chocolate into a shallow bowl. Working with one orange segment at a time, drop it into the chocolate, then use a fork (a lobster fork is good for this) to carefully turn it over so that it is completely coated in chocolate.

Use the fork to remove the segment, tap it lightly on the rim of the bowl to remove excess chocolate, and place it on the baking sheet. Repeat with the remaining segments, working fast so that the chocolate doesn't harden. You might want to keep the bowl on a heating pad turned to low to keep the chocolate fluid.

Refrigerate the segments until the chocolate hardens. You can serve them right from the refrigerator, but I think they are best at room temperature.

These should be eaten within 12 hours of making them.

3. Chocolate for Breakfast

Chocolate Caramel Sticky Buns

Chocolate Chip Muffins

Icy Mexican Chocolate Smoothie

Chocolate Chip Pancakes with Chocolate Butter

Sunnyside Muffins

Chocolate-Filled Monkey Bread

Instant Chocolate Croissant

IN FRANCE the idea of bread and chocolate for breakfast is considered as normal as a bowl of cold cereal or a bagel with cream cheese is in this country. Nutella (a hazelnut-infused milk-chocolate spread) is smeared on baguettes and chocolate is tucked inside warm, flaky croissants. These folks have it right. Why wait until lunch or even dinner to anticipate a dessert that might have chocolate in it? With luck and a little planning you can start your day off right.

Many of the following recipes can be started the night before and completed just before serving, including pancake batter and doughs that, in fact, benefit from rest in the refrigerator. Some can be frozen after completion, defrosted overnight, and popped into the oven for a quick reheat.

If you have children who run out the door without breakfast, offering chocolate-filled muffins instead of cereal might make them reconsider and look much more fondly at the first meal of the day.

Chocolate Caramel Sticky Buns

Makes 16 buns

If breakfast in your house is a bowl of cereal gulped down standing at the counter trying to read the paper, pack the kids' lunch boxes, and feed the dog while you empty the dishwasher, then you certainly deserve a break. With a little planning you can make the dough for these gooey, over-the-top breakfast treats ahead of time (up to 3 days stored in the refrigerator or 3 months in the freezer), put them together the night before, let them rise in the refrigerator, then pop them in the oven and treat yourself to a superlative breakfast the next morning.

Think of these when you want something showy for brunch, as well.

For the dough

3 cups (15 ounces) all-purpose flour, plus more if necessary

3 tablespoons sugar

3 tablespoons Lora Brody's Dough Relaxer (optional) for a richer, more workable dough (see Sources, page 271)

1 tablespoon active dry yeast (*not* rapid-rise)

1½ teaspoons salt

1 extra-large egg

1 extra-large egg yolk

3 tablespoons (1.5 ounces) unsalted butter, at room temperature

For the topping

6 tablespoons (3 ounces) unsalted butter

½ cup (4 ounces) dark brown sugar, packed

½ cup (4 ounces) honey

2 cups (10 ounces) toasted pecans, coarsely chopped

For the pan preparation and filling

Unsalted butter for preparing the pan

4 tablespoons (2 ounces) unsalted butter, melted and slightly cooled

1⅔ cups (8 ounces) semisweet chocolate chips

2 tablespoons sugar mixed with ½ teaspoon ground cinnamon

(CONTINUED ON NEXT PAGE)

Bread Machine Method

Place the flour, ⅓ cup (3 ounces) of water, the sugar, dough relaxer (if using), yeast, salt, egg, egg yolk, and the 3 tablespoons of soft butter in the bread machine. Program for the dough or manual cycle. Check the dough after the first few minutes of the first knead cycle, adding flour or water as necessary to make a soft, supple ball. Allow the dough to have one rise.

Stand Mixer Method

Fit the mixer with the dough hook and place the flour, ⅓ cup (3 ounces) of water, the sugar, dough relaxer (if using), yeast, salt, egg, egg yolk, and the 3 tablespoons of soft butter in the bowl. Knead for 5 to 7 minutes, or until the dough forms a soft, supple ball. Add flour or water as necessary. Remove the dough hook, cover the bowl with plastic wrap, set it in a warm place, and allow the dough to rise until doubled in bulk.

Food Processor Method

Fit the processor with the dough blade and place the flour, ⅓ cup (3 ounces) of water, the sugar, dough relaxer (if using), yeast, salt, egg, egg yolk, and the 3 tablespoons of soft butter in the work bowl. Pulse on and off for 30 seconds to combine the ingredients into a lax dough. Process for 40 seconds, let the dough rest for 5 minutes, then process for another 30 seconds. With the cover on, allow the dough to rise in the processor until doubled in bulk. If you think your food processor is too small to handle the volume of risen dough, transfer it to a lightly oiled mixing bowl and cover with plastic wrap, and set in a warm place to rise until almost doubled in bulk.

While the dough is rising, make the topping. (This mixture will go in the bottom of the pan to bake; when the buns are inverted it will become the topping.) Place the 6 tablespoons of butter, the brown sugar, honey, and pecans in a large skillet. Bring the mixture to a boil over medium heat, stirring constantly. Reduce the heat and let the mixture simmer for 5 minutes, stirring occasionally. Set aside.

When the dough has doubled in bulk, generously butter a 10-inch springform pan. Wrap the outside of the pan with a double layer of aluminum foil to prevent oven leakage or place the pan on a heavy-duty rimmed baking sheet. Scrape the topping into the bottom of the prepared pan.

Transfer the dough to a lightly floured work surface and roll it into a rectangle that is 24 inches long and 8 inches wide. Brush the dough surface with 2 tablespoons of the melted butter. Scatter the chocolate chips over the dough, leaving a 1-inch border without chips along the long edges. Sprinkle the cinnamon sugar over the chips. Starting with a long edge, roll the dough, jelly-roll style, into a 24-inch-long roll. Try not to stretch the dough as you roll. Use a knife or a dough scraper to cut the roll into 16 equal slices. Place each slice cut-side down in the prepared pan on top of the pecan mixture. Space the slices as evenly as possible, leaving a little space between the sides of the pan and the outer circle of slices. Cover the pan with plastic wrap and allow the dough to rise in a warm place until almost doubled in bulk.

Preheat the oven to 350°F. with the rack in the center position. Brush the top surface of the rolls with the remaining 2 tablespoons of melted butter. Bake the rolls for 35 to 40 minutes, until the crust is well browned and the pecan mixture is bubbling up around the rolls. The buns should have an internal temperature of 200°F. on an instant-read thermometer. Remove the pan from the oven and carefully invert it onto a slope-sided heat-proof platter. Remove the sides of the pan and the base. Scoop any topping left in the pan onto the buns. Let them cool for 15 to 20 minutes before serving.

NOTE
To make bigger, higher buns, cut the roll into twelve 2-inch slices. In this case you will need to use a pan that is 3 inches deep.

Chocolate Chip Muffins

Makes 12 regular or 6 jumbo muffins

Chocolate for breakfast can take many forms. These muffins are inspired by similar ones served at the Green Street Café Bakery in Northampton, Massachusetts. The bakery is gone now, but the memory of those muffins lingers. They made life's problems seem a little less serious with every bite when eaten in the company of a sympathetic friend and a cup of good, strong coffee. These muffins are just a springform pan away from being a coffee cake; the choice is yours.

For the tin preparation and topping

Unsalted butter for preparing the muffin tin

$^1\!/_2$ cup (2.5 ounces) all-purpose flour

$^1\!/_3$ cup (3 ounces) light brown sugar, packed

$^1\!/_3$ cup (1.3 ounces) toasted pecans, coarsely chopped

$1^1\!/_2$ tablespoons unsweetened natural cocoa powder

3 tablespoons sweetened shredded coconut (optional)

4 tablespoons (2 ounces) unsalted butter, at room temperature

For the muffins

2 cups (10 ounces) all-purpose flour

1 teaspoon baking powder

1 teaspoon baking soda

$^1\!/_2$ teaspoon salt

1 stick (4 ounces) unsalted butter, at room temperature

1 cup (8 ounces) sugar

2 extra-large eggs

2 teaspoons vanilla extract

1 cup (8 ounces) sour cream

$1^1\!/_2$ cups (7.5 ounces) semisweet chocolate chips

Preheat the oven to 400°F. with the rack in the center position. Butter the cups of a 12-cup regular muffin tin or a 6-cup jumbo muffin tin.

To prepare the topping, in a medium bowl, stir together the flour, light brown sugar, pecans, cocoa powder, and the coconut, if using. Add the butter and mash with a fork or use your fingers, so that the butter is well distributed. Set aside.

For the muffins, sift the flour, baking powder, baking soda, and salt into a medium bowl. Place the butter and sugar in a large mixing bowl. With an electric mixer on high speed, beat them until light and fluffy, about 2 minutes. Reduce the mixer speed to medium and add the eggs, one at a time, beating well after each addition. Reduce the speed to low and mix in the vanilla. Keep the speed on low and add half the flour mixture. When that is combined, add half the sour cream. Repeat with the remaining flour mixture and sour cream. Scrape the sides of the bowl well as you mix. Mix in the chocolate chips.

Scrape the batter into the prepared muffin tin. Spoon about 1½ tablespoons of topping on each muffin, pushing the topping gently onto the surface of the batter. (You may have a little topping left over if you added the coconut.) Bake regular muffins for 20 to 22 minutes, until they have risen nicely and a tester inserted into the center of a muffin comes out clean. Jumbo muffins will bake in 28 to 30 minutes. Cool muffins in the tins for 5 minutes, then either serve them warm while the chocolate chips are still gooey, or remove them to a wire rack to cool.

VARIATION

To make Chocolate Chip Coffee Cake, butter and flour a 9½-inch springform pan. Preheat the oven to 350°F. Prepare the topping without the coconut. Scrape the batter into the prepared springform pan, add the topping, and bake for 40 minutes, or until a cake tester inserted into the center of the cake comes out clean. Let the coffee cake cool in its pan, then remove the sides of the pan and serve, preferably while the cake is still warm.

Icy Mexican Chocolate Smoothie

Makes 2 smoothies

Counting Cheryl and Bill Jamison among my dearest friends means I get to have more fun than most people. Best-selling cookbook and travel writers based in Santa Fe, they set the standard when it comes to celebrating life in all ways. To hear Bill laugh over breakfast is to hear total joy, and to hear Cheryl's wit and humor and to taste her cooking is to get about as close to heaven as this girl can. When I asked them for a chocolate recipe for this book, they suggested this smoothie recipe from their latest book, *A Real American Breakfast*; it's great for breakfast or any time you are looking for a quick chocolate fix.

1 cup (8 ounces) milk

1 cup (8 ounces) plain yogurt

2 tablespoons unsweetened natural cocoa powder

1 to 2 tablespoons light brown sugar, packed

1/2 teaspoon almond extract

1/2 teaspoon vanilla extract (optional)

1/4 teaspoon ground cinnamon

1 small banana, cut into slices

Orange slices and/or cinnamon sticks for garnish (optional)

Combine the milk, yogurt, cocoa powder, 1 tablespoon of the brown sugar, the almond extract, vanilla (if using), and cinnamon in a blender and purée until smooth. Add the sliced banana and blend again until well combined; add more brown sugar and/or almond extract, if desired. Pour into 2 tall glasses. Garnish with orange slices and/or cinnamon sticks, if desired.

VARIATION

Mocha Smoothie:
To the Icy Mexican Chocolate Smoothie add 1 teaspoon or more of instant espresso powder or granules, or up to 1/2 cup brewed coffee, and blend. For leisurely weekends, a splash of brandy or Kahlúa can add a special note to the smoothie.

Chocolate Chip Pancakes with Chocolate Butter

Makes twelve 4-inch pancakes

What could be better than pancakes for breakfast? Chocolate chip pancakes, of course! Even better is a stack of chocolate chip pancakes with a lovely pat of chocolate butter melting on top.

For the chocolate butter

1 stick (4 ounces) unsalted butter, at room temperature

1/3 cup (1.5 ounces) confectioners' sugar

2 tablespoons unsweetened Dutch-processed cocoa powder

Pinch of salt

For the pancakes

1 1/2 cups (7.5 ounces) all-purpose flour

4 teaspoons baking powder

2 tablespoons sugar

1/2 teaspoon salt

2 extra-large eggs

1 cup (8 ounces) milk

6 tablespoons (3 ounces) unsalted butter, melted

1/2 cup (2.5 ounces) semisweet mini chocolate chips

2 to 3 tablespoons unsalted butter, softened, for greasing the cooking surface

To make the chocolate butter, place the butter, confectioners' sugar, cocoa powder, and salt in the bowl of a food processor. Process until well mixed. Scrape the mixture onto a piece of plastic wrap and use the wrap to help shape the butter into a 1-inch-diameter roll. Wrap well and chill until firm, about 2 hours, or freeze for 30 minutes.

When you are ready to make the pancakes, preheat the oven to 200°F. Have ready a large baking sheet or ovenproof platter.

Sift the flour, baking powder, sugar, and salt together into a large mixing bowl. In a medium mixing bowl, stir the eggs to break them up, then stir in the milk and melted butter. Add the egg mixture to the flour mixture; stir with a wooden spoon just until the flour mixture is moistened and no large lumps remain. Stir in the chocolate chips.

Place about 1 tablespoon of the softened butter in a heavy, 12-inch skillet or griddle. Heat the skillet over medium-high heat until the butter melts and foams. Reduce the heat to medium and drop the batter into the skillet in 1/4-cup portions, leaving some space between the pancakes so that the edges will crisp. (You should be able to cook 4 pancakes at a time.) Cook the pancakes until the edges are brown and crisp, the top surfaces are covered with tiny bubbles, and the bottoms are golden. Turn the pancakes over and cook for another 2 minutes, or until the bottoms are golden brown. Transfer the pancakes in a single layer to the baking sheet or platter and place in the oven. Add more butter to the skillet as needed and continue to cook the remaining batter.

Serve the pancakes with the chocolate butter.

Sunnyside Muffins

Makes 12 regular muffins

Commercially made muffins have become so sweet, it's hard to tell if they are breakfast food or cupcakes. While I have no problem eating dessert for breakfast, I like to make sure that it does have some mildly redeeming nutritional benefit. The idea of chocolate chip–carrot muffins started out as a joke (gee, what else can we add chocolate to?), but these quickly became a new favorite. You can leave them plain and serve them as muffins, or add the white chocolate–cream cheese frosting that follows and call them cupcakes.

Unsalted butter for preparing the muffin tin, if needed

1½ cups (7.5 ounces) all-purpose flour

¾ teaspoon baking powder

¾ teaspoon baking soda

1½ teaspoons ground cinnamon

1 teaspoon ground ginger

¾ teaspoon ground nutmeg

¼ teaspoon salt

3 extra-large eggs

½ cup (4 ounces) canola oil

½ cup (4 ounces) dark brown sugar, packed

½ cup (4 ounces) granulated sugar

1½ teaspoons vanilla extract

1½ cups grated peeled carrots (about 3 medium carrots)

1 cup (4 ounces) walnuts, roughly chopped

¾ cup (4 ounces) golden raisins

1 cup (5 ounces) semisweet mini chocolate chips

Preheat the oven to 400°F. with the rack in the center position. Coat the cups of a 12-cup muffin tin with butter, or line the cups with paper or aluminum-foil muffin liners. Set aside.

To make the muffins, sift the flour, baking powder, baking soda, cinnamon, ginger, nutmeg, and salt into a medium bowl.

Place the eggs, oil, brown and granulated sugars, and the vanilla in a large mixing bowl. With an electric mixer on medium-high speed, beat the mixture until it is well combined, about 2 minutes. Reduce the mixer speed to low and add the flour mixture. Mix until all the flour is incorporated. Use a wooden spoon to stir in the carrots, walnuts, raisins, and chocolate chips. Divide the batter among the prepared muffin cups. Bake the muffins for 15 to 17 minutes, or until they have risen and a cake tester inserted into the center of the muffins comes out clean. Let the muffins cool in the tin for 10 minutes, then transfer them to a wire rack to cool completely.

The unfrosted muffins can be kept, covered, at cool room temperature for up to 1 week.

White Chocolate–Cream Cheese Frosting

Makes about 2 cups

2 ounces white chocolate, coarsely chopped

8 ounces cream cheese, at room temperature

4 tablespoons (2 ounces) unsalted butter, at room
temperature

2 cups (8 ounces) confectioners' sugar

3/4 cup (3 ounces) sweetened shredded coconut, toasted
(see page 20)

Melt the chocolate in a metal bowl set over, but not touching, a
pan of simmering water, or in a microwave-safe bowl in a
microwave oven. When it has melted, stir it well and remove
the bowl from over the water. Set aside. Place the cream
cheese and butter in a medium bowl. With an electric mixer,
beat them together on high speed for about 4 minutes, until
the mixture is light and fluffy. Reduce the mixer speed to low
and gradually mix in the confectioners' sugar. Increase the
mixer speed to medium and beat for 2 minutes. Add the
melted white chocolate and beat until well blended. Refrigerate the frosting, covered, until it is firm enough to spread on
the muffins, which are now cupcakes.

Swirl a generous amount of frosting on the cupcake tops.
Sprinkle each cupcake with about 1 tablespoon of toasted
coconut.

The frosted cupcakes can be kept, covered, at cool room temperature for up to 2 days.

Chocolate-Filled Monkey Bread

Makes one 10-inch loaf

This makes an absolutely gorgeous, fancy, showstopping loaf that's worthy of a blue ribbon at the state fair.

Making, serving, and eating this bread is more fun than a barrel of monkeys, which is one theory about the origin of its strange name. Individual chocolate-filled balls of sweet yeast dough are layered in either a loaf pan or a tube pan, then they rise into one magnificent coffee cake. To serve, you pull the balls apart instead of slicing the bread. If you eat the bread while it's still warm you get to revel in the creamy chocolate center—an experience I strongly recommend.

For the dough

4^1/$_2$ cups (22.5 ounces) all-purpose flour

^{1}/$_4$ cup (2 ounces) sugar

3 tablespoons Lora Brody's Dough Relaxer (optional), for a softer crumb and crust

1 tablespoon active dry yeast (*not* rapid-rise)

1^1/$_2$ teaspoons salt

3 extra-large eggs

1^1/$_2$ sticks (6 ounces) unsalted butter, at room temperature

To assemble the loaf or loaves

Unsalted butter for preparing the pan

25 to 30 ^{1}/$_2$-ounce pieces of milk chocolate, preferably in 1-inch squares

1 stick (4 ounces) unsalted butter, melted and cooled slightly

^{1}/$_2$ cup (4 ounces) sugar

Hand Mixing Method

Place the flour, sugar, dough relaxer (if using), yeast, salt, eggs, ^{2}/$_3$ cup (6 ounces) of warm water, and the butter in a large mixing bowl. With a wooden spoon, stir the ingredients together, then transfer the dough to a lightly floured work surface and knead until a soft, shiny ball has formed, about 10 minutes. Return the dough to the mixing bowl and cover the top with plastic wrap. Let the dough rise in a warm place until doubled in bulk. Gently deflate the dough, re-cover the bowl, and refrigerate for at least 4 hours and as long as 24 hours.

Stand Mixer Method

Place the flour, sugar, dough relaxer (if using), yeast, salt, eggs, ^{2}/$_3$ cup (6 ounces) of warm water, and the butter in the bowl of a stand mixer fitted with the dough hook. Knead on low speed until a ball starts to form, then increase the speed to medium and knead for 5 to 7 minutes, adding more flour if necessary to form a soft, supple ball of dough. Turn off the mixer, remove the dough hook, leave the dough in the bowl, and cover with plastic wrap. Let the dough rise in a warm place until doubled in bulk. Gently deflate the dough, re-cover the bowl, and refrigerate for at least 4 hours and as long as 24 hours.

Food Processor Method

Place the flour, sugar, dough relaxer (if using), yeast, salt, eggs, ^{2}/$_3$ cup (6 ounces) of warm water, and the butter in the work

(CONTINUED ON NEXT PAGE)

bowl of a food processor fitted with the dough blade. Pulse on and off for 30 seconds to combine the ingredients into a sticky mass. Process for 40 seconds, then rest for 5 minutes. Process for 30 seconds more, adding more flour if necessary to form a soft, supple ball. Transfer the dough to a lightly oiled bowl or a large resealable heavy-duty plastic bag and allow it to rise in a warm place until doubled in bulk, then gently deflate it. Cover the bowl or close the bag, pushing out the air, and refrigerate the dough for at least 4 hours and as long as 24 hours.

Bread Machine Method

Place the flour, sugar, dough relaxer (if using), yeast, salt, eggs, 2/3 cup (6 ounces) of warm water, and the butter in the bread machine. Program for dough or manual. Allow the machine to go through one knead and one rise, checking during the first few minutes of the first knead cycle to make sure the dough has formed a soft, supple ball. When the dough has doubled in bulk, transfer the dough to a lightly floured work surface, deflate it gently, and knead it gently. Place the dough in a bowl, cover it with plastic wrap, and refrigerate the dough for at least 4 hours and as long as 24 hours.

Coat a 10 × 5 × 3-inch loaf pan (or a similar pan with an 8-cup capacity, such as an angel food pan) with butter. Gently deflate the risen, refrigerated dough without kneading it—this will keep it relaxed and easy to roll. Place it on a lightly floured work surface, and roll it into a 1/4-inch-thick circle. Use a 2 1/2-inch round cookie cutter or other similar circle to cut 25 to 30 circles of dough, re-rolling and cutting any scraps. Place a piece of chocolate in the center of each circle. Paint the edges of the dough with a little water, then gently stretch and mold the dough around the chocolate to enclose it. Pinch the edges together to form a neat package. Dip each ball into the melted butter and then roll it in the sugar before placing it seam-side down in the bottom of the pan. Make two rows, then a second layer of two rows resting on the spaces between the bottom pieces. Place any leftover balls of dough on top to make a third layer. Drizzle any remaining melted butter over the balls of dough and sprinkle on any remaining sugar. Let the loaf rise, uncovered, at room temperature for 30 to 40 minutes, or until almost doubled in bulk.

Preheat the oven to 375°F. with the rack in the center position. Bake the bread for 60 minutes, or until an instant-read thermometer inserted in the center reads 200°F. It's essential to bake this bread long enough for the insides to be thoroughly cooked, so if the top starts getting too dark before the cooking time is done, tent the pan loosely with foil.

Remove the pan from the oven and cool for 10 minutes on a cake rack before unmolding. Serve warm or at room temperature. This bread is best enjoyed the day it's baked.

Instant Chocolate Croissant

Makes 1 croissant

I find that the chocolate that goes into commercially made chocolate croissants isn't nearly as good as what you might add yourself—if you were, in fact, making a chocolate croissant from scratch. The knowledge that you can easily turn a plain croissant into a very good chocolate croissant in the twinkling of an eye might never have occurred to you, in which case I've done my good deed for the day.

1 large fresh croissant

1 ounce semisweet, bittersweet, milk, or gianduja chocolate, coarsely chopped

Preheat the oven to 350°F. with the rack in the center position. Use a small, sharp knife to make a horizontal pocket in back of the croissant, cutting all the way to the front of the croissant and being careful not to cut into the narrow "arms." Stuff the chocolate pieces into the incision. Place the croissant on a baking sheet and sprinkle the top with a few drops of water. Bake for 5 minutes, or until the croissant is heated through and the chocolate has softened. Cool briefly, then serve. (Alternatively, the stuffed croissant may be heated in a microwave oven. Do not sprinkle the croissant with water. Heat at full power for 30 seconds, or until the chocolate is melted.)

Chocolate Cream Pie

Boston Cream Pie

White Chocolate–Coconut Cream Pie

Chocolate Mousse

Silky Soy Chocolate Pudding

4. Comfort Me with Chocolate

Chocolate Flan

Chocolate Tapioca Pudding Brûlée

White Chocolate–Coconut Milk Crème Brûlée

Jennie's Amazing Chocolate Rice Pudding

Whoopie Pies

Mint "Girl Scout" Cookies

Cream-Filled Chocolate Cupcakes

Tunnel of Fudge Cake

Chocolate Cherry Upside-Down Cake

Woodstocks

Chinese Noodle Nut Clusters

Coke Cake

Never-Never Cake

Satin Mocha

THOSE OF US who truly adore chocolate know that it is the ultimate comfort food. It has the power to make us feel that even though things are pretty awful at any given minute, eventually equilibrium will be restored. And when you pair chocolate with a nostalgic reminder of sweeter, simpler times, it has an even more powerful effect.

When your teenage daughter is rejected by the "in" clique, doesn't get invited to the prom, is the recipient of the "worst haircut in the world!," doesn't score what she thought she should on the SATs, or has her heart broken, invite her into the kitchen to make Whoopie Pies. She may just sit there, eyes red and swollen, a miserable look on her face, and her only communication with you may be an occasional groan of self-pity and a series of snuffles, but when they come out of the oven, rest assured she will pour herself a glass of milk and dig in.

Pudding. Even the word, homey as can be, brings comfort. It goes down easy and soothes the most ragged soul. Make that *chocolate* pudding and the world suddenly seems a better place. Make it chocolate mousse and things look downright rosy. The comfort that a chocolate dessert brings has as much to do with the taste and texture as it does with the implied love and caring that goes along with it. Even if you're both the giver and the recipient it means you've taken the time to treat yourself as you deserve to be treated, and in a spoonful or two, you'll be feeling that things are going to be just fine.

Chocolate Cream Pie

Makes 8 servings

I never had birthday cakes growing up because my dessert of choice—one that I could have eaten the other 364 days of the year too—is my mother's Chocolate Cream Pie. Not so beautiful to look at, but oh, so achingly exquisite to eat, topped with creamy, homemade chocolate pudding and massive amounts of whipped cream (never from the can!); it beats any layer cake hands down. Don't wait for a birthday to serve it.

For the crust

24 Oreo cookies, crumbled

6 tablespoons (3 ounces) unsalted butter, melted

For the filling

4 extra-large egg yolks

1 cup (8 ounces) sugar

1/4 cup (1.25 ounces) all-purpose flour

3 tablespoons (1 ounce) cornstarch

2 1/2 cups (20 ounces) whole milk

4 ounces semisweet chocolate, coarsely chopped

2 ounces unsweetened chocolate, coarsely chopped

1 tablespoon vanilla extract

For the garnish

1 cup (8 ounces) heavy cream

3 tablespoons confectioners' sugar

Grated semisweet chocolate (optional)

Preheat the oven to 350°F. with the rack in the center position.

To make the crust, place the crumbled cookies in the work bowl of a food processor fitted with the metal blade. Pulse until the cookies are quite finely ground. Drizzle the butter over the crumbs and pulse again until the crumbs are well coated. Scrape the mixture into a 9-inch pie pan. Press the crumbs over the bottom and evenly up the sides of the pan. Bake for 13 to 15 minutes, until the crust is firm to the touch. Remove the pie plate from the oven and let cool completely on a wire rack.

To make the filling, place the egg yolks, sugar, flour, and cornstarch in a medium metal bowl. Whisk them together, then add 1 or 2 tablespoons of the milk to make a paste. Pour the remaining milk into a medium saucepan and bring it almost to a bare simmer over medium-high heat. Carefully whisk the hot milk into the egg-yolk mixture. Transfer the mixture back into the saucepan and set it over medium heat. Whisk constantly until the mixture boils and thickens, scraping the sides and bottom of the pan to prevent burning. Cook for 1 full minute. Remove the pan from the heat and stir in the semisweet chocolate, unsweetened chocolate, and vanilla. Stir until the chocolate has melted and the mixture is smooth. Scrape the filling into the prepared crust. At this point the pie can be covered with plastic wrap and refrigerated for 24 hours.

Just before serving, pour the heavy cream into a chilled metal bowl and whip with chilled beaters until soft peaks form. Add the confectioners' sugar and beat for 15 seconds more. Spread the whipped cream over the pie filling. Decorate, if desired, with grated chocolate. Serve immediately.

Boston Cream Pie

Makes one 9$^1/_2$-inch cake; 8 servings

Okay, okay. It's not a pie; it's a cake, and how it came to be associated with my adopted city, where it is now "The Official Dessert," beats me. Culinary historians say that colonists baked pies and cakes in the same pan and that's where the confusion started. All I know is that it's delicious and is supposed to look a tad messy, which is always a plus as far as I'm concerned.

    A lovely chocolate custard filling oozes out between two yellow cake layers, and the whole thing is topped with a rather informal chocolate glaze that should run down the sides a bit. If you like the combination of chocolate and bananas, try adding the sliced fruit to the custard before you put on the top layer.

For the cake

Unsalted butter and flour for preparing the pan

2 cups (9.4 ounces) cake flour

2$^1/_2$ teaspoons baking powder

$^1/_2$ teaspoon salt

1$^1/_2$ sticks (6 ounces) unsalted butter, at room temperature

1$^1/_4$ cups (10 ounces) sugar

2 extra-large eggs

2 teaspoons vanilla extract

$^3/_4$ cup (6 ounces) whole milk

For the pastry cream

3 extra-large egg yolks

$^1/_4$ cup (2 ounces) sugar

3 tablespoons all-purpose flour

1 teaspoon vanilla extract

$^1/_4$ teaspoon salt

1$^1/_3$ cups (11 ounces) milk

4 ounces bittersweet chocolate, coarsely chopped

2 tablespoons (1 ounce) unsalted butter

2 tablespoons Bailey's Irish Cream liqueur

For the glaze

6 ounces bittersweet chocolate, coarsely chopped

2 tablespoons (1 ounce) unsalted butter

1 tablespoon plus 1 teaspoon light corn syrup

$^1/_4$ teaspoon salt

Preheat the oven to 350°F. with the rack in the center position. Coat the interior of a 9½-inch springform pan with butter. Line the bottom of the pan with a circle of parchment paper. Butter the parchment, then dust with flour, knocking out the excess.

To make the cake, sift the cake flour, baking powder, and salt into a medium bowl. Set aside. Place the butter and the sugar in a large mixing bowl. With an electric mixer on high speed, beat until light and fluffy. Reduce the mixer speed to medium and add the eggs, one at a time, beating well after each addition. The mixture may appear curdled, but this is okay. Beat in the vanilla. Reduce the mixer speed to low and add the flour mixture alternately with the milk, beginning and ending with the flour. Mix to combine them well. Pour and scrape the batter into the prepared pan.

Bake for 35 to 40 minutes, or until the top is golden brown, the cake has begun to pull away from the sides of the pan, and a cake tester inserted into the middle of the cake comes out clean. Transfer the cake, in its pan, to a wire rack; let it cool completely in the pan.

To make the pastry cream, whisk the egg yolks, sugar, flour, vanilla, and salt together in a medium metal bowl. Place a large sieve over another medium metal bowl and set aside. Pour the milk into a medium saucepan and bring to a simmer over medium-high heat. Whisk about half the hot milk into the egg-yolk mixture, then pour the egg-yolk mixture into the remaining hot milk. Whisk constantly over medium heat until it thickens and boils. Use the whisk to reach all over the bottom of the pan so that the pastry cream doesn't burn. Let the mixture boil for 30 seconds, then remove from the heat. Strain the mixture through the sieve; use a rubber spatula to push the pastry cream through the sieve. Add the chocolate and butter, stirring until the chocolate has melted completely, then stir in the Bailey's Irish Cream. Press a piece of plastic wrap onto the surface of the pastry cream and refrigerate until firm, about 1 hour.

To make the glaze, place the chocolate, butter, 2 tablespoons of water, the corn syrup, and salt in a medium metal bowl set over, but not touching, a pan of simmering water. Stir the mixture until the chocolate has melted and the glaze is smooth. If you are not ready to assemble the cake at this point, let the glaze cool, then refrigerate it. Reheat the glaze over simmering water, stirring, until it is smooth and pourable.

To assemble the cake, release the sides of the pan, invert the cake onto a wire rack, and remove the pan base and the parchment paper. Re-invert the cake. Use a long, serrated knife to split the cake layer in half horizontally. Place the bottom half, cut-side up, on a serving plate. Spread the pastry cream on the cake, then top with the second split layer, cut-side down. Pour the glaze onto the top of the cake; use an offset metal spatula to smooth the glaze over the top of the cake so that it spills over the sides. Don't spread it on the sides; let it spill naturally.

The cake can be kept, loosely covered, in the refrigerator for up to 3 days.

White Chocolate–Coconut Cream Pie

Makes one 9-inch pie

I've always been a huge fan of the circular, many-tiered rotating glass showcases that feature prominently in the entryway of many delis and coffee shops. Lacking one of those, a glass- or plastic-domed pie stand sitting right on the counter is a pretty good second choice. One of the things I look for when judging the quality of an eatery is the presence of coconut cream pie, which is a clear indication that someone back there cares about serving a great dessert. The version in the revolving cases usually features a creamy, light coconut custard resting in a flaky crust, all topped with mounds of whipped cream. This version improves on the former, with its cookie crust and toasted coconut garnish. And the whipped cream? It's in the filling!

For the crust

5 ounces (40 cookies) vanilla wafer cookies, crumbled

6 tablespoons (3 ounces) unsalted butter, melted

¼ cup (2 ounces) sugar

For the filling

½ cup (4 ounces) sugar

2 tablespoons cornstarch

¼ teaspoon salt

2 cups (16 ounces) heavy cream

½ cup (4 ounces) unsweetened coconut milk

3 extra-large egg yolks

4 ounces white chocolate, coarsely chopped

1 teaspoon vanilla extract

1¼ cups (5 ounces) sweetened shredded coconut, toasted (see page 20)

Preheat the oven to 350°F. with the rack in the center position. To make the crust, place the crumbled cookies in the work bowl of a food processor fitted with the metal blade. Pulse until the cookie pieces are reduced to small crumbs, then add the melted butter and sugar. Pulse until the butter is evenly dispersed among the crumbs. Press the crust mixture into the bottom and up the sides of a 9-inch pie plate. Bake the crust for 18 to 20 minutes, or until it is fragrant and light brown, and is slightly firm to the touch. Remove the plate to a wire rack to cool. Turn off the oven. (The crust can be made up to 2 days ahead. Cover well with plastic wrap and store at room temperature.)

To make the filling, combine the sugar, cornstarch, and salt in a 2-quart, heavy saucepan. Whisk the mixture together, then whisk in 1 cup of the cream and the coconut milk. Add the egg yolks and whisk vigorously to combine. Set the saucepan over medium heat. Stir or whisk constantly, making sure to reach into the corners of the pan, as the mixture thickens and comes to a boil. Remove the pan from the heat and stir or whisk the mixture very well, then return the pan to the heat. Simmer the mixture, whisking constantly, for 1 minute. Remove the custard from the heat and stir in the white chocolate and vanilla. Stir until the chocolate melts. The mixture will be very thick and slightly oily looking. Transfer the mixture to a large metal bowl, press a piece of plastic wrap onto the top, and refrigerate until cold.

When the custard is cold, beat it with an electric mixer on high speed for 1 minute, until it is smooth. Add the remaining 1 cup of heavy cream and beat on high speed until the mixture is thick and fluffy like whipped cream. Fold in 1 cup of the toasted coconut. Pour and scrape the filling into the prepared crust. Sprinkle the top with the remaining 1/4 cup toasted coconut. Refrigerate the pie until ready to serve.

The pie can be stored in the refrigerator, covered, for up to 4 days.

Chocolate Mousse

Makes 8 to 10 servings

When I was a child my parents had season tickets to the Metropolitan Opera in New York City. It was at the old Met, not the new one at Lincoln Center, that I cut my eyeteeth on four-hour performances of *Der Rosenkavalier* and *Don Giovanni.* We always ate before the opera, and if I had my way, dinner would be at La Comédie, a huge French restaurant that was located where the new Lincoln Center sits today. The best part of the meal, for me anyway, was dessert. A very formal waiter in a cutaway coat would wheel a silver cart to the table. There was your tarte tatin, your œufs à la neige, and your baba au rhum. You could have strawberries with crème anglaise, or profiteroles. My choice was always the same. I loved to watch the waiter dip the silver ladle into the swimming-pool-size bowl of chocolate mousse and dexterously maneuver it onto a dessert plate.

La Comédie is gone, as is the old Met, but memories of that mousse and that grand house live on.

This recipe is one of a few in this book that calls for raw eggs. To avoid salmonella, it's essential to use clean eggs that come from a reputable farm. It is also a recipe that is even better made with one of the butters with a high fat content. These can be found in many supermarkets and gourmet groceries.

3 cups (24 ounces) heavy cream

3 tablespoons instant espresso powder or granules

10 ounces bittersweet chocolate, coarsely chopped

2 ounces unsweetened chocolate, coarsely chopped

1 stick (4 ounces) unsalted butter, cut into 8 pieces, at room temperature

3 extra-large eggs, at room temperature, separated

1/2 cup (4 ounces) sugar

Unsweetened whipped cream, for garnish

Place the cream in a 2-quart saucepan. Set the pan over medium heat and bring the cream to a simmer. Reduce the heat and continue barely simmering the cream until it is reduced to 2 cups. Remove the cream from the heat and stir in the espresso powder.

Place both chocolates in the work bowl of a food processor fitted with the metal blade. With the motor running, pour the hot cream through the feed tube. Process until the mixture is completely smooth, about 30 seconds. With the motor running, add the butter, one piece at a time, waiting for each to be completely combined before adding the next. With the motor still running, add the egg yolks, one at a time, processing until they are incorporated.

Using very clean beaters and a very clean bowl, beat the egg whites until foamy. Add the sugar gradually, and continue beating until the mixture holds stiff peaks, but do not let them become dry. Pour the chocolate mixture into the beaten whites and fold gently but thoroughly until no whites remain.

If you want to serve the mousse in individual dishes, portion out the mousse, then cover and refrigerate the filled dishes. If you want to serve it from a serving bowl, pour and scrape it into the bowl, cover it, then refrigerate.

The mousse can be made up to 1 day ahead, but do not keep it for more than 48 hours, as it contains raw eggs. Serve with a generous dollop of unsweetened whipped cream.

Silky Soy Chocolate Pudding

Makes 6 to 8 servings (3$^1/_2$ cups)

Soy milk (now available in most supermarkets) makes a perfectly lovely base for this "health-conscious" adaptation of the classic chocolate pudding recipe. This is a light(ish) dessert, and one that soy-loving or lactose-intolerant folks will appreciate.

$^3/_4$ cup (6 ounces) sugar

$^1/_3$ cup (1 ounce) unsweetened Dutch-processed cocoa powder

$^1/_4$ cup (1 ounce) cornstarch

$^1/_4$ teaspoon salt

3 cups (24 ounces) chocolate soy milk

1$^1/_2$ teaspoons vanilla extract

In a heavy-bottomed 3-quart saucepan, combine the sugar, cocoa powder, cornstarch, and salt. Pour in the soy milk in a slow, steady stream, whisking constantly. Bring the mixture to a boil over medium-high heat, whisking constantly. When the mixture comes to a boil, lower the heat to the lowest setting, cover the saucepan, and simmer gently for 7 minutes. Remove from the heat and whisk in the vanilla.

Pour into individual serving cups or into a medium bowl. Cover the pudding with plastic wrap, pressing it directly onto the surface of the pudding. Pierce the plastic in one or two places with a sharp knife to allow steam to escape. Refrigerate for several hours, until the pudding is thoroughly chilled and set.

The pudding can be refrigerated, covered, for up to 2 days.

Chocolate Flan

Makes 6 servings

For a generation raised on crème brûlée, it will be news that there is a dessert out there that tastes just as good as—and, when made right, even better than—that now-ubiquitous standard. Flan (or caramel custard) requires you to make a simple caramelized sugar syrup before you make the custard, but the reward goes far beyond that small expenditure of time and effort. Instead of a brittle, mirror-like shell on top of the custard, you get a built-in burnt-sugar sauce. This preparation eliminates the probability of your dinner partner reaching over to tap and then consume half of the "special" part of your dessert.

   Flan is a classic Spanish dessert and most likely does not appear in this chocolate form in homes and restaurants from Barcelona to Cancún, but this version, which I think transcends its more pallid distant cousins, is eminently exportable.

Unsalted butter for preparing the ramekins

For the caramel

1¼ cups (10 ounces) sugar

For the custard

5 ounces semisweet chocolate, coarsely chopped

2 cups (16 ounces) heavy cream

1 tablespoon strong brewed coffee, or 1 teaspoon instant espresso powder or granules dissolved in 1 tablespoon hot water

1 teaspoon vanilla extract

4 extra-large egg yolks

2 tablespoons sugar

Preheat the oven to 350°F. with the rack in the center position. Coat six 4-ounce ovenproof ramekins with butter and set aside. Have ready a roasting pan large enough to hold the ramekins. Bring a large kettle or pot of water to a boil, and keep it hot while you prepare the custards.

To make the caramel, place the sugar and ⅓ cup (3 ounces) of water in a small, heavy saucepan. If you are going to use a candy thermometer, attach it to the side of the pan now. Make sure that the end of the thermometer does not touch the bottom of the pan. Set the pan over medium-low heat and stir with a wooden spoon until the sugar dissolves. Increase the heat to high and bring to a rapid boil without stirring. Reduce the heat to medium-high and use a pastry brush dipped in water or a damp paper towel to brush sugar down from the sides of the pan to prevent sugar crystals from forming. Cook, without stir-ring, until the sugar is caramelized and golden and the candy thermometer registers 320°F. (The time for making the caramel will vary; it will probably take 10 to 12 minutes.) Very carefully pour some of the caramel into the prepared ramekins, one by one, and tilt them a bit to coat the bottoms and partially up the sides, dividing it equally. Work quickly, as the caramel sets rapidly. It is not necessary to use all the caramel. Set the pre-pared ramekins aside while you prepare the custard.

To make the custard, melt the chocolate in a metal mixing bowl set over, but not touching, a pan of simmering water, or in a microwave-safe bowl in a microwave oven. Stir the chocolate with a wooden spoon as it melts. When the chocolate has melted, remove it from over the water and set it aside.

Place the cream, coffee, and vanilla in a medium saucepan. Place the pan over medium-high heat and heat the mixture until almost boiling. Remove from the heat. Place the egg yolks and sugar in a large metal mixing bowl and whisk together for about 2 minutes, until slightly thickened and lighter in color. Whisk in the melted chocolate, then gradually pour in the warm cream mixture, whisking vigorously. Strain the mixture through a sieve into a large, spouted cup or pitcher, then pour the custard into the prepared ramekins. Place the filled ramekins in the roasting pan, and place the pan in the oven. Pour in enough hot water to come halfway up the sides of the ramekins. Bake the custards for 20 to 25 minutes, or until a skewer inserted into the center comes out clean. The custards should no longer be liquid but should wobble slightly when gently shaken. Carefully transfer the ramekins from the water bath to a wire rack. Let cool completely, then refrigerate.

To unmold each custard, run a small, sharp knife around the edges of the ramekin to loosen the custard. Place a small rimmed serving plate over the top of the ramekin, hold it to the plate securely, and invert the whole thing quickly. Gently shake the ramekin, then lift it away from the plate, freeing the custard and the caramel, which will form a lovely golden reservoir around the custard. Serve immediately.

Chocolate Tapioca Pudding Brûlée

Makes 6 servings

Just watching those tall, pudding-filled dessert dishes go round and round in a slowly turning display case at the deli or diner, or seeing them lined up on the shelf over the counter along with the coconut cream pie and carrot cake, makes me want to skip the club sandwich and proceed directly to dessert. This is a particularly grown-up version of tapioca pudding that has slightly less sugar, and, of course, more chocolate, than you may be used to. In addition, it has a crisp burnt-sugar topping that elevates it to the level of high comfort food.

1 extra-large egg

1 extra-large egg white

3 tablespoons quick-cooking tapioca

7 tablespoons granulated sugar

2 cups (16 ounces) whole milk

3 ounces unsweetened chocolate, finely chopped

1/3 cup (3 ounces) dark brown sugar, packed

Have ready six 4-ounce ovenproof ramekins or dessert dishes.

Separate the whole egg; place the white in a very clean mixing bowl and put the yolk in a heavy, medium saucepan. Add the second white to the bowl with the first.

Place the tapioca, 4 tablespoons of the granulated sugar, and the milk in the saucepan with the yolk. Whisk the mixture to combine, then let rest for 5 minutes to soften the tapioca.

Place the saucepan over medium heat. Bring the mixture to a full boil, scraping the sides and bottom of the pan constantly with a wooden spoon or heat-proof spatula to prevent burning. When the mixture has come to a full boil, remove the pan from the heat. Stir in the chocolate. Stir until the chocolate has melted.

With an electric mixer with very clean beaters, beat the two egg whites on medium speed until foamy. Increase the mixer speed to high and gradually add the remaining 3 tablespoons of sugar. Continue beating until soft peaks form. Fold the beaten egg whites into the warm chocolate mixture, then divide the pudding among the ramekins or dishes. Cover with plastic wrap and refrigerate until cold.

To make the crust, place the chilled dishes of pudding on a heavy-duty baking sheet or in a roasting pan. Preheat the broiler to high with a rack positioned so that the tops of the dishes will be about 4 inches from the heating element. In a

(CONTINUED ON NEXT PAGE)

small bowl, whisk together the brown sugar and 1 to 2 tablespoons of hot water to form a smooth, thick paste. Divide the mixture evenly over the tops of the puddings, using the back of a teaspoon to spread it smooth. (If you are using wide, shallow dishes, you may need to make additional topping to cover the surfaces.)

Place the pan holding the puddings under the broiler. Watch carefully as the topping melts, then bubbles. Cook the topping only until the entire surface bubbles and begins to turn dark, 1 to 2 minutes at the most. The surface won't cook uniformly, and may have light and dark areas. Watch the puddings carefully. Remove the pan from under the heat as soon as the surface is cooked.

Refrigerate the puddings until the topping hardens—15 to 20 minutes—before serving.

White Chocolate–Coconut Milk Crème Brûlée

Makes 8 servings

During her stint as a pastry chef in one of Boston's most upscale restaurants, Lesley Abrams-Schwartz devoted herself to perfecting this recipe that tastes like a cross between heaven and a miracle. I particularly love the smooth, easy way the custard glides down.

Unsalted butter for preparing the ramekins

2¹/₂ cups (12 ounces) heavy cream

²/₃ cup (5 ounces) unsweetened coconut milk

1 vanilla bean

8 ounces white chocolate, coarsely chopped

6 extra-large egg yolks

³/₄ cup (6 ounces) sugar, plus extra for caramelizing the custard tops

Preheat the oven to 325°F. with the rack in the center position. Coat the interiors of eight 4-ounce ovenproof ramekins with a little butter. Place the ramekins in a roasting pan and set aside. Bring a large kettle or pot of water to a boil and keep it hot.

Place the cream and coconut milk in a small saucepan. Split the vanilla bean lengthwise with a small, sharp knife and scrape the seeds into the cream mixture. Add the scraped bean to the saucepan. Heat the mixture slowly until it just starts to bubble around the edges. Remove the vanilla bean and discard it. Stir in the chopped chocolate until it has melted.

Place the egg yolks and the ³/₄ cup sugar in a large metal mixing bowl. Use an electric mixer with a whisk attachment to beat the yolks with the sugar on high speed until the mixture is light yellow and thickened; it should form a ribbon when the mixer is stopped and the mixture is allowed to drip from the beaters. Slowly pour the hot cream mixture into the yolk mixture, whisking constantly until all the cream is added. Pour the custard mixture into the prepared ramekins. Pull out the oven rack and place the roasting pan with the ramekins on it. Carefully pour enough boiling water into the roasting pan to come halfway up the sides of the ramekins. Push in the rack and bake the custards for 40 to 45 minutes, or until the custards are set on the outer edges but still soft in the centers. Remove the custards from the water bath and place them on a rack to cool for 20 minutes, then refrigerate them until cold.

When ready to serve, place the custards on a rimmed baking sheet or in a roasting pan. Sprinkle the top of each custard with a generous teaspoon of sugar. Caramelize the tops either by placing them under a hot broiler for 2 to 4 minutes or with a kitchen torch until the topping bubbles and turns golden brown.

Jennie's Amazing Chocolate Rice Pudding

Makes 6 servings

There's an involuntary low moan that someone eating homemade chocolate pudding makes. In fact there are very few things in life as satisfying as a perfectly made chocolate rice pudding, served warm with a puddle of heavy cream on top. My friend Jennie Pakradooni knows her pudding and I promise that her version transcends anything you've ever eaten before.

While this down-home dessert is fine chilled, nothing beats the texture and mouth feel of warm pudding.

3 cups (24 ounces) light cream

1/3 cup (2 ounces) raw Arborio (short-grain) rice

2 1/2 tablespoons sugar

1/4 teaspoon salt

5 ounces bittersweet chocolate, finely chopped

2 tablespoons (1 ounce) unsalted butter, cut into small pieces

Heavy cream, for garnish (optional)

Place the light cream, rice, sugar, and salt in a heavy 2-quart saucepan. Place over medium-high heat and bring the mixture to a boil. Simmer the mixture vigorously, stirring frequently for 15 to 20 minutes, or until the rice is very tender (but not breaking apart) and the pudding is still soupy but thicker than heavy cream. Stir in the chopped chocolate and butter; the pudding will start to thicken.

Divide the warm pudding among six serving dishes (martini glasses work well). Serve the pudding warm, at room temperature, or chilled. Before serving, pour a few tablespoons of heavy cream over each serving, if desired.

The pudding may be prepared and put into serving dishes up to 3 days ahead; cover the servings with plastic wrap, allowing the wrap to contact the surfaces, and refrigerate. Add the heavy cream just before serving.

Whoopie Pies

Makes 9 large pies

Chances are that the reaction of the first person who bit into one of these oversize cream-filled chocolate cake sandwiches was "Whoopie!" It's not just the size, but the generosity of the sugary filling that make this an "I-wanna-be-a-kid-again" sort of dessert.

This is an adaptation of a recipe that comes from my friend and baker sublime P. J. Hamel, who puts together the King Arthur Flour Company's Baker's Catalogue and is the senior editor of its *Baking Sheet,* a bimonthly newsletter that anyone who loves to bake should check out.

For the cake

2 cups (5 ounces) all-purpose flour

3/4 cup (2.4 ounces) unsweetened natural cocoa powder

1/2 teaspoon baking powder

1 teaspoon baking soda

3/4 teaspoon salt

1 cup (8 ounces) whole milk

1 tablespoon lemon juice

2 teaspoons vanilla extract

1 stick (4 ounces) unsalted butter, at room temperature

1 cup (8 ounces) dark brown sugar, packed

1 extra-large egg

For the filling

1 stick (4 ounces) unsalted butter, at room temperature

1/2 cup (2 ounces) confectioners' sugar

2 cups Marshmallow Fluff or marshmallow cream

1 1/2 teaspoons vanilla extract

Preheat the oven to 350°F. with 2 racks close to the center. Line two heavy-duty baking sheets with parchment paper.

Sift the flour, cocoa powder, baking powder, baking soda, and salt into a medium bowl. In a small spouted cup, combine the milk, lemon juice, and vanilla. Set aside. The mixture will thicken and curdle.

Place the butter, brown sugar, and egg in a large mixing bowl. With an electric mixer, beat the mixture on medium-high speed until it is light and fluffy. Reduce the mixer speed to low and add some of the flour mixture, then pour in some of the milk mixture. Continue to add the two mixtures alternately, and mix until the batter is smooth. Use a 1/4-cup measure or ice cream scoop to drop the batter onto the prepared baking sheets, leaving 2 inches between cakes. Tap the sheets gently on the work surface to flatten the cookies slightly.

Bake the cakes for about 15 minutes, or until they are firm to the touch. Switch the sheets top to bottom and front to back after 8 minutes. Remove them from the oven and let them cool completely, on the sheets, on a wire rack.

To make the filling, place the butter, confectioners' sugar, and Marshmallow Fluff in a medium bowl. Use an electric mixer on medium-high speed to beat the mixture until blended, then stir in the vanilla. Spread half the chocolate cakes with filling, then top with the remaining cakes.

Wrap each whoopie pie tightly in plastic wrap and store at room temperature for up to 1 week.

Mint "Girl Scout" Cookies

Makes 28 cookies

Sure, it's easier to call your local Girl Scout or Brownie and order a couple dozen boxes, but unless you buy a case and store them out of sight of family members who think nothing of polishing off a box at one sitting, you can indulge your passion for these classic thin, mint- and chocolate–covered wafers only once a year. My favorite way to eat both these and the purchased kind is straight from the freezer.

A stand mixer is needed for making these cookies.

For the cookies

Unsalted butter and flour for preparing the baking sheets, if you use parchment paper as lining material

$1^1/_2$ cups (7.5 ounces) all-purpose flour

$1^1/_4$ cups (4 ounces) unsweetened Dutch-processed cocoa powder

$1/_2$ teaspoon salt

$1^1/_2$ sticks (6 ounces) unsalted butter, at room temperature

1 cup plus 2 tablespoons (11 ounces) sugar

1 extra-large egg

$1/_2$ teaspoon mint extract

For the chocolate coating

10 ounces mint chocolate chips (see Note)

$1/_3$ cup (3 ounces) solid vegetable shortening

Preheat the oven to 325°F. Place 2 oven racks as close to the center of the oven as possible. Line 2 heavy-duty baking sheets with parchment paper or silicone pan liners. If you use parchment paper, you must coat the parchment lightly with butter then dust it with flour, knocking off the excess.

Sift the flour, $3/_4$ cup of the cocoa powder, and the salt into a medium bowl. Set aside. Place the butter and sugar in a large mixing bowl. With an electric mixer on medium-high speed, beat the butter and sugar until light and fluffy. Reduce the mixer speed to low and add the egg, 1 tablespoon of water, and the mint extract. Beat on medium speed for 2 minutes, scraping down the sides of the bowl with a rubber spatula as you work. The mixture may look curdled at this point, but that is fine. Reduce the mixer speed to low and add the flour mixture, $1/_2$ cup at a time, mixing well to incorporate all the flour. The dough will be stiff; it may be necessary to raise the mixer speed, or even finish mixing the dough with a wooden spoon.

To form the cookies, place the remaining $1/_2$ cup of cocoa powder in a shallow bowl. (You may find you need a little more cocoa powder, depending on how generously you dust the dough.) Use a teaspoon to scoop up walnut-size pieces of dough. Roll them into balls with your fingers. Drop them into the cocoa and use a spoon to roll them in the cocoa to coat them completely. Place the balls on the baking sheets, leaving $1^1/_2$ inches between balls. Cover the balls of dough with deli wrap or wax paper. Use a flat-bottomed drinking glass to gently press the balls into disks that are 2$\frac{1}{2}$ inches in diameter. Try to keep the edges the same thickness as the centers so that the cookies will bake evenly.

Bake the cookies for 16 minutes, switching the sheets front to back and top to bottom halfway through the baking time. Remove the sheets from the oven, but maintain the oven temperature. Use a wide spatula to gently flip the cookies over. Return the sheets to the oven and bake for another 4 to 5 minutes, until the cookies are completely dry on both sides. Transfer the cookies to a wire rack.

Let the baking sheets cool completely, then reline with clean parchment (unbuttered) or clean silicone pan liners.

To make the coating, melt the mint chocolate chips with the shortening in a metal bowl set over, but not touching, a pan of simmering water, or in a microwave-safe bowl in a microwave oven. Stir the mixture until it is melted and smooth, then strain it through a sieve into a small, microwave-safe deep bowl. The mixture should be completely smooth, on the thin side, and free-flowing, which will make it easier to coat the cookies.

Place one cookie at a time in the melted chocolate, then use a rubber or metal spatula to flip the cookie over. Lift the coated cookie with the spatula and tap the spatula gently on the side of the pan, allowing the excess chocolate to slide back into the bowl. Transfer the cookie to the prepared cooled baking sheets. Repeat with all the cookies. Depending on how efficiently you coat the cookies and tap off the excess chocolate, you should have just enough to coat both sides of all the cookies. If the melted chocolate starts to thicken, set the bowl over the pan of hot water until it thins out again, or microwave for 10 seconds.

Let the chocolate coating harden at room temperature, then store the cookies between sheets of wax paper or deli wrap in a tightly covered container at room temperature for up to 3 weeks.

NOTE
Mint chocolate chips are available in many grocery stores and from the King Arthur Flour Company's Baker's Catalogue (see Sources, page 271).

Cream-Filled Chocolate Cupcakes

Makes 24 cupcakes

Before we knew the difference between real chocolate and any old brown dessert that had enough sugar to make it attractive to our undeveloped palates, finding one of those commercially-made cream-filled cupcakes with the distinctive white squiggle across its smooth icing surface in our lunch box was the high point of the school (or camp) day. Other kids watched with envy as we first nibbled back the icing and then poked a hole into the creamy white filling with our tongues, scooping the filling up and grinding the slightly gritty sweetness into our fluoride-protected teeth. Now we know that the shelf life on those babies is measured in half-lives; with all the additives and preservatives they contain, who in his or her right mind would offer that sort of cupcake to a kid? The rational (and much better-tasting) alternative is to make your own.

In this version, created by Susan Schwartz, the chocolate-studded cream-cheese filling oozes up from the middle when the cupcakes are baked and forms a wonderful cheesecake-like topping.

Softened unsalted butter for preparing the tins

For the filling

8 ounces cream cheese, at room temperature

$1/3$ cup (3 ounces) sugar

1 extra-large egg

Pinch of salt

1 cup (5 ounces) semisweet chocolate chips

For the cupcakes

2 cups (10 ounces) all-purpose flour

$1/2$ cup (1.6 ounces) unsweetened natural cocoa powder

1 teaspoon baking powder

$1/2$ teaspoon baking soda

$1/2$ teaspoon salt

$11/2$ sticks (6 ounces) unsalted butter, at room temperature

2 cups (16 ounces) sugar

3 extra-large eggs

$1/2$ cup (4 ounces) sour cream

$3/4$ cup (6 ounces) milk

Preheat the oven to 350°F. with the rack in the center position. Coat the cups of two 12-cup muffin tins with butter, or lightly butter only the flat top of the tin and line the cups with paper or foil liners. Set aside.

For the filling, place the cream cheese, sugar, egg, and salt in the bowl of a food processor and process until the mixture is smooth. Add the chocolate chips and pulse once, just to distribute the chips uniformly through the cream-cheese mixture.

To make the cupcakes, sift the flour, cocoa powder, baking powder, baking soda, and salt into a medium bowl. Place the butter and sugar in a large mixing bowl. With an electric mixer on medium speed, beat the butter and sugar until light and fluffy. With the mixer still on medium speed, add the eggs, one at a time, beating well after each addition. Beat in the sour cream, scraping down the sides of the bowl with a rubber spatula as you work. Reduce the mixer speed to low and add about a third of the flour mixture. Mix well, then add about half the milk, and mix well. Continue adding the flour and milk, mixing well after each addition, ending with flour.

Use a large spoon or an ice cream scoop to fill each prepared muffin cup halfway with batter. Drop about 1 tablespoon of the cream-cheese filling on the cupcake batter. Bake the cupcakes for 25 to 30 minutes, until the cakes have risen somewhat, the tops spring back when lightly pressed, and a tester inserted into a cupcake center comes out clean. Let the cupcakes cool in the pan for 10 minutes, then transfer them to a wire rack to cool completely.

The cooled cupcakes can be stored in an airtight container at room temperature for up to 3 days.

Tunnel of Fudge Cake

Makes one 9½-inch tube cake; 12 servings

This is a classic dessert that has somehow been overlooked by several generations of chocolate-loving citizens. It used to appear at every church bazaar and school bake sale. Our version boasts a tender chocolate cake outside and a super-rich creamy chocolate filling. It makes a beautiful presentation that will satisfy any chocolate cravings one might have. Once you get into the spirit of the project, try flavoring the fudge filling with all sorts of lovely things, such as raspberry, coffee, or orange. Serving it warm from the oven with a scoop of vanilla ice cream is an act of kindness that will be repaid many times over.

For the fudge filling

½ cup (4 ounces) heavy cream

8 ounces bittersweet or semisweet chocolate, coarsely chopped

For the cake

Unsalted butter and flour for preparing the pan

4 ounces unsweetened chocolate, coarsely chopped

2 ounces semisweet chocolate, coarsely chopped

2½ cups (12.5 ounces) all-purpose flour

½ cup (1.6 ounces) unsweetened cocoa powder, preferably Dutch-processed

1 teaspoon baking powder

1 teaspoon baking soda

¾ teaspoon salt

2 sticks (8 ounces) unsalted butter, at room temperature

1¼ cups (10 ounces) granulated sugar

3 extra-large eggs

1½ cups (12 ounces) buttermilk

Confectioners' sugar, for garnish

Preheat the oven to 350°F. with the rack in the center position.

To make the filling, place the heavy cream in a medium saucepan. Heat the cream over medium heat until almost boiling, then remove the pan from the heat and add the semisweet chocolate. Stir until the chocolate is melted and smooth. Let the mixture cool in the pan to room temperature. Draw a 6-inch circle on a piece of wax paper (a salad plate makes a good guide). Place the wax paper on a small, flat pan. Scoop the chocolate mixture onto the wax paper, using the circle to form a ring of chocolate approximately 1½ inches wide. Place the chocolate ring on its pan in the freezer while you prepare the cake.

To make the cake, coat the interior of a 9½-inch Bundt pan with butter. Dust with flour, knocking out the excess. Set aside. Melt the unsweetened and semisweet chocolates in a medium metal bowl set over, but not touching, a pan of simmering water, or in a microwave-safe bowl in a microwave oven. Remove the bowl from over the water.

Sift the flour, cocoa powder, baking powder, baking soda, and salt into a medium bowl. Place the butter in a large mixing bowl. With an electric mixer on medium speed, beat the butter until it is light and fluffy, about 1 minute. With the mixer still on medium speed, gradually add the granulated sugar. Add the eggs one at a time, beating well after each addition. With the mixer on low speed, add a third of the flour mixture, then a third of the buttermilk. Mix well after each addition, and continue to add the flour mixture alternately with the buttermilk. Scrape in the melted chocolate and mix until no streaks of chocolate are visible.

Scrape about 2 cups of the batter into the prepared pan. Remove the pan with the frozen chocolate ring from the freezer and turn the ring out onto the batter. Discard the wax paper. Spoon the remaining batter over the ring. Bake the cake for 45 minutes, or until the cake has risen, the surface is cracked, and the cake has just begun to pull away from the sides of the pan. Place the cake, in the pan, on a rack to cool for 20 minutes. This is important, as it allows the filling to settle. Place a serving plate over the cake pan and invert the cake onto the plate.

The cake is delicious served warm, sprinkled with confectioners' sugar. It can be stored, tightly covered, at room temperature for 3 days.

FILLING VARIATIONS

Raspberry:
Add ⅓ cup seedless raspberry jam to the cream when you heat it to make the fudge filling. Add the chocolate and proceed with the filling as directed in the recipe above.

Coffee:
Add 1 tablespoon instant espresso powder or granules to the cream when you heat it to make the fudge filling. Add the chocolate and proceed with the filling as directed in the recipe above.

Orange:
Add ¼ teaspoon orange oil to the hot cream along with the chocolate when you make the fudge filling. Proceed with the filling as directed in the recipe above.

Chocolate Cherry Upside-Down Cake

Makes one 9-inch cake; 8 servings

While I can be happy eating maraschino cherries fished out of Manhattans, I prefer the rainbow of cherries that takes center stage in this chocolate-accented version of a beloved classic: the typical candied cherries and canned pineapple are replaced with cherries of all hues, textures, and flavors. Not only is the result so much better than the original, but the flavors (including chocolate) meld and flow together in such a way that it's hard to stop after only one piece.

Serve this cake warm or even hot from the oven with a scoop of the very best quality vanilla (or Ben & Jerry's Cherry Garcia) ice cream melting alongside. If you have trouble finding Royal Ann cherries, which have a lovely golden-pink skin, use all Bing cherries to top the cake.

Unsalted butter for preparing the cake pan

1/2 cup (3 ounces) dried cherries, roughly chopped

3 tablespoons Kirsch

1/2 cup (4 ounces) light brown sugar, packed

6 tablespoons (3 ounces) unsalted butter

1 (15-ounce) can Royal Ann cherries in heavy syrup

1 (15-ounce) can Bing cherries in heavy syrup

3 extra-large eggs

3/4 cup (6 ounces) granulated sugar

1 teaspoon almond extract

1 stick (4 ounces) unsalted butter, melted and cooled

1 cup (5 ounces) all-purpose flour

1 teaspoon baking powder

1/2 teaspoon salt

1 cup (5 ounces) semisweet mini chocolate chips

Preheat the oven to 350°F. with the rack in the center position. Coat the interior of a 9-inch round cake pan with butter.

Place the dried cherries in a small bowl and pour the Kirsch over them. Set aside, stirring occasionally, until somewhat softened, about 15 minutes. Drain the cherries; discard the Kirsch.

Place the brown sugar and the 6 tablespoons of butter in a small skillet and set over medium-high heat. Cook, stirring constantly, until the sugar and butter have melted and the mixture comes to a simmer. Pour the mixture into the prepared pan. Drain the Royal Ann and Bing cherries separately; discard the syrup. Place each type of cherry on a different plate and check for pits. Place a ring of Royal Ann cherries around the outside of the brown sugar and butter mixture in the cake pan, leaving about a 1/2 inch between cherries. Place a ring of Bing cherries inside the first ring, and continue to form rings, alternating the light-colored rings with the dark, until you reach the center.

To make the cake batter, place the eggs in a medium mixing bowl. Add the granulated sugar and almond extract. Beat with an electric mixer on medium-high speed until the mixture is light and fluffy and doubled in volume, about 4 minutes. Scrape down the sides of the bowl with a rubber spatula as you work. Reduce the mixer speed to low and mix in the melted butter until it is just combined. Place a sieve over the

(CONTINUED ON NEXT PAGE)

mixing bowl and sift the flour, baking powder, and salt onto the batter. Fold the flour into the batter, then fold in the drained dried cherries and the chocolate chips. Scrape the batter into the prepared pan.

Bake for 30 to 35 minutes, or until the edges of the cake are bubbling, the top is brown and risen, and a cake tester inserted into the middle of the batter comes out dry. Transfer the cake to a wire rack and let it rest in the pan for 10 minutes. Place a serving plate over the cake pan and carefully invert the cake onto the plate. If any cherries have stuck, place them back on the cake.

The cake is best eaten warm from the oven, but it can be cooled and stored, covered, at room temperature, for up to 3 days.

Woodstocks

Makes 12 large bars or 16 smaller squares

I was all set to go to Woodstock until my husband pointed out that the projected due date for our first child was that same weekend. I was there in spirit, however, and the images of the constant rain and resultant mud made me just as happy to have spent the weekend doing the Lamaze thing in the hospital. The twenty-fifth anniversary of Woodstock was pretty much a bust except for the fact that it inspired this crunchy granola–ice cream dessert. If you were one of those kids who loved to play with your ice cream, turning it into soup before you slurped it down, then making these will project you back in time.

Nutella is a milk chocolate–hazelnut spread that is now available in many supermarkets and most Italian specialty stores.

1 (13-ounce) jar Nutella

1 (12-ounce) jar creamy peanut butter

1 pound (approximately 4 cups) granola of your choice

1 quart best-quality chocolate ice cream, softened

NOTE
To avoid scratching your metal pan when cutting the bars, use a dough scraper (bench knife) to cut straight down to the bottom of the pan. You may also make the recipe in a disposable foil pan.

Soften the Nutella and peanut butter: Remove the lids and place the jars in the microwave oven on high for 30 to 40 seconds each. Place the granola in a large mixing bowl. Scrape the Nutella and peanut butter over the granola and mix well with a wooden spoon or large rubber spatula until the granola is completely coated.

Scrape half the mixture into a 9-inch square metal pan and press it firmly and evenly into the pan using your fingers or a rubber spatula. Spoon the softened ice cream over the granola mixture and level it with a rubber spatula. If the ice cream seems too soft to support the top crust at this point, place the pan in the freezer for 15 to 20 minutes to firm the ice cream. Spoon the remaining granola mixture onto the ice cream and press it evenly over the ice cream. Cover the pan with aluminum foil and freeze for at least 1 hour, until the ice cream is completely frozen.

To serve, cut into twelve $2^{1}/_{4} \times 3$-inch bars, or into sixteen $2^{1}/_{4}$-inch squares.

Chinese Noodle Nut Clusters

Makes about 30 clusters

The combination of salty, sweet, crunchy, and smooth gives these confections a special place in my heart. That, added to the fact that they made an appearance at every bridge and mahjongg game my mother ever hosted, elevates their status to serious nostalgia food. They are fun to make (especially for kids) and are a great gift, since everyone seems to love them. "Betcha can't eat just one" will take on a whole new dimension when you are facing a plateful.

Using chocolate chips here instead of bar or block chocolate makes a more viscous "batter," which makes the clusters easier to form. This chocolate does not have to be tempered. You can find cans of Chinese chow-mein noodles in the Asian food section of the supermarket. The ones you want are cooked and ready to eat like crackers.

2 cups (10 ounces) semisweet chocolate chips

2 tablespoons (1 ounce) unsalted butter

2 cups (about 4 ounces) Chinese chow-mein noodles, broken into 1/2-inch to 1-inch pieces (vary the sizes)

1 1/4 cups (5 ounces) dry-roasted salted peanuts, shaken in a sieve to remove excess salt

Line a baking sheet with wax paper, parchment paper, or aluminum foil. Set aside.

Melt the chocolate chips and butter together in a metal bowl set over, but not touching, a pan of simmering water, or in a microwave-safe bowl in a microwave oven. Stir the mixture until it is smooth. In a large mixing bowl, toss the noodles and peanuts together. Pour the melted chocolate mixture over them. Working quickly before the chocolate hardens, use a rubber spatula to mix and coat the noodles and nuts with chocolate.

Use 2 soup spoons (or teaspoons, depending on how large you want your clusters) to scoop up portions of the mixture. Set the clusters on the prepared sheet. Set the baking sheet in a cool place (not in the refrigerator) until the chocolate hardens.

The clusters can be stored in an airtight container at room temperature for up to 1 month.

Coke Cake

Makes one 9 × 13-inch cake; 12 servings

I get a bad feeling in my stomach when just as I've delivered a forkful of chocolate cake to my mouth, I hear the fateful words, "Bet you can't guess what's in it." Oh no! Please, God, not zucchini, not beets, not three tablespoons of red food coloring! I felt almost the same way when someone suggested that I check out this chocolate cake made with Coca-Cola. But upon reading the ingredient list I didn't see anything so weird that I wouldn't eat on its own, so I gave the recipe a whirl. I was delighted with the results.

If you're from the South you probably know and perhaps love this cake. But if you don't know from grits for breakfast, you're just going to have to make that leap of faith and try it. Chances are good that you'll like it.

This is the kind of cake that guys like—sweet and moist with a great big in-your-face chocolate impact. Think of it at Super Bowl time when folks who espouse macrobiotic diets need an energy boost to get them through halftime.

For the cake

Unsalted butter and flour for preparing the pan

2 sticks (8 ounces) unsalted butter

1 cup (8 ounces) Coca-Cola (not diet, but the caffeine-free version is okay)

3/4 cup (1.5 ounces) marshmallows

2 ounces unsweetened chocolate, coarsely chopped

2 1/3 cups (11.65 ounces) all-purpose flour

3/4 cup (2.4 ounces) unsweetened Dutch-processed cocoa powder

1 1/2 teaspoons baking powder

1 teaspoon baking soda

1/2 teaspoon salt

2 cups (16 ounces) sugar

1/2 cup (4 ounces) vegetable oil

2 teaspoons vanilla extract

3 extra-large eggs

3/4 cup (6 ounces) buttermilk

For the frosting

2 ounces unsweetened chocolate, coarsely chopped

1 stick (4 ounces) unsalted butter, at room temperature

1/4 cup (2 ounces) Coca-Cola

1 teaspoon vanilla extract

2/3 cup (2 ounces) unsweetened Dutch-processed cocoa powder

2 1/2 cups (10 ounces) confectioners' sugar

To make the cake, preheat the oven to 350°F. with the rack in the center position. Coat the interior of a 9×13-inch baking pan with butter. Dust with flour, knocking out the excess.

Place the butter and cola in a medium saucepan and simmer over medium heat until the butter is melted. Add the marshmallows, reduce the heat to low, and stir until the marshmallows are melted. Add the chocolate and stir over low heat until the chocolate is melted. Set the mixture aside to cool for about 10 minutes.

Meanwhile, sift the flour, cocoa powder, baking powder, baking soda, and salt into a medium mixing bowl. Place the sugar, oil, and vanilla in a large mixing bowl. Beat well with an electric mixer on medium speed. Add the eggs, one at a time, beating well after each addition. Scrape down the sides of the bowl as you work. Add the cooled chocolate mixture and beat on low speed until combined. Add half the flour mixture, then the buttermilk, then the rest of the flour mixture; mix well after each addition.

Pour and scrape the batter into the prepared pan. Bake for 40 to 45 minutes, until a cake tester inserted into the center of the cake comes out clean. Remove the pan to a rack and let the cake cool completely in the pan.

To make the frosting, melt the unsweetened chocolate in a metal bowl set over, but not touching, a pan of simmering water, or in a microwave-safe bowl in a microwave oven. Remove the bowl from over the water and let the chocolate cool slightly. Place the butter, cola, and vanilla in the large bowl of an electric mixer. With the mixer on low speed beat the mixture until blended. Increase the mixer speed to medium-high and gradually add the cocoa powder and then the melted chocolate. Beat in the confectioners' sugar, scraping the bowl well as you work. Mix until the sugar is completely mixed in and the frosting is smooth and shiny. Immediately spread the frosting on the cooled cake. (Alternatively, the frosting can be made in a food processor. Melt the chocolate, then place all the frosting ingredients in the work bowl of a food processor. Pulse until the frosting is thickened, shiny, and smooth.)

The unfrosted cake can be stored, wrapped airtight in plastic wrap, at room temperature for 24 hours, refrigerated for 2 days, or frozen for up to 3 months. The frosted cake can be stored in a cake saver at room temperature for up to 3 days.

Never-Never Cake

Makes one 10 × 14-inch or 9 × 13-inch sheet cake; can be made as a two-layer cake (see below)

The whole time I was making this cake, "never" is the word I kept muttering to myself. Our contractor would *never* finish the house we were building. The plumber would *never* show up to fix the leak from the washing machine that was dripping through my brand-new kitchen ceiling. I was *never* going to figure out how to make the kind of layer cake I had been dreaming about.

Tired of yelling at the contractor, I simply took my aggression out on the cake, and started throwing ingredients into a bowl, barely taking the time to measure them. All the while I continued to mutter, "never, never, never"; there was no way this was going to work and I'd end up throwing the whole mess out. I realized I hadn't found the right size pan to bake it in. A new neighbor had graciously brought over a lasagne the night before and her large Pyrex pan was sitting there waiting to be returned, so that's what I used. Then I went to put the thing in the oven and realized I had forgotten to preheat it. Well, it wasn't going to work anyway, so why not a cold oven?

I poured myself a shot of brandy (it was nearly evening by now) and sat down to listen to the sound of water dripping onto my just-installed kitchen counter, feeling completely sorry for myself. After a while a very lovely and very chocolaty aroma began to flutter, then waft, out of the oven. It was my never-never cake, rising so beautifully, so perfectly—a true baking miracle if ever there was one.

I made this cake in a very large (10 × 14 × 2-inch) pan. You can use a slightly smaller pan (no less than 13 × 9 × 2-inch) to make a higher cake, but be sure to increase the baking time by 5 to 10 minutes. The frosting is best made in a food processor, and it should be made just before you are ready to frost the cooled cake.

For the cake

Unsalted butter and flour for preparing the pan

2 extra-large eggs

2 tablespoons (1 ounce) fresh lemon juice

1 tablespoon vanilla extract

Approximately 1²/₃ cups (13 ounces) whole milk

3¹/₂ cups (17.5 ounces) all-purpose flour

1³/₄ cups (14 ounces) sugar

²/₃ cup (2 ounces) unsweetened natural cocoa powder

1 teaspoon baking soda

¹/₄ teaspoon salt

2 sticks (8 ounces) unsalted butter, melted and slightly cooled

For the frosting

9 ounces milk chocolate, coarsely chopped

4 tablespoons (2 ounces) unsalted butter, at room temperature

1 pound (4 cups) confectioners' sugar, sifted

1 cup (8 ounces) sour cream

Coat the interior of a 10 × 14 × 2-inch baking pan (preferably ovenproof glass) with butter. Line the bottom with parchment paper, then butter the parchment. Dust the pan with flour, knocking out the excess. Position a rack in the center of the oven, but do not turn the oven on.

Place the eggs, lemon juice, and vanilla in a 2-cup glass measuring cup. Break the eggs up with a fork, then pour in enough milk so that the mixture measures 2 cups. The mixture will curdle. Set aside. In a large mixing bowl, combine the flour, sugar, cocoa powder, baking soda, and salt. Whisk them together well. Pour in the milk mixture and then the melted butter. Whisk the batter just until it is smooth and lump-free. Do not overbeat the batter, as it will make the cake tough. Pour and scrape the batter into the prepared pan; smooth the top with a rubber spatula. Place the pan in the cold oven. Set the oven to 350°F. Bake for 40 minutes (bake for 45 to 50 minutes if you are using a 9 × 13-inch pan), or until a cake tester inserted into the center of the cake comes out dry. Cool the cake in the pan for 15 minutes, then turn it out onto a wire rack to cool completely before frosting. (If you wish to make a two-layer cake, cut the cooled cake in half, parallel to the short sides, then trim the uncut ends with a long, serrated knife to even up the layers.)

When you are ready to frost the cake, make the frosting. Melt the chocolate in a metal bowl set over, but not touching, a pan of simmering water, or in a microwave-safe bowl in a microwave oven. Stir the chocolate until it is smooth. Place the butter and confectioners' sugar in the work bowl of a food processor; pulse for 30 seconds. The mixture will be granular and powdery. Add the melted chocolate and pulse for 30 seconds more. The mixture will still appear granular and powdery. Add the sour cream and process until smooth, about 30 seconds, stopping to scrape down the sides of the work bowl several times. Spread the frosting (there will be a generous amount) over the top and sides of a one-layer cake. For a two-layer cake, spread one third of the frosting on the top of the first layer, top it with the second layer, and then frost the top and sides.

The cake can be stored at room temperature in a cake saver or wrapped in plastic wrap for up to 3 days.

Satin Mocha

Makes 16 servings

This seductive combination of ricotta cheese, bittersweet chocolate, almonds, and cream is swoon-inducing. The presentation is splendid, and this is one dessert that will feed a crowd. If you want to make a big splash for a lot of people, this is the dessert for you. Of course, they have to be the sort of people who don't order decaf after sunset, since there's a serious caffeine hit in the filling.

For the crust

Unsalted butter for preparing the pan

8 ounces amaretti cookies, crumbled if large

4 ounces (18 wafers) chocolate wafers, crumbled

1/2 cup (3 ounces) slivered almonds

1 stick (8 ounces) unsalted butter, melted

For the filling and garnish

3 1/2 teaspoons unflavored gelatin

1/4 cup instant espresso powder or granules dissolved in 1 cup (8 ounces) boiling water, or 1 cup (8 ounces) brewed espresso (see Note)

9 ounces bittersweet chocolate, coarsely chopped

2/3 cup (5.5 ounces) plus 2 tablespoons sugar

2 pounds (32 ounces) whole-milk ricotta cheese

2 cups (16 ounces) heavy cream

1 teaspoon almond extract

Reserved crumbs from crust recipe

Preheat the oven to 400°F. with the rack in the center position. Coat a 9- or 10-inch springform pan with butter.

To make the crust, place the amaretti cookies and the chocolate wafer pieces in the work bowl of a food processor fitted with the metal blade. Pulse to reduce the mixture to crumbs. Add the almonds and process until the almonds are ground, about 30 seconds. Remove 1/3 cup of this crumb mixture for garnish; set aside. Add the butter to the mixture in the food processor and process until the butter is thoroughly incorporated, about 20 seconds. Transfer the butter and crumb mixture to the prepared pan and use your fingers to pat it into the bottom and three-quarters of the way up the sides of the pan. Bake the crust for 5 minutes. Transfer the pan to a wire rack and let cool completely.

To make the filling, place 3 tablespoons plus 1 teaspoon of cold water in a small bowl and sprinkle the gelatin over the top. Allow it to dissolve without stirring.

Place the dissolved espresso powder mixture or the brewed espresso in a small saucepan. Set the pan over low heat. Add the chopped chocolate and whisk until smooth. Remove the pan from the heat and whisk in the dissolved gelatin and the 2/3 cup sugar. Let the mixture cool to room temperature; do not refrigerate. Place the ricotta in the cleaned food processor and process for 30 seconds. With the motor running, add the chocolate mixture through the feed tube; pause to scrape down the sides of the work bowl after 15 seconds. Process for 15 to 20 seconds more, until the mixture is completely combined.

In a large chilled bowl with chilled beaters, beat 1 cup of the heavy cream until stiff peaks form. Fold in the ricotta mixture gently and thoroughly. Pour and scrape the ricotta filling into the cooled crust and smooth the top with a rubber spatula. Refrigerate the cake, uncovered, for at least 4 hours, then cover with foil. (It is important to store anything chocolate far away from strong-smelling foods in the refrigerator.)

Just before serving, run a small sharp knife around the inside of the springform pan. Remove the sides. Make the garnish by beating the remaining cup of heavy cream with the remaining 2 tablespoons of sugar and the almond extract; beat until stiff peaks form. Transfer the whipped cream to a piping bag fitted with a medium star tip. Pipe rosettes of whipped cream around the rim of the cake, then sprinkle the cake with the reserved crumb mixture.

NOTE
You may make a reduced-caffeine version of this recipe by using 1 cup brewed decaf espresso.

Best Birthday Cake

Dominos

Chocolate Birthday Rolls

Milk Chocolate Cheesecake Cups with Kahlúa

5. Celebrations, Holidays, and Other Special Occasions for Eating Chocolate

White Chocolate–Heath Bar Cheesecake

Reverse Marble Cake

Marble Milano Cake

Rocky Road Cake

Chocolate Cherry Torte

Chocolate Hazelnut Torte

Chocolate-Pecan Torte with Chocolate Espresso Glaze

Mint Chocolate–Mascarpone Striped Cake

Chocolate Ice Cream Roll

Chocolate Refrigerator Cake

Black and White Semifreddo with Strawberry Sauce

IN OUR FAMILY I try to make sure that every joyous event is marked with a special chocolate dessert. Sometimes my best intentions run amok. The winter that our son Max had his bar mitzvah, we threw a big dessert open-house for family, friends, and neighbors. It took me almost as much time and energy to bake for the party as it had taken Max to prepare for his big day. During the party the house pulsed with activity. Kids ran around on a sugar high, adults balanced a dessert-laden dish in one hand and a champagne glass in the other. The jewel-in-the-crown of the dessert table was an eight-foot-long ice-cream-filled chocolate jelly roll made in sections laid end to end to form a long log. In milk chocolate icing I had written the name of each guest. Since the cake was filled with ice cream before it was frosted, I had to do the writing outside on the deck in the sub-zero-degree weather. The cake was safely stashed in the freezer until it came time to serve it. What a sight it made with candles twinkling down the eight-foot length. The guests oohed and ahhed and pushed close to the table, each trying to find his or her own name. My handwriting is terrible to begin with; standing out in sub-freezing weather, speed-writing in frosting on an ice-cream-filled cake made it even worse. Starting at one end, I began slicing fast, trying to get the cake served before it dissolved into a puddle.

"Oh, this is Jeremy's piece," wailed the little girl in the black velvet dress as she pushed the plate back toward me. "I want the piece that says 'Rebecca.'" She wasn't the only one. Every guest, it seemed, wanted to consume his or her own name, as if eating someone else's constituted a form of cannibalism. Even the adults gave me a hard time. I ended up doing a slow jig around the table, cutting into the center of one log so that Paul could eat the piece with his name, then down to the other end of the table so that Alison could eat the piece with hers. By the time Grandma Ida got her piece she spooned it up from a bowl, but she was thrilled because it was the piece with her name on it.

What's the moral here? Beats me; I'm finished with bar mitzvahs, and when it comes time to make Max's wedding cake it will be made without ice cream and decorated with something other than the guests' names.

Best Birthday Cake

Makes one 9-inch layer cake; 12 servings

Remember when you were a kid, going to birthday parties and being jammed around a crinkly theme-paper-covered dining room table, watching as the mom cut the cake, wishing with all your might (or asking right out loud if you were nervy enough) to get the piece with the biggest frosting flower? Remember how you looked forward to your own birthday so you could get one of the prime pieces? And then when you did get it, remember the greasy feeling of the frosting as it hit your mouth, and the crunch of the sugar as it reached your molars? Remember being disappointed that pink was not a flavor and that the red flower tasted exactly the same as the blue and yellow flowers?

I actually loved that frosting and even the soft white cake it rested on, until I grew up and developed a modicum of culinary discretion. Now my birthday cake of choice is chocolate, and the icing is made from ingredients that taste just as good on their own (well, maybe not the sugar).

This is a beautiful cake—you'll be proud to bring it to the table. So get out the camera and remember to snap before you cut.

For the cake

Unsalted butter and flour for preparing the cake pans

2¼ cups (18 ounces) sugar

1¾ cups (8.25 ounces) cake flour (*not* self-rising flour)

1¼ cups (4 ounces) unsweetened natural cocoa powder

2¼ teaspoons baking soda

1¼ teaspoons baking powder

½ teaspoon salt

3 extra-large eggs

1 stick (4 ounces) unsalted butter, melted and cooled

1 tablespoon vanilla extract

1½ cups (12 ounces) buttermilk

1 teaspoon instant espresso powder or granules, dissolved in ¾ cup boiling water, cooled

For the frosting

4 ounces white chocolate, coarsely chopped

16 ounces (1 pound) cream cheese, at room temperature

1 stick (4 ounces) unsalted butter, at room temperature

4 cups (1 pound) confectioners' sugar

Semisweet chocolate shavings (optional)

(CONTINUED ON NEXT PAGE)

Preheat the oven to 350°F. with the rack in the center position. Coat the interiors of two 9-inch round cake pans with butter. Line each pan with a 9-inch circle of parchment. Lightly butter the parchment. Dust with flour, knocking out the excess.

In a large mixing bowl, sift together the sugar, cake flour, cocoa powder, baking soda, baking powder, and salt. Set aside. Place the eggs in a medium mixing bowl. With an electric mixer on medium speed, beat the eggs well, then beat in the melted butter and vanilla. With the mixer still on medium speed, beat in the buttermilk and espresso, and beat only until they are combined. The mixture will appear curdled. Scrape the liquid mixture into the flour mixture, and beat on medium speed just until all traces of the flour mixture disappear. Scrape down the bowl with a rubber spatula as you mix. Pour and scrape the batter into the prepared pans, dividing it equally.

Bake the cakes for 30 to 35 minutes, or until the cakes pull away from the sides of the pans and a cake tester inserted into the center of the cakes comes out clean. Transfer the cake pans to a wire rack and cool the cakes in the pans for 20 minutes. Invert the cakes onto another rack, remove the cake pans and parchment, then invert the layers again so that they are right side up. Allow them to cool completely before frosting.

To make the frosting, melt the white chocolate in a metal bowl set over, but not touching, a pan of simmering water, or in a microwave-safe bowl in a microwave oven. When the chocolate has melted, remove the bowl from over the water and let the chocolate cool while you continue with the frosting. Place the cream cheese and butter in a large mixing bowl. With an electric mixer, beat them together on high speed for about 4 minutes, or until the mixture is light and fluffy. Reduce the mixer speed to low and gradually mix in the confectioners' sugar. Increase the mixer speed to medium and beat for 2 minutes. Add the melted white chocolate and beat until well blended. Refrigerate the frosting, covered, until it is firm enough to spread on the cakes.

When you are ready to frost the cakes, use a long, serrated knife to split each cake layer in half horizontally. Place the bottom half of one split layer on a serving plate, cut-side up. Use an offset spatula or kitchen knife to spread about 3/4 cup of frosting on the exposed surface. Frosting the cut surface will loosen many chocolate crumbs, but don't worry about that. Top this layer with its other half, smooth-side up. Frost this layer the way you did the first, then stack and frost both halves of the second split layer in the same way, ending with the smooth layer up. Frost the top and sides. Scatter semisweet chocolate shavings on the top of the cake, if desired.

The cake can be made 1 day ahead. Refrigerate the cake, in a cake saver. Let the cake sit at room temperature for 1 hour before serving.

Dominos

Makes about 48 cookies

A great chocolate chunk cookie can make a bad day much, much better. It can make the world seem a nicer place. It can bring a smile to the face of the meanest curmudgeon. I've even seen it mend a broken heart. In this particular, very excellent chocolate chunk cookie, the ratio of batter to "stuff" (white chocolate chips and pecans) is perfect—just enough to hold the cookie together and just enough to melt in your mouth as you eat these warm from the oven.

8 ounces bittersweet chocolate, chopped

2 tablespoons (1 ounce) unsalted butter

3 tablespoons all-purpose flour

1/4 teaspoon baking powder

Pinch of salt

2 extra-large eggs

2/3 cup (5 ounces) sugar

2 teaspoons vanilla extract

1 1/2 cups (9 ounces) white chocolate chips

2 cups (8 ounces) pecans, coarsely chopped

Preheat the oven to 350°F. with the rack in the center position. Line 2 heavy-duty baking sheets with parchment paper, silicone pan liners, or aluminum foil.

Melt the bittersweet chocolate and butter in a medum metal bowl set over, but not touching, a pan of simmering water, or in a microwave-safe bowl in a microwave oven.

Sift the flour, baking powder, and salt into a small bowl. Place the eggs, sugar, and vanilla in a large mixing bowl or the bowl of an electric mixer. Beat them together on high speed until thick and light in color, about 2 minutes. Reduce the speed to low and add the melted chocolate mixture and the flour mixture, mixing only until incorporated. Use a rubber spatula or a wooden spoon to stir in the white chocolate chips and pecans.

Use a tablespoon to drop rounded mounds of batter onto the baking sheets, spacing them about 1 inch apart; these cookies do not spread very much. Bake the cookies, one sheet at a time, for 12 minutes, or until the tops look shiny and slightly cracked. The cookies will remain quite wet in the centers. Remove the baking sheets to cooling racks and let the cookies cool completely on the sheets, then carefully peel them from the pan lining material.

The cookies should cool for at least 15 minutes before eating, since they tend to fall apart if they are too warm when handled. Store at room temperature in an airtight container for up to 2 weeks .

Chocolate Birthday Rolls

Makes 16 rolls

My friend Susan Schwartz wears many hats: she's a lawyer, she's a mom with four school-age children, and she has time and energy to develop and test recipes for me.

This is a recipe she makes for all of her children's birthdays, at their request. She says, "As far as Perry, Jeffrey, Jamie, and Joshua are concerned, birthdays and half-birthdays just can't start without these rolls for breakfast." Now, in my opinion anyone lucky enough to have a mother who celebrates half-birthdays is a lucky child indeed. "These are very easy to make the night before the celebration," says Susan. "They take about forty minutes to put together and shape (including a twenty-minute rest for the dough), then I put the formed rolls in the refrigerator overnight. On the big morning, I just take the rolls out of the refrigerator and bake them. These also freeze beautifully after they are baked. The hardest thing about making these is waiting until the chocolate inside is cool enough not to burn your mouth!"

For the rolls

1¹⁄₃ cups (11 ounces) whole or low-fat milk, brought to a simmer and then cooled to 105° to 115°F.

¹⁄₄ cup (2 ounces) sugar

4 tablespoons (2 ounces) unsalted butter, melted

1 extra-large egg

1 teaspoon vanilla extract

1 teaspoon salt

1 tablespoon (1 package) active dry yeast

2¹⁄₂ to 3 cups (12.5 to 15 ounces) all-purpose flour

1¹⁄₂ cups (8 ounces) semisweet chocolate chips

For the egg wash and topping

1 extra-large egg beaten with 1 tablespoon cream or milk

1-ounce chunk of milk or dark chocolate for grating over the rolls

Line a baking sheet with a silicone pan liner, parchment paper, or buttered aluminum foil.

To make the rolls, place the milk, sugar, butter, egg, vanilla, salt, yeast, and 1 cup of the flour in the bowl of an electric mixer fitted with the paddle attachment (which works better than a dough hook in this recipe) or in a large mixing bowl. Beat on medium speed or stir vigorously with a wooden spoon for 1 minute. Add ¹⁄₂ cup more of the flour, then beat or stir again for 1 minute. Add the remaining flour, ¹⁄₄ cup at a time, until you form a soft and supple dough. Turn the dough onto a lightly floured surface and knead until smooth and elastic, 1 to 2 minutes. Cover the dough with a clean towel and let rest for 20 minutes.

Divide the dough in half. Leave one half of the dough covered by the towel; roll the other into a 12-inch circle. With a sharp knife or a pizza wheel, cut the dough circle into 8 equal wedges. Place a generous line of chips along the wide end of each wedge. Starting from the wide end, roll each dough wedge all the way to the narrow end, so that the chocolate is enclosed. Repeat with the remaining wedges. Roll out the second portion of dough and make 8 more rolls. Place the rolls about 2 inches apart on the prepared baking sheet.

(CONTINUED ON NEXT PAGE)

If you are going to bake the rolls within the hour, cover them loosely with plastic wrap and let them rise for 30 minutes at room temperature. (If you are going to bake the rolls the next day, place the covered rolls in the refrigerator to rise overnight. Remove them from the refrigerator 30 minutes before baking.)

Preheat the oven to 375°F. with the rack in the center position. Just before placing the rolls in the oven, brush generously with the egg wash. Bake the rolls for about 12 minutes, or until they are golden and browned on the top and bottom. Transfer the baked rolls to a wire rack, grate chocolate on top of each one, and allow them to cool for at least 10 minutes before eating.

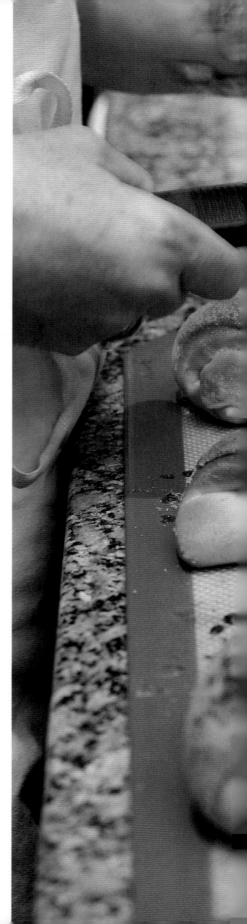

Milk Chocolate Cheesecake Cups with Kahlúa

Makes 12 cheesecake cups

You'll never look at cupcakes the same way once you've bitten into one of these chocolate-crumb-crusted mini chocolate cheesecakes. They are rich, rich, rich, so consider either skipping dinner altogether, sharing one with a friend, or looking around for a doggie bag.

While the recipe calls for coffee liqueur, brewed espresso may be used instead. These cakes freeze beautifully (directions follow).

For the crust

Nonstick vegetable cooking spray for coating foil cup liners

4½ ounces (about 20 wafers) chocolate wafers, crumbled

4 tablespoons (2 ounces) unsalted butter, at room temperature

For the cheesecake filling

8 ounces milk chocolate, coarsely chopped

16 ounces (1 pound) cream cheese, at room temperature

½ cup (4 ounces) light brown sugar, packed

2 extra-large eggs

¼ cup (2 ounces) Kahlúa or other coffee-flavored liqueur, ¼ cup brewed espresso, or 2 teaspoons instant espresso powder or granules dissolved in ¼ cup boiling water

Unsweetened natural cocoa powder or confectioners' sugar, for garnish (optional)

Preheat the oven to 350°F. with the rack in the center position. Coat twelve 2½-inch foil baking cups with cooking spray. Place the oiled baking cups in a 12-cup muffin tin. Select a baking dish large enough to hold the muffin tin, and have ready a large pot of water that has been brought to a boil.

To make the crust, place the crumbled chocolate wafers in the bowl of a food processor and pulse until the wafers form fine crumbs, about 30 seconds. Place the crumbs in a medium mixing bowl and add the butter. Use a wooden spoon or a rubber spatula to combine the crumbs and butter evenly. Place a generous 2 tablespoons of crumbs into each foil baking cup and press the crumbs firmly into the bottoms of the cups.

To make the filling, melt the chocolate in a medium metal bowl set over, but not touching, a pan of gently simmering water, or in a microwave-safe bowl in a microwave oven. Stir the chocolate with a wooden spoon as it melts. Remove the bowl from over the water and set aside.

Place the cream cheese and brown sugar in the bowl of an electric mixer. Beat on medium speed until smooth. Add the eggs, Kahlúa or espresso, and the melted chocolate; continue to beat on medium speed until well combined. Scrape down the sides of the bowl with a rubber spatula several times as you work. Divide the mixture among the prepared baking cups; the cups will be quite full. Place the muffin tin in the baking dish and place the dish in the oven. Carefully pour in enough hot water to come halfway up the sides of the muffin tin. Bake for about 20 minutes, or until the tops look dry, the cakes have puffed, and a cake tester inserted into the center of a cake has a little moist batter on it. Remove the muffin tin from the baking dish and place it on a wire rack. Cool for 30 minutes.

You may leave the cheesecakes at room temperature for up to 6 hours; otherwise, cover the cheesecakes with plastic wrap and refrigerate. Serve the cheesecakes chilled or at room temperature. To serve, remove the foil baking cups, place the cheesecakes on individual serving plates, and garnish, if desired, with sifted cocoa powder or confectioners' sugar.

The cooled cheesecakes can be frozen for up to 3 months. Wrap them in several layers of plastic wrap before placing them in an airtight container or in a freezer-strength resealable plastic bag. Label with a waterproof marker. Defrost them, in their wrapping, in the refrigerator overnight or at room temperature for 2 to 3 hours.

White Chocolate–Heath Bar Cheesecake

Makes one 9½-inch cheesecake; 12 servings

I was never a huge fan of Heath Bars (I always munched on Junior Mints in the movie theater) until the new wave of ice cream parlors started doing "mix-ins," where they would smoosh all manner of crumbled and chopped candies and fruits into the ice cream of your choice. One dish of ice cream with Heath Bars and I was hooked. The crunchy sweetness of the inner toffee buffeted by the outer shell of chocolate makes for some fine eating. Head recipe tester and developer Emmy Clausing's idea of putting crushed Heath Bars in a cheesecake was an over-the-top idea that landed squarely in the winner's circle.

For the crust

Unsalted butter, for preparing the pan

5.5 ounces (about 11 whole crackers) graham crackers, crushed, or 5.5 ounces (1¾ cups) packaged graham cracker crumbs

6 tablespoons (3 ounces) unsalted butter, melted

For the filling

8 (1.4-ounce) chocolate-covered toffee bars, such as Heath Bar or Skor, to yield 2 cups of pieces

6 ounces white chocolate, coarsely chopped

24 ounces (1.5 pounds) cream cheese, at room temperature

1 cup (8 ounces) sugar

3 extra-large eggs

1 tablespoon vanilla extract

For the topping

1 cup (8 ounces) sour cream

3 tablespoons sugar

1 teaspoon vanilla extract

Cocoa powder, for garnish (optional)

Preheat the oven to 350°F. with a rack in the center position. Butter the sides and bottom of a 9½-inch springform pan. Place the pan on a 12-inch square piece of aluminum foil, and press the foil around the sides of the pan, to catch any leakage during baking.

To prepare the crust, place the graham cracker crumbs and melted butter in a small mixing bowl and stir with a fork to combine. Use your fingers to press the mixture into the bottom of the springform pan, pressing the crumbs about ½ inch up the sides of the pan. Bake until the crumbs are lightly browned and firm, 10 to 12 minutes. Remove from the oven to cool while you prepare the filling. Maintain the oven temperature.

To make the filling, place the toffee bars, in their wrappers, on a work surface. Crush them with a rolling pin to break them up, but do not crush them fine. You want irregular chunks of toffee bar. Unwrap the bars, and, if some pieces are still too big, crush them a little more between sheets of wax paper. You should have 2 cups. Set aside. (The bars may be pulsed in a food processor, but be very careful not to over-process them.)

Melt the chocolate in a medium metal mixing bowl set over, but not touching, a pan of gently simmering water, or in a microwave-safe bowl in a microwave oven. When it has melted, turn off the heat and leave the chocolate over the water. Place the cream cheese and sugar in the bowl of an electric mixer. Beat on high speed until light and fluffy, about 2 minutes. Add the eggs, one at a time, and beat well after each addition. Beat in the vanilla. Scrape in the melted chocolate and beat on medium speed until well combined.

Scatter half the crushed toffee bars over the prepared crust. Carefully pour half the white chocolate filling over the crushed bars, being careful not to dislodge them too much. Scatter the remaining crushed bars over the filling, and top with the remaining filling. Use an offset spatula to spread the filling evenly over the toffee. Bake the cheesecake for 45 minutes, or until the top is very light brown in spots and the edges are firm but the center 3 inches move when the cake is shaken gently. Remove the cheesecake from the oven to a wire rack to cool for 20 minutes, but maintain the oven temperature.

To make the topping, stir the sour cream, sugar, and vanilla together in a small bowl. When the cake has cooled for 20 minutes, use an offset spatula to spread the topping over the top of the cake; spread it all the way to the edges of the pan. Return the cheesecake to the oven and bake for 5 minutes. Place the cheesecake on a wire rack. Run a dull knife around the sides of the cake to loosen it from the sides of the pan. Let it cool completely.

To serve, remove the sides of the pan. Cut the cheesecake in small slices (this is a rich cake!) and sift a little cocoa powder over each slice, if desired.

The cooled cheesecake can be refrigerated, covered with plastic wrap or in an airtight container, for up to 4 days. It can also be frozen, on its pan base, for up to 3 months. Cover it with plastic wrap and place in an airtight container or a jumbo (2-gallon) resealable plastic bag. Defrost it in its wrapping in the refrigerator overnight or at room temperature for 3 to 4 hours.

Reverse Marble Cake

Makes 1 loaf cake; 10 to 12 servings

And now for something new and different: for those of us who think that there's not enough ripple in Fudge Ripple or fudge icing on a yellow cake, this dessert is made to order. Here the "vanilla" part of the marble cake is swirled through the chocolate part, making a mostly chocolate cake with a gorgeous contrasting swirl running through it.

For the cake

Unsalted butter for preparing the cake pan

1$^1/_2$ cups (7.5 ounces) all-purpose flour

1 teaspoon baking powder

$^1/_2$ teaspoon salt

$^1/_4$ teaspoon baking soda

2 sticks (8 ounces) unsalted butter, at room temperature

1$^1/_2$ cups (12 ounces) sugar

2 extra-large eggs

1 cup (8 ounces) sour cream

1$^1/_2$ teaspoons vanilla extract

$^1/_2$ cup (1.6 ounces) unsweetened Dutch-processed cocoa powder

For the glaze

$^1/_4$ cup (.75 ounce) unsweetened Dutch-processed cocoa powder

$^1/_2$ cup (4 ounces) sugar

Pinch of salt

$^1/_2$ teaspoon vanilla extract

To make the cake, preheat the oven to 350°F. with a rack in the center position. Coat the interior of a 6-cup loaf pan with butter.

Sift the flour, baking powder, salt, and baking soda into a small bowl. Place the butter and sugar in a medium mixing bowl. With an electric mixer, beat on high speed until fluffy, about 2 minutes. With the mixer still on high speed, add the eggs, one at a time, beating for a minute after each addition. Reduce the mixer speed to low and mix in half the flour mixture, then mix in the sour cream and vanilla. Scrape down the sides of the bowl with a rubber spatula as you work. Add the remaining flour mixture and mix just until blended. Scoop one third of the batter into a small mixing bowl and set it aside. Add the cocoa to the larger portion of batter and mix it in thoroughly.

Spoon the chocolate batter into the prepared loaf pan. Drop spoonfuls of the vanilla batter on top of the chocolate batter and use two butter knives to cut down and across to gently swirl the vanilla batter into the chocolate. Don't overdo this; the vanilla batter should remain visible throughout the chocolate batter.

Bake the cake for 55 to 60 minutes, or until a cake tester inserted into the center comes out clean. The cake will still look moist on top. Remove the cake from the oven and transfer it to a wire rack. Let the cake cool in the pan for about 20 minutes while you make the glaze.

For the glaze, place the cocoa powder, sugar, and salt in a small saucepan. Whisk them together, then whisk in ¼ cup (2 ounces) of water. Set the saucepan on medium heat and bring the glaze just to a boil, stirring constantly. Remove the pan from the heat and stir in the vanilla.

Remove the cake from the pan and set it on a serving platter. Use a cake tester, toothpick, or thin skewer to poke tiny holes about 3 inches deep over the surface. Brush or drizzle the cake with the warm glaze. You should use up all the glaze, and this may mean waiting a few minutes for it to soak in between applications.

The cooled glazed cake can be stored, covered, at room temperature for up to 1 week.

Marble Milano Cake

Makes one 9-inch cake; 10 servings

I was looking for ingredients for a not-your-usual-streusel topping that was worthy of this luscious and oh-so-beautiful coffee cake, and, in the recesses of my pantry, I happened upon a package of Milanos, those delicate, oblong sandwich cookies made by Pepperidge Farm. Someone had dropped a large can of stewed tomatoes on it, and, on careful inspection, I saw there wasn't an intact cookie in the bunch. The crumbs reminded me of the very streusel topping I was seeking. I sprinkled some on top of the cake just before I put it in the oven, and the rest, as they say, is history. This cake quickly became the rave of the family, and then the neighborhood. It was the hit of bake sales, birthday parties, and my mother's weekly bridge game. Everyone who tasted it wanted the recipe, and then felt free to weigh in with his or her own version; that's how many different flavors of Milanos there are. I love mint Milanos, while my husband goes for the double chocolate.

This is a beautiful cake inside and out. Its moist interior is a rich white sour-cream cake, punctuated with swirls of dark chocolate. The topping makes it look quite fancy.

Unsalted butter for preparing the pan

7.5 ounces (about 22 cookies) Pepperidge Farm Milano cookies, the flavor of your choice

2¼ sticks (9 ounces) unsalted butter, very soft

2 ounces unsweetened chocolate, coarsely chopped

1¾ cups (8.75 ounces) all-purpose flour

1½ teaspoons baking powder

½ teaspoon salt

¼ teaspoon baking soda

1¼ cups (10 ounces) sugar

4 extra-large eggs, at room temperature

1 cup (8 ounces) sour cream

2 teaspoons vanilla extract

Preheat the oven to 350°F. with the rack in the center position. Butter the bottom and sides of a 9-inch-diameter and 3-inch-deep springform pan. Line the bottom with a circle of parchment, then butter the parchment.

Working over a medium bowl, break the cookies into roughly ½-inch pieces. Use your fingers to knead in 6 tablespoons of the butter, so that the cookie pieces are just coated. Set aside.

Melt the chocolate in a small bowl set over, but not touching, a pan of simmering water, or in a microwave-safe bowl in a microwave oven. When it is melted, turn off the heat under the chocolate, but leave it in the bowl. It needs to be warm when it is added to the batter later, so that the batter will marbleize readily.

Sift the flour, baking powder, salt, and baking soda into a medium bowl. Set aside. Place the remaining 1½ sticks of butter and the sugar in a large mixing bowl. With an electric mixer on medium-high speed, beat the mixture until light and fluffy. Add the eggs, one at a time, beating well after each addition. Scrape down the sides of the bowl with a rubber spatula as you work. The mixture will have small lumps, which is fine. Beat in the sour cream and vanilla. Reduce the mixer speed to low and mix in the flour mixture. Mix until the flour is just incorporated.

Scrape three-fourths of the batter into the prepared pan. Smooth the top with a rubber spatula. Quickly stir the warm melted chocolate into the remaining fourth of the batter until there are no white streaks remaining. Drop the chocolate batter by tablespoonfuls over the surface of the white batter. Use two butter knives in a crisscross motion to cut the chocolate batter into the white batter to create a marbled effect. Sprinkle the reserved cookie topping over the batter and use your hands or a rubber spatula to gently press it onto the batter.

Bake for 1 hour, until the cake has risen, the top is brown, and the cake just begins to pull away from the sides of the pan. Transfer the pan to a wire rack to cool for 20 minutes before removing the sides of the pan. Let the cake cool completely on the rack.

The cake can be stored at room temperature, well covered or in a cake saver, for up to 1 week.

Rocky Road Cake

Makes 12 to 15 servings

I don't know about you, but it just about kills me when I go into one of those upscale coffee dens dying for a chocolate fix, fork over a tidy sum for a yummy-looking this or that, and realize, after taking one bite, that it doesn't taste nearly as good as it looks, and I could have made a whole pan of these cookies, bars, or squares for what they charged me for one. Enough complaining. My intrepid recipe developer, Susan Schwartz, came up with her very own, truly excellent version of what Starbucks calls Caramel Topped Chocolate Cake, and what we call Rocky Road Cake.

You don't need a mixer to make this cake.

For the cake

Unsalted butter for preparing the pan

1¼ cups (6.25 ounces) all-purpose flour

¾ cup (2.4 ounces) unsweetened Dutch-processed cocoa powder

¼ teaspoon salt

8 ounces semisweet chocolate, chopped

1½ sticks (6 ounces) unsalted butter

3 extra-large eggs

1½ cups (12 ounces) sugar

1 teaspoon vanilla extract

1 cup (8 ounces) buttermilk

½ teaspoon baking soda

For the caramel sauce and finishing the cake

2 cups sugar

1¼ cups (10 ounces) heavy cream

¾ teaspoon vanilla extract

1 cup mini marshmallows

Preheat the oven to 325°F. with the rack at the center position. Coat the interior of a 9 × 13-inch baking pan with butter. Set aside.

Sift the flour, cocoa, and salt into a medium bowl. Set aside. Melt the chocolate and butter in a metal bowl set over, but not touching, a pan of simmering water. Stir occasionally until the mixture is smooth, then remove from over the water and set aside to cool slightly. (The chocolate and butter may also be melted together in a microwave-safe bowl in a microwave oven.) In a large bowl, whisk together the eggs, sugar, and vanilla. Whisk in the warm chocolate mixture until it is well combined. In a small bowl, stir together the buttermilk and the baking soda, then whisk it into the chocolate batter. Whisk in the flour mixture until the batter is smooth and glossy. Pour and scrape the mixture into the prepared baking pan.

Bake for 40 minutes, or until a cake tester inserted into the center of the cake comes out clean, the cake is puffed and looks dry on top, and it has just begun to pull away from the sides of the pan. Transfer the cake to a wire rack and let cool completely in the pan.

To make the caramel sauce, place the sugar and ½ cup (4 ounces) of water in a heavy, medium saucepan. Place over low heat and stir until the sugar dissolves. Raise the heat to medium-high and bring the mixture to a boil, without stirring.

Wash down the insides of the pan with a small brush dipped in water. Boil until the mixture is deep golden brown. Remove the pan from the heat and carefully pour in the cream. The mixture will bubble up and harden. Place the pan over medium heat and stir until the sauce is smooth. Stir in the vanilla, remove the pan from the heat, and let cool to lukewarm. (The sauce can be prepared a day ahead. Before serving, reheat the sauce in a double boiler or microwave until it is warm and thick but pourable.)

To assemble the cake, loosen the cooled cake from the sides of the pan with a table knife. Cut a piece of parchment larger than the cake and place the parchment over the top of the cake pan. Place a cutting board over the parchment, then invert the pan onto the parchment-lined cutting board. Tap the cake pan, if necessary, to release the cake, then remove the cake pan. Position the cake with a long side in front of you. With a serrated knife, cut off a 9 × 4-inch piece of cake, leaving a 9-inch square cake. Cut the 9 × 4-inch portion into $1/2$-inch chunks, and set them aside.

Use a long, serrated knife to cut the 9-inch square cake in half horizontally. Remove the top half using a removable tart pan bottom, a flat baking sheet, or a large, thin spatula to support it. Set the top half aside. Pour about one third of the warm caramel sauce over the bottom half of the cake. Replace the other cake half and pour half of the remaining sauce over the top layer. Scatter the reserved cake chunks and the marshmallows evenly over the caramel. Drizzle the remaining sauce over the chunks and marshmallows. Let the caramel cool and set.

To serve, cut the cake into serving portions with a serrated knife.

To store the cake, wrap it loosely in foil and store at room temperature for up to 4 days.

Chocolate Cherry Torte

Makes one 9- or 10-inch cake; 10 to 12 servings

This was the first of my recipes that Craig Claiborne published in the *New York Times*. It was an indescribably enormous thrill. This terribly sophisticated cake was then and still is one of my very favorite chocolate desserts. It has everything going for it: it's easy to make; it has unique but not-impossible-to-find ingredients; and it has a divine combination of textures and tastes, from the slightly crunchy chocolate almond layers to the buttery marzipan layer to the smooth-as-silk glaze. It looks like a million dollars as well.

Pitted Morello cherries are available in many gourmet food stores and even some super-markets. You want the kind in light syrup, not the kind with liqueur added. Even though the label indicates that these are pitted, it is essential to stick your finger into the center of each, looking for that lone pit that remains. Your teeth will thank you.

For the torte

Unsalted butter and flour for preparing the pan

1 (24-ounce) jar pitted Morello or other canned or bottled sour cherries in light syrup (or 6 ounces recon-stituted dried sour cherries)

6 ounces bittersweet chocolate, coarsely chopped

1$^{1}/_{2}$ sticks (6 ounces) unsalted butter

$^{2}/_{3}$ cup (5 ounces) granulated sugar

3 extra-large eggs

1 teaspoon vanilla extract

$^{1}/_{2}$ teaspoon almond extract (or $^{1}/_{2}$ teaspoon bitter almond extract, if available)

$^{1}/_{2}$ cup (2 ounces) finely ground almonds

$^{2}/_{3}$ cup (3.3 ounces) all-purpose flour

8 ounces almond paste (see Note)

2 tablespoons confectioners' sugar

For the glaze

$^{1}/_{2}$ cup (4 ounces) heavy cream

8 ounces bittersweet chocolate, coarsely chopped

NOTE

Very good quality almond paste is available through the King Arthur Flour Company's Baker's Catalogue (see Sources, page 271).

Preheat the oven to 350°F. with the rack in the center position. Coat the inside of a 9- or 10-inch cake pan or springform pan with butter. Line the bottom with a circle of parchment. Butter the parchment. Dust the pan with flour, knocking out the excess.

To make the torte, empty the jar of cherries into a strainer and set them aside to drain. Melt the chocolate in a metal bowl set over, but not touching, a pan of simmering water, or in a microwave-safe bowl in a microwave oven. Stir the chocolate as it melts, then remove the bowl from the heat. Place the butter and sugar in a large mixing bowl. With an electric mixer, beat the mixture on medium-high speed until it is light and fluffy. Add 2 of the eggs and beat well. Reduce the mixer speed to low and mix in the vanilla and almond extracts. Scrape in the melted chocolate, then add the nuts and flour, mixing only until they are incorporated. Mix in the remaining egg, and again mix only until well incorporated.

Pour and scrape the batter into the prepared pan. Scatter the drained cherries over the batter, but keep them away from the very edge of the cake, near the rim. Press them down gently with your fingers so that only the very tops show. Bake for 45 to 50 minutes, or until the cake looks dry on top but remains quite moist inside. (Check the interior with a cake tester; it should have moist crumbs attached when removed.) Remove the cake from the oven and allow it to cool for 10 minutes in the pan. Invert the cake onto a wire rack, remove the pan, invert the cake again so it is right-side up, and let it cool completely.

Knead the almond paste on a work surface to make a flat, round cake. Place a 15- to 16-inch length of wax paper on the work surface and dust it with some of the confectioners' sugar. Place the paste on the wax paper and dust it with more of the confectioners' sugar. Cover it with another piece of wax paper. Use a heavy rolling pin to roll the almond paste into a circle approximately the same diameter as the cake and $1/8$ inch thick. Use the cake pan as a guide. When the circle of almond paste is large enough, remove the top piece of wax paper. If the almond paste tears, just patch it together. Use the cake pan as a guide and use a small, sharp knife to cut a circle the size of the pan. Invert the rolled circle onto the top of the cake, and remove the wax paper. Leave the cake on the rack to glaze, or place it on a flat plate with four narrow strips of wax paper under the edges of the cake to protect the plate from drips.

To make the glaze, pour the cream into a small saucepan and heat it almost to a boil. Remove the pan from the heat. Stir in the chocolate and continue to stir until the glaze is smooth. Pour the glaze over the cake and spread it smoothly over the top and sides of the cake with an off-set spatula. Remove the strips of wax paper before the glaze hardens on it.

Store the torte, well covered with plastic wrap or in a cake saver, at room temperature for up to 3 days.

Chocolate Hazelnut Torte

Makes 10 to 12 servings

This deceptively simply dessert is quite easy to make and tastes and looks as if you've spent all day slaving away in the kitchen. The combination of toasted hazelnuts with their almost smoky flavor, the bright accent of raspberry jam, and the silky-smooth chocolate glaze paint a picture as beautiful for the eye as the flavor is for the palate.

For the cake

Unsalted butter and flour for preparing the pan

8 ounces bittersweet or semisweet chocolate, coarsely chopped

1½ sticks (6 ounces) unsalted butter, at room temperature

¾ cup (6 ounces) sugar

6 extra-large eggs, at room temperature, separated

1½ cups (6 ounces) hazelnuts, toasted, skinned, and ground

⅓ cup (3 ounces) seedless raspberry jam or preserves

For the glaze

3 tablespoons light corn syrup

2 tablespoons unsalted butter

6 ounces bittersweet or semisweet chocolate, cut in small pieces

2 ounces unsweetened chocolate, cut in small pieces

Fresh raspberries or unsweetened whipped cream, for garnish (optional)

Preheat the oven to 350°F. with the rack in the lower third of the oven, but not at the very bottom. Butter the interior of a 9-inch-diameter × 3-inch-high cake pan or springform pan. Line the bottom with a circle of parchment. Butter the parchment. Dust the pan with flour, knocking out the excess.

To make the cake, melt the chocolate in a metal bowl set over, but not touching, a pan of simmering water, or in a microwave-safe bowl in a microwave oven. When the chocolate has melted, remove it from over the water and set aside to cool slightly.

Place the butter and sugar in a large bowl. With an electric mixer, beat them together on medium-high speed until the mixture is very light and fluffy. Beat in the egg yolks, one at a time, beating well after each addition. Reduce the mixer speed to low and mix in the melted chocolate and nuts until they are just incorporated.

In a clean mixing bowl, with clean beaters, beat the egg whites until they hold soft peaks. Do not overbeat. Scoop a large spoonful of whites into the chocolate batter to lighten it, then scrape the remaining whites onto the chocolate batter and fold them in thoroughly. The batter will deflate considerably. Pour and scrape the batter into the prepared pan and level it off with a rubber spatula. Bake for 50 to 60 minutes, or until the top is puffed and crusty and the cake feels firm when pressed in the center. It is important not to overbake this cake. Remove the pan from the oven and let the cake cool in the pan for 15 minutes. Turn the cake out onto a wire rack and remove the parchment, but leave the cake bottom-side up.

When you are ready to assemble the cake, place the preserves in a small saucepan and bring them to a boil over medium heat. Place the cooled cake with the flat (bottom) side up on a flat serving plate with four strips of wax paper under the cake to catch drips from the glaze. Pour the preserves over the top of the cake and smooth with an offset spatula. Use only enough to cover the top, but not the sides, of the cake. Let the preserves set while you prepare the chocolate glaze.

Place 3 tablespoons of water, the corn syrup, and the butter in a small saucepan and bring the mixture to a boil, stirring occasionally. Remove from the heat and add the bittersweet or semi-sweet chocolate and the unsweetened chocolate. Stir gently, then set aside to thicken slightly as it sets. When it is slightly thickened, pour the glaze over the cake and smooth over the top and sides with a cake spatula. Remove the protective wax paper strips. Garnish the cake with the fresh berries, or serve with a bowl of unsweetened whipped cream.

Store the cake, covered, at room temperature for up to 4 days.

Chocolate-Pecan Torte with Chocolate Espresso Glaze

Makes one 9 1/2-inch cake; 10 to 12 servings

This lovely example of chocolate nirvana has a moist, slightly crumbly interior and a glaze so shiny you'll practically see your expectant smile in its sheen. Cut small pieces, as it's rich. Thanks to the ground nuts, the shelf life is quite long (in cake years), so you'll be able to savor it over a few days.

For the cake

Unsalted butter and flour for preparing the cake pan

9 ounces bittersweet chocolate, coarsely chopped

1 1/2 cups (6 ounces) pecans, toasted and finely ground

2 tablespoons all-purpose flour

6 extra-large eggs, at room temperature

1 1/2 sticks (6 ounces) unsalted butter, at room temperature

3/4 cup (6 ounces) plus 3 tablespoons sugar

For the glaze

1/2 cup (4 ounces) heavy cream

1 tablespoon instant espresso powder or granules

5 ounces bittersweet chocolate, finely chopped

Preheat the oven to 350°F. with the rack in the lower third of the oven, but not at the bottom of the oven. Coat the interior of a 9 1/2- or 10-inch springform pan with butter. Line the bottom of the pan with a circle of parchment. Butter the parchment. Dust with flour, knocking out the excess.

To make the cake, melt the chocolate in a medium metal bowl set over, but not touching, a pan of simmering water, or in a microwave-safe bowl in a microwave oven. Set aside to cool slightly.

Combine the ground nuts and flour in a medium bowl; toss together with a fork to mix well. Set aside. Separate the eggs: place the whites in a clean, medium, metal bowl and place the yolks in a small, shallow bowl.

Place the butter in a large mixing bowl. With an electric mixer on medium-high speed, beat the butter until it is light and fluffy, about 2 minutes. With the mixer still on medium-high, gradually add the 3/4 cup sugar and beat for 1 minute more. Maintain the mixer speed and add the egg yolks, one at a time, mixing well after each addition. Reduce the mixer speed to low and mix in the melted chocolate and finally the nut mixture.

With very clean beaters, beat the egg whites on medium speed until foamy, then increase the mixer speed to medium-high. Gradually add the remaining 3 tablespoons of sugar and beat until stiff but soft peaks form. Stir a large dollop of the egg whites into the chocolate batter, then carefully and thoroughly fold in the rest of the whites. Pour and scrape the batter into the prepared pan and smooth the top.

Bake the cake for 35 to 40 minutes, until the top is puffed and forms a crust and the edges have begun to pull away from the sides of the pan. A cake tester inserted close to the edge will come out dry, but a tester inserted in the center of the cake will have moist crumbs attached. Remove the cake in its pan to a wire rack and let cool for 15 minutes. Invert the cake onto a wire rack, remove the parchment, and let the cake cool completely; leave it bottom-side up.

While the cake is cooling, prepare the glaze. Heat the cream in a small saucepan set over medium heat. When it comes to a simmer, add the espresso powder and whisk until it dissolves completely. Remove the pan from the heat and add the chocolate. Whisk gently until the mixture is completely smooth. Let the glaze cool at room temperature until it is thick but pourable.

When you are ready to glaze the cake, move it gently on the rack to be sure you can move it later. Leave the cake on the rack and place a piece of wax paper under the rack. Pour the glaze in a steady stream over the cake, allowing it to fill in the center cavity and any cracks that may have appeared. Use a rubber spatula or an offset metal spatula to smooth the glaze over the cake so that the glaze falls over the sides. Smooth the glaze over the sides of the cake. Gently tap the wire rack on the counter to settle the glaze smoothly. Use two wide spatulas to carefully transfer the glazed cake to a flat serving plate. Refrigerate the cake to help the glaze harden a bit.

The glazed cake can be stored at room temperature, carefully covered, for up to 4 days.

Mint Chocolate–Mascarpone Striped Cake

Makes 6 to 8 servings

This is a grown-up version of the very first cake I learned to make. My mother and I used to make it following the recipe on the back of the box of Nabisco Famous Chocolate Wafers and serve it to someone special like a teacher who came to lunch. The combination of sweet, semifrozen cream and slightly soggy wafers is indescribably delicious. This updated version puts a whole new spin on this well-loved standard. Using mascarpone and whipped cream makes it more substantial and a tad more sophisticated. If you object to mint flavor, leave it out completely, substitute almond extract, or add the finely grated zest of one large orange or $1/4$ teaspoon of orange oil.

2 cups (about 16 ounces) mascarpone cheese

$1^{1}/_{2}$ cups (12 ounces) heavy cream

2 teaspoons peppermint extract

1 teaspoon vanilla extract

$1/_{2}$ cup (2 ounces) confectioners' sugar

48 (one 9-ounce package) chocolate wafer cookies

Semisweet chocolate curls, for garnish (optional)

Peppermint candies, crushed, for garnish (optional)

Place the mascarpone cheese and heavy cream in a large mixing bowl. With an electric mixer, beat on medium speed until combined. Add the peppermint and vanilla extracts and mix to combine. Slowly add the confectioners' sugar and beat until the mixture is soft and creamy.

Use a small spatula or a butter knife to spread a $1/4$-inch-thick layer of mascarpone filling on one chocolate wafer. Place the covered wafer on a work surface and top it with another wafer with an identical layer of mascarpone mixture, wafer side down. Continue to spread wafers with cheese mixture and stack them until you have stacked 11 covered wafers. End the stack with a plain wafer, so that you have used 12 wafers. Build 3 more identical stacks. Choose a serving platter large enough to hold the 4 stacks in a row. Lay the 4 stacks side by side and adjust them so that there are continuous stripes of filling and wafer across the top of the cake. Frost the sides and top of the cake with the remaining mascarpone mixture.

Place toothpicks at regular intervals in the top of the cake so that about an inch of each protrudes from the cake. Cover the cake with plastic wrap; the toothpicks will keep the plastic wrap from touching the cake. Refrigerate for 2 hours or longer before serving.

To serve, remove the plastic wrap and toothpicks; garnish the cake with the chocolate curls and crushed peppermint candies, if using.

For a semifreddo (partially frozen) dessert, freeze the cake 2 hours before you plan to serve it, then serve with the garnish, if desired.

The ungarnished cake can be made ahead and frozen for up to 1 month. Wrap the cake securely in plastic wrap, place in an airtight container or a 2-gallon resealable plastic bag, label, and freeze. Thaw the cake, in its wrapping, in the refrigerator for 1 hour before serving, then carefully remove the wrapping and place the cake on a serving plate. To serve, cut 6 to 8 slices on a slight diagonal and place each slice cut-side down on a dessert plate.

Chocolate Ice Cream Roll

Makes one 17-inch cake; 8 to 10 servings

This is the famous bar-mitzvah cake. The terrific hot fudge sauce that accompanies the roll comes to you through the gracious generosity of Cappy Feuer, who spoils us and her lucky husband, Stuart, with a continuous stream of delicious things from her kitchen.

For the cake and filling

Unsalted butter for preparing the pan

8 extra-large eggs, at room temperature

1 cup (8 ounces) sugar

1/3 cup (1 ounce) unsweetened natural cocoa powder, sifted, plus 3 tablespoons for dusting the cake

2 tablespoons all-purpose flour

2 pints best-quality chocolate ice cream or chocolate frozen yogurt, or one of the ice cream recipes on pages 135, 136, or 140

For the sauce

4 ounces unsweetened chocolate

2 tablespoons unsalted butter

2 cups (16 ounces) sugar

2 heaping tablespoons light corn syrup

2 teaspoons vanilla extract

To make the cake, preheat the oven to 350°F. with the rack in the center position. Line the bottom of an 11×17-inch heavy-duty jelly-roll pan with parchment. Coat the parchment lightly but thoroughly with butter. (Alternatively, you can use a silicone pan liner, in which case it is not necessary to use any butter in the pan.)

Carefully separate the eggs. Place the yolks in a 4-quart mixing bowl and place the whites in another, very clean 4-quart metal mixing bowl. With an electric mixer on medium speed, beat the yolks until they are broken up. Increase the speed to high and sprinkle in 1/2 cup of the sugar; beat until the mixture is thick and light yellow, 6 to 8 minutes. Scrape down the sides of the bowl with a rubber spatula as you work. Reduce the mixer speed to low and mix in the 1/3 cup of cocoa powder and the flour. Set the mixture aside.

Wash the beaters thoroughly and dry them well. Beat the egg whites on medium speed until they are foamy, then increase the mixer speed to high. Gradually add the remaining 1/2 cup of sugar, and beat the whites until they hold soft peaks, but be careful not to beat them until they are stiff and dry.

Quickly scoop one-third of the whites into the chocolate batter. Use a rubber spatula to gently mix the whites with the batter. Scoop the remaining egg whites into the batter, and use the rubber spatula to fold the two together until there are no longer any traces of egg white. Pour and scrape the batter into the prepared pan and spread it evenly. Bake for 15 to 18 minutes, reversing the pan front to back after 8 minutes. The cake is done when it has puffed in the pan, the outer 2 inches of batter look rather dry, and a cake tester inserted into the center of the cake comes out clean.

Remove the cake from the oven and transfer the pan to a cooling rack. To keep the cake from drying out and cracking, rinse a clean dish towel with water and wring out as much water as you possibly can, so that it is barely damp. Drape the towel over the cake and let it sit until the cake is completely cool. The cake will deflate somewhat as it cools. Remove the towel. Release the edges of the cake by cutting around the sides of the pan with a small, sharp knife. Dust the surface of the cake with the 3 tablespoons of cocoa powder. Cut two 20-inch lengths of plastic wrap and lay them, overlapping, lengthwise on the cake so that the plastic wrap extends beyond all sides of the cake. Place a large cookie sheet or lightweight tray on top of the cake and invert everything so that the baking pan is on top and the cookie sheet and plastic wrap are under the cake. Carefully lift off the baking pan and peel off the pan lining material. Trim off the dry edges of the cake with scissors.

If you are going to fill the cake now, cover the cake with the damp towel while you let the ice cream soften. You can do this by leaving the carton or cartons at room temperature for about 30 minutes, or you can microwave the ice cream for about 15 seconds on high. Gently spread the ice cream to within 1 inch of the cake's borders. Position the cake so that a long side is facing you. Using the plastic wrap to help, start rolling the cake away from you to form a long roll. Wrap the cake in the plastic wrap, then wrap the cake in a layer of aluminum foil. Freeze the cake for at least 2 hours before serving. (The filled cake may be frozen for up to 3 months.)

To make the hot fudge sauce, melt the chocolate and butter together in a small, heavy saucepan over medium-low heat. Add $^2/_3$ cup (6 ounces) of hot water and stir rapidly until the mixture is thick. Add the sugar; stir until smooth. Stir in the corn syrup and vanilla and stir well. Stir over low heat for 10 minutes, or until the sauce is no longer gritty. (The sauce can be stored, covered, in the refrigerator for several weeks. Stir the sauce over low heat before serving.)

To serve the cake roll, use a long, sharp serrated knife to slice the cake into 1$^1/_2$-inch slices. Drizzle the slices with the hot fudge sauce and serve.

Chocolate Refrigerator Cake

Makes 8 servings

Once upon a time every hostess worth her salt knew how to make a refrigerator cake. It usually involved first making ladyfingers. Thankfully nowadays you can buy them in the supermarket. Those cakes sported several layers of contrasting flavors and colors, and were usually stabilized with gelatin. This version with its three layers of chocolate—bittersweet, milk, and white—gets its mousse-like consistency from the addition of mascarpone, a soft Italian cream cheese. Since this cake contains no gelatin it can be made ahead and frozen.

30 to 36 soft ladyfinger cookies, each about 3½ inches long and 1 inch wide

2 ounces bittersweet chocolate, coarsely chopped

2 ounces milk chocolate, coarsely chopped

2 ounces white chocolate, coarsely chopped

1½ cups (12 ounces) heavy cream

1 cup (about 7 ounces) mascarpone cheese

2 tablespoons granulated sugar

Confectioners' sugar, for dusting

Grated chocolate or chocolate shavings, for garnish (optional)

Place a large mixing bowl and the beaters of an electric mixer in the freezer to chill while you prepare the cake pan and melt the chocolate. Line a 10 × 5 × 3-inch loaf pan with plastic wrap so that the entire interior is covered. It's all right if some extends beyond the edges of the pan. Line the bottom and then the sides of the pan with ladyfingers, placing the raised sides against the pan bottom and walls. You may need to trim some of the ladyfingers to fit the pan neatly.

Place the bittersweet chocolate, milk chocolate, and white chocolate each in a separate metal bowl. Place each bowl over, but not touching, a pan of simmering water. Stir the chocolate in each bowl with a separate wooden spoon as it melts. When the chocolates are melted, remove each bowl from over the water and set it aside. (If you don't have 3 saucepans to hold the bowls, the chocolates may be melted one after another, using the same saucepan. The chocolates may also be melted in separate microwave-safe bowls in a microwave oven.)

Place the cream in the chilled bowl. Use an electric mixer with the chilled beaters to beat the cream on high speed until soft peaks form. Add the mascarpone cheese and the granulated sugar and continue to beat on high speed until medium peaks are formed and the cream mixture is visibly thicker and smooth. Scrape down the sides of the bowl with a rubber spatula as you work. Divide the cream mixture evenly among the 3 bowls containing the chocolates; use separate rubber spatulas to fold the cream into the chocolates.

Use an offset spatula or a rubber spatula to spread the bittersweet chocolate–cream mixture evenly into the bottom of the prepared pan. Cover the pan with plastic wrap and place it in the freezer for 10 minutes. Remove it from the freezer, remove the plastic wrap, and spread the white chocolate cream mixture over the bittersweet layer. Cover with plastic wrap, freeze for 10 minutes, then remove the plastic wrap and spread the milk chocolate–cream mixture over the white layer. Cover the top of the cake with plastic wrap. Cut a piece of stiff cardboard to fit the top of the cake, and place it on the plastic wrap. Place a 1-pound weight (such as a 16-ounce can of tomatoes) on the cardboard, and refrigerate the cake for at least 2 hours or as long as 48 hours. (At this point the cake can be frozen for up to 3 months; remove the cardboard and weight and wrap in several layers of plastic wrap and then in foil. Defrost the cake without removing the wrappings.)

When you are ready to serve the cake, remove it from the refrigerator and remove the weight, cardboard, and top layer of plastic wrap. Spread any visible plastic wrap lining away from the top of the cake and place a serving plate over the top of the pan. Invert the cake onto the plate. Carefully remove the pan lining. Dust the cake with confectioners' sugar and top with grated chocolate, if desired. Serve by cutting thin slices with a sharp, serrated knife.

Leftover cake should be well wrapped in plastic wrap and refrigerated.

Black and White Semifreddo with Strawberry Sauce

Makes 8 servings

Think frozen chocolate mousse, think light as a cloud, think smooth as silk, and you're thinking semifreddo. This is the happy place where ice cream meets mousse, and the results are smiles and chocolate mustaches all around. Some semifreddo recipes are built on a layer of sponge cake and fruits; this one has a bottom layer of white chocolate with crunchy toasted almonds and a top layer of dark chocolate.

4 ounces white chocolate, coarsely chopped

4 ounces bittersweet chocolate, coarsely chopped

1¹/₂ cups (12 ounces) heavy cream

2 extra-large eggs

¹/₃ cup (3 ounces) sugar

¹/₂ cup (2 ounces) slivered almonds, toasted

¹/₂ teaspoon almond extract

1 teaspoon vanilla extract

Strawberry Sauce (recipe follows)

Line an 8¹/₂ × 4¹/₂ × 2¹/₂-inch metal loaf pan with plastic wrap so that the plastic wrap extends about 4 inches over each end. Place the pan in the freezer while you prepare the semifreddo.

Melt the white and bittersweet chocolates separately in metal bowls set over, but not touching, pans of simmering water, or in microwave-safe bowls in a microwave oven. (If you only have one appropriate saucepan, you can melt the chocolates one after another.) While the chocolate is melting, place the heavy cream in a medium, well-chilled bowl and beat it with an electric mixer until soft peaks form. Place the whipped cream in the refrigerator until ready to use.

Place the eggs and sugar in a medium metal bowl. Set the bowl over a pan of simmering water. Beat the eggs and sugar with an electric mixer on medium-high speed until the mixture is pale yellow, has tripled in volume, and falls back on itself in a discernible ribbon when the beaters are lifted over it.

Fold half of the egg mixture into the melted white chocolate. Fold in the almonds and the almond extract; be sure that the chocolate is well incorporated with the other ingredients. Pour and scrape the white chocolate mixture into the prepared pan. Fold the remaining egg mixture and the vanilla into the melted bittersweet chocolate. Fold until no light streaks remain. Carefully pour and scrape the bittersweet mixture onto the white chocolate layer in the prepared pan. Cover the semifreddo with the plastic wrap extensions, then cover securely with another piece of plastic wrap.

Place the semifreddo in the freezer for at least 8 hours, or overnight. To serve, peel the plastic wrap away from the top and unmold the semifreddo onto a serving platter. Carefully remove all the plastic wrap. Cut it into slices and serve with strawberry sauce.

Strawberry Sauce

Makes about 1 cup

1 (12-ounce) package frozen unsweetened strawberries, thawed

6 to 8 tablespoons sugar, to taste

2 to 3 teaspoons fresh lemon juice, to taste (optional)

Place the berries and their juice in the work bowl of a food processor or in a blender. Add 6 tablespoons of sugar and process or blend until smooth. Taste, and add lemon juice and/or more sugar if necessary. Pass the sauce through a fine-mesh sieve into a bowl. Cover and refrigerate for up to 2 weeks.

6. Soda-Fountain Favorites

Bittersweet Chocolate Ice Cream

Malted Milk Chocolate Ice Cream

Chocolate Granita

Chocolate Sorbet

Bailey's Chocolate Chunk Ice Cream

Black Satin Fudge Sauce

Easy Fudge Sauce

Chocolate Sauce

Classic Chocolate Frappé

Espresso Frappé

Chocolate Pizzelles

The Big Dig

Chocolate Ice Cream Soda

THERE IS SOMETHING absolutely magical about watching a baby tasting ice cream for the very first time. The mouth opens willingly, the tongue boldly extends, eagerly connecting with the extended spoon or cone, and then Whoa!—the look of total astonishment as the brain registers the brand-new experience of sweet and cold at the same instant. Here's a convert, hooked at first bite, to the delight of the adult holding the spoon.

There's no denying the instant gratification factor with commercially made ice cream. You pick out one of a dozen brands and five times as many flavors, race home, grab a spoon, pry open the carton, and there you are. But homemade ice cream is in a whole other league from that stuff you bring home from the store. First of all, the store stuff is so darn sweet you can't taste any flavor. Next, unless you are buying the super-premium brands, the amount of overrun—that's the air that is whipped into ice cream to keep it from being simply an impenetrable block of frozen custard—is so high that there's no real substance to the ice cream and, if you let it melt, it dissolves into a pile of foam. Finally, while I do like "stuff" mixed into my ice cream, I need only one, or at the most, two kinds of "stuff," not the long list in many brands. Having all those flavors and textures duking it out in my mouth isn't my idea of a good time.

I like to think we've broken some new ground here in the chocolate ice cream department. Take the Bittersweet Chocolate Ice Cream on page 135. One of the recipe testers described eating it as "falling headfirst into a deep, incredibly dark, velvet-lined tunnel that ends in a lake of chocolate." When's the last time store-bought ice cream inspired such a remark?

Now, take a scoop of that "this must be heaven" (as we were inspired to call it) ice cream and use it to top off the Chocolate Ice Cream Soda on page 147, or to make the Classic Chocolate Frappé on page 143. If you are looking for something a wee bit more sophisticated, pass Go and head directly to the Chocolate Sorbet on page 139. It looks smashing served in a martini glass.

Home ice cream makers are a relatively inexpensive kitchen appliance. Kids can use them without risking burns, strangulation, electrocution, or drowning. Your spouse no longer will have to venture out in search of a fix, and you'll attain a new, higher consciousness of ice cream happiness every time you crank it up.

Bittersweet Chocolate Ice Cream

Makes about 1 quart

Perhaps you are too old to walk around with a chocolate ice cream mustache, but hopefully you can remember back to a time when, several hours after you wolfed down a double dip cone, you were delighted to find the remnants on your upper lip or perhaps on your chin. A friend who tasted this recipe declared it "the chocolate ice cream of my youth."

Super-creamy and just rich enough to allow you to go for seconds, it's heavenly by itself and even better when used in the ice cream soda recipe on page 147.

2 cups (16 ounces) light cream

¼ cup (.75 ounce) unsweetened Dutch-processed cocoa powder

5 extra-large egg yolks

½ cup (4 ounces) light brown sugar, packed

2 tablespoons light corn syrup

5 ounces bittersweet chocolate, finely chopped

Set a fine-mesh sieve over a medium metal bowl. Have ready a second, larger bowl filled with ice water.

Place the cream and cocoa powder in a heavy-bottomed, medium saucepan set over medium-high heat. Whisk until the cocoa dissolves and the mixture comes to a gentle simmer. While the cream is heating, place the egg yolks, sugar, and corn syrup in the bowl of an electric mixer and beat on high for 3 to 4 minutes, or until the mixture is thickened and light yellow in color.

Ladle about a half cup of the hot cream mixture into the egg mixture and mix on low speed just to blend. Pour and scrape the egg mixture into the saucepan with the remaining hot cream mixture and cook over medium heat, stirring constantly with either a wooden spoon or a heatproof rubber spatula, taking care to scrape the sides and bottom of the pan to prevent the mixture from burning. Without allowing it to boil, cook until the mixture begins to thicken enough to coat the spoon or spatula. Immediately pour it through the sieve, add the bittersweet chocolate, and stir until it has melted and the mixture is completely smooth. Place the bowl containing the ice cream base in the bowl with the ice water and stir occasionally until the ice cream base is cold. Pour and scrape into an ice cream maker and freeze according to the manufacturer's directions.

Malted Milk Chocolate Ice Cream

Makes 1 quart

"Mmmmm, what's in this? It tastes like something from my childhood," said my mother, as she polished off a second helping of ice cream. In her youth, malted milk shakes and ice cream were as ubiquitous as non-fat, sugar-free, soft-serve ice cream is now. Somehow malt went the way of raspberry lime rickies; a shame, since these soda-fountain treats taste as great today as they did back then.

Malt, which is made from slowly roasted sprouted barley, adds a sweet, almost dusky "old-fashioned" flavor to this ice cream. For those who favor a less assertive chocolate punch, this is the perfect dessert. Malt powder is available in supermarkets and through the King Arthur Flour Company's Baker's Catalogue (see Sources, page 271).

1 cup (8 ounces) heavy cream

3 extra-large egg yolks

1/2 cup (4 ounces) sugar

5 ounces milk chocolate, coarsely chopped

1/2 cup (1.6 ounces) malt powder

2 cups (16 ounces) half-and-half

1 teaspoon vanilla extract

1 cup malted milk balls, crushed (optional)

Place the heavy cream in a medium saucepan over medium heat and heat until tiny bubbles form around the edge of the pan. Turn off the heat. Place the egg yolks in a small mixing bowl and whisk them until they are smooth and light in color. Add the sugar and continue to whisk until the mixture is very light in color and smooth. Slowly whisk 1/4 cup of the scalded cream into the yolk mixture, then whisk the yolk mixture into the hot cream in the saucepan. Place the saucepan over medium heat and cook, stirring constantly with a wooden spoon, until the mixture thickens enough to coat the back of the spoon and a finger drawn through the mixture on the spoon leaves a visible track.

Remove the pan from the heat and add the chocolate. Let the mixture sit for 3 minutes, then stir. Add the melting chocolate into the cream. Add the malt powder and stir well. Stir in the half-and-half and vanilla. Strain the mixture into a large metal bowl, cover the bowl with plastic wrap, and refrigerate until very cold, at least 4 hours. If you are going to use the crushed malted milk balls, put them in a freezer-proof container and put them in the freezer now.

Pour the ice cream mixture into the container of an ice cream maker and freeze according to the manufacturer's instructions. About 5 minutes before the ice cream is finished, add the frozen crushed malted milk balls.

Chocolate Granita

Makes 1 generous quart

There is something so sophisticated about this easy-to-make dessert that I feel like throwing on an evening gown and a pair of diamond earrings and lighting up the old silver candelabra before I eat it. If your idea of going for the gold is producing an unadulterated chocolate taste, then this is the recipe for you. There's little to get between you and your cacao bean.

3/4 cup (6 ounces) sugar

1/3 cup (1 ounce) unsweetened natural cocoa powder

3 ounces semisweet chocolate, coarsely chopped

1/2 teaspoon vanilla extract

Place the sugar and 3 cups (24 ounces) of water in a medium saucepan. Set the saucepan over medium heat and stir the mixture until it comes to a boil. Reduce the heat and simmer for 5 minutes, stirring occasionally. Whisk in the cocoa powder and mix until the cocoa is dissolved and the mixture is smooth. Remove from the heat and stir in the chopped chocolate. Let the mixture stand for 3 minutes, then stir well to combine the chocolate thoroughly. Stir in the vanilla.

Scrape the mixture into a 9 × 13-inch metal pan. Cool the granita mixture to room temperature, then place the dish in the freezer. When the granita begins to freeze (about 30 minutes), use a fork to scrape the icy parts from around the edges of the pan into the center. Push the unfrozen center portion to the outsides. Continue this scraping process every 10 to 15 minutes, until the mixture is frozen. Scrape the granita with a fork, then scoop the loosened granita into serving dishes and serve immediately.

If you are not going to serve the granita immediately, leave it in the pan, in the freezer. If it becomes too frozen to be readily scraped and served as described above, break it into rough chunks with a knife. Chop the chunks in a blender until the granita is the texture of crushed ice. Serve immediately.

Chocolate Sorbet

Makes about 3 cups

Bruce Weinstein, chocolate aficionado and author of many cookbooks, including *The Ultimate Ice Cream Book,* generously shared this recipe for a sublimely simple and sinfully deep and dark frozen delight.

1 cup (8 ounces) sugar

1 cup (3.2 ounces) unsweetened natural cocoa powder

Place 2 cups (16 ounces) of water and the sugar in a heavy saucepan. Set the pan over medium heat and stir until the sugar dissolves completely. Whisk in the cocoa powder and bring the mixture to a simmer. Simmer for 3 minutes, stirring constantly.

Remove the pan from the heat and pour the mixture through a fine sieve into a bowl. Refrigerate the sorbet mix for about 2 hours, or until it is completely cold. Stir it again, then freeze in an ice cream machine according to the manufacturer's instructions.

When finished, the sorbet will be soft, but ready to eat. For a firmer sorbet, transfer it to a freezer-safe container and freeze for at least 2 hours.

Bailey's Chocolate Chunk Ice Cream

Makes 1 generous quart

This reminds me of a Frozen Mud Slide—that bar drink that tastes more like dessert than a libation for those of drinking age—that you can eat with a spoon. It's a perfect companion for Boston Cream Pie (page 64).

3 cups (24 ounces) light cream

6 extra-large egg yolks

1/2 cup (4 ounces) sugar

1/2 cup (4 ounces) Bailey's Irish Cream liqueur

2 teaspoons vanilla extract

8 ounces milk chocolate, broken into 1/2-inch pieces, chilled

Prepare an ice-water bath in a large bowl or roasting pan, and place a medium metal bowl in the bath; place a fine-mesh sieve over that bowl. Set aside.

Place the cream in a 2-quart saucepan and set the pan over medium heat. While the mixture is heating, combine the egg yolks and sugar in a medium mixing bowl. Beat the yolks and sugar with a wire whisk or with an electric mixer until the mixture is pale yellow and falls in a thick ribbon when the whisk or beaters are raised from the bowl. Gradually whisk the hot cream into the yolk mixture, then pour the mixture back into the saucepan. Cook over medium-low heat, stirring constantly with a rubber spatula or a wooden spoon, until the mixture thickens slightly and coats the back of the spatula or spoon. Do not let the mixture boil, or it will curdle. Pour the custard through the sieve into the bowl in the water bath.

Stir occasionally until the custard is lukewarm, then stir in the Bailey's liqueur and the vanilla. Refrigerate the custard until it is very cold. Freeze in an ice cream machine according to the manufacturer's directions. Add the chilled chocolate chunks at the end of the freezing process.

Black Satin Fudge Sauce

Makes 3½ cups

The name says everything.

This sauce is thin when it is finished cooking and needs to be chilled a bit before using if you want a thicker consistency. One of the best things about it is that if you use it on ice cream while it is still warm (and thin), it acts like Ice Cap—the hard chocolate coating that soft-serve ice cream gets dipped into. It won't get quite as hard, but then again it tastes a whole lot better.

4 cups (32 ounces) heavy cream

8 ounces bittersweet chocolate, chopped

2 ounces unsweetened chocolate, chopped

3 tablespoons (1.5 ounces) unsalted butter, cut into pieces

⅓ cup (3 ounces) honey

2 to 3 tablespoons dark rum (optional)

Heat the heavy cream in a 2-quart saucepan over medium heat. Bring the cream to a gentle simmer (don't let it boil over!) and cook until reduced by half. This will take 20 to 30 minutes. Stir the cream occasionally with a wooden spoon or wire whisk. When it has reduced, remove it from the heat and stir in the bittersweet and unsweetened chocolates and the butter. Stir or whisk until everything has melted and the mixture is smooth. Stir in the honey and the rum, if desired.

Serve warm over ice cream, or, for a thick sauce, stir over a bowl of ice water until the sauce reaches the desired consistency. Store in the refrigerator in an airtight container for up to 1 month. The sauce may be frozen in an airtight container for up to 3 months. Reheat in a microwave or in a double boiler before serving.

Easy Fudge Sauce

Makes 1½ cups

Whenever you feel that longing for something chocolate and gooey to pour over ice cream, you can quickly turn wishes into something substantial enough to eat with this simple but oh-so-satisfying fudge sauce.

4 tablespoons (2 ounces) unsalted butter

1½ ounces unsweetened chocolate

½ cup (4 ounces) light cream or whole milk

¾ cup (6 ounces) sugar

¼ cup (.75 ounce) unsweetened cocoa powder

Pinch of salt

1 teaspoon vanilla extract

Place the butter and chocolate in a heavy 1-quart saucepan. Set the pan over medium-low heat and melt the butter with the chocolate, stirring until smooth. Stir in the cream. In a small bowl whisk together the sugar, cocoa powder, and salt. Stir the sugar mixture into the chocolate and butter mixture. Bring the sauce to a boil, stirring constantly, then remove it from the heat. Stir in the vanilla.

Cool the sauce to room temperature, then store it, covered, in the refrigerator. Reheat the sauce over low heat or in the microwave.

Chocolate Sauce

Makes 1 cup

One summer when the raspberry crop failed and there wasn't enough fruit to make jam, I gave everyone on my list a jar of homemade hot fudge sauce instead. I didn't get a single complaint. Be sure to make up a few jars for yourself; it's irresistible.

This recipe can be doubled or tripled.

½ cup (4 ounces) sugar

¼ cup (.75 ounce) unsweetened natural cocoa powder

½ cup (4 ounces) light corn syrup

¼ cup (2 ounces) half-and-half or evaporated milk

2 tablespoons (1 ounce) unsalted butter

½ teaspoon vanilla extract

In a 1-quart saucepan, place the sugar, cocoa powder, corn syrup, and half-and-half. Stir to blend, then set the pan over medium heat and bring the mixture to a full boil. Immediately reduce the heat to medium-low and simmer, stirring occasionally, for 3 minutes. Remove the pan from the heat and add the butter and vanilla. Stir until the butter melts.

Cool the sauce in the pan to room temperature, then store, covered, in the refrigerator for up to 3 months, or freeze for up to 6 months. Reheat the sauce over low heat or in the microwave. Serve warm or at room temperature.

Classic Chocolate Frappé

Makes 2 servings

Where I live, if you ask for a milk shake you'll get milk and syrup in a tall glass because in Massachusetts you need to ask for a frappé in order to get ice cream in your shake. Keys to making a great shake (or frappé) are: *whole* milk that is very, very cold; premium ice cream; and some decent chocolate syrup, because otherwise you're just adding bulk and diluting flavor. You also need a machine to aerate the shake; ideally this is one of those old-time soda-fountain wonders with two twirling metal rods that end with frilly disks that you stick into an ice-cold metal container, but second choice is a really good blender that comes with a metal container that can be stored in the freezer until called into action for the shake seeker.

1 pint (2 cups) premium chocolate ice cream

2 cups (16 ounces) whole milk, well chilled

1/3 cup (3 ounces) premium chocolate syrup

Place the ice cream, milk, and syrup in the container of a blender. Cover and blend until smooth and foamy. Pour the mixture into 2 tall glasses. Serve immediately.

Espresso Frappé

Makes 2 servings

In Provincetown, Massachusetts, there is an institution by the name of Spiritus. Inside, ice cream orders are taken by a waitress with blue hair and a dazzling assortment of nose rings. You will, I might imagine, reel as I did the first time I encountered a milk shake that cost six dollars. Trust me, it's worth it. Almost too thick to suck up through a straw, it has a consistency exactly like that of melted premium coffee and chocolate ice creams that have been gently softened with two shots of hot espresso. A direct-hit caffeine buzz will light up your life almost as much as being in Provincetown will.

1/2 pint (1 cup) premium coffee ice cream

1/2 pint (1 cup) premium chocolate ice cream

2 shots (2 ounces) espresso (see Note)

2 cups (16 ounces) whole milk, well chilled

Whipped cream

Place the coffee and chocolate ice creams, espresso, and milk in the container of a blender. Cover and blend until smooth and foamy. Pour the mixture into 2 tall glasses. Top each with some whipped cream and serve immediately.

NOTE
Instead of espresso, you can use 2 rounded tablespoons of instant espresso powder diluted in 3 tablespoons boiling water

Chocolate Pizzelles

Makes 30 cookies, each 4 inches in diameter; 30 cones; 30 bowls; or 15 ice cream sandwiches

Oniomania is a noun that means compulsive shopping or an excessive, uncontrollable desire to buy things. This is what happens to me when I see a baking utensil I don't already own. I knew that if I bought a pizzelle maker, I would find a great use for it other than making the traditional anise-flavored wafer-thin crisp Italian cookies, thus justifying my purchase. These pizzelles are as thin as a socialite, as crisp as a fall afternoon, and as chocolaty as a dream come true. They make the world's most elegant ice cream cones.

   Pizzelle makers are available in most gourmet shops and online (see Sources, page 271).

2 cups all-purpose flour

1 teaspoon baking powder

½ cup (1.6 ounces) unsweetened natural cocoa powder

1 stick (4 ounces) unsalted butter, melted and cooled

1 cup (8 ounces) granulated sugar

3 extra-large eggs

½ cup (4 ounces) milk

½ teaspoon vanilla extract

Confectioners' sugar, for sprinkling (optional)

Preheat a pizzelle maker according to the manufacturer's directions. Meanwhile, sift the flour, baking powder, and cocoa powder together into a medium bowl. Set aside. In a large bowl, place the butter and granulated sugar. Whisk or stir together until well combined. Add the eggs, milk, and vanilla; whisk until combined. Add the reserved flour mixture and mix until very smooth.

Use 1 teaspoon of batter for each pizzelle. Open the pizzelle maker and drop the measured batter onto each exposed hot griddle section. Use the catch to hook the griddle plates together. Cook for about 45 seconds (adjust the time for your pizzelle maker).

To make cookies: Remove the finished cookies to a wire rack. Continue cooking the remaining batter in the same way. Dust the cookies with confectioners' sugar, if desired, while they are still warm.

To make ice cream cones: Remove the finished cookies from the pizzelle maker one at a time, leaving the remaining cookie(s) on the open griddle while you work. Beginning with the outside edge of a cookie, roll it into a cone shape with your fingers. Gently press the seam against the work surface until the cone holds its shape, 5 to 10 seconds. Repeat the shaping process with the remaining cookies. Continue cooking the remaining dough in the same way.

To make bowls: Have ready 2 or 4 shallow heat-proof bowls or ramekins, depending on how many cookies your pizzelle maker makes at a time. Remove the finished cookies from the pizzelle maker one at a time, leaving the remaining cookie(s) on the open griddle while you work. Gently press each cookie into a bowl or ramekin, pleating the top edges of the cookie and pressing the cookie against the bottom of the bowl. Allow the cookies to remain in the bowls or ramekins until the next batch of cookies is ready. Remove the shaped cookies from the bowls or ramekins and let them continue to cool upside down on the work surface.

To make ice cream sandwiches: Bake the dough as described for cookies, above, but do not use the catch to hook the griddle plates together. The finished cookies will be slightly puffy. Remove the cookies from the griddle and stack them on top of each other to cool. To make sandwiches, use a serrated knife to cut pints of ice cream horizontally, still in the cylindrical cartons, into 5 equal slices. You can vary the flavors as you wish. Remove the carton material from around each slice, and place the ice cream slice on a cookie. Top with a second cookie. (If the ice cream slices are smaller than the cookies, you may wish to trim the cookies a bit before making the sandwiches. Use the lid of the ice cream carton as a template and trim with a small, sharp knife, or use a round cookie cutter in the appropriate size.) Serve immediately or wrap sandwiches individually in plastic wrap, then place each one in a sandwich-size resealable plastic bag. Label and freeze for up to 1 month.

The Big Dig

Makes 12 to 20 servings, depending on age and appetite

Tradition can be a good or not-so-good thing. A now-infamous construction project called The Big Dig has had the streets of Boston ripped up for so long that it's become a tradition in the worst sense of the word. I used to be able to park right in front of my favorite gelato place in the North End and run in to get a quick fix of their best flavor (rum chocolate), but I haven't seen a parking place in downtown Boston in ten years. (Yes, that's how long this "tradition" has paralyzed the city.)

We gripe and joke about The Big Dig, even write poems and short stories about it. Now some enterprising soul has gone to a delicious Big Dig extreme. I couldn't believe my eyes when I walked into a book store in Harvard Square and saw an eight-ounce chocolate bar called The Big Dig. The wrapper depicted the beautiful chain of green spaces that will replace the soon-to-be-buried ancient elevated highway that now runs through the city.

"Sweetening" the mega-project with chocolate was an inspired idea. The least I could do, I felt, was to buy a couple of bars and use some to construct my own big dessert. Keeping in mind images of giant excavation sites, gargantuan tunneling equipment, mounds of rubble, and the resulting "god-awful mess," I built this incredibly informal, reserved-for-family-and-good-friends-only-to-bowl-'em-over-with concoction.

Assembling this completely American dessert is a lot like The Big Dig's seemingly hang-loose construction. It relies almost completely on the artistic impulses of the architect (that's you), so feel free to go your own route once you get the hang of it. You'll need a very large bowl (a punch bowl if you have one—does anyone anymore?), or a big (really big) serving bowl. Of course, you can divide the dessert between two bowls if need be.

3 cups (24 ounces) heavy cream

1/2 cup (4 ounces) superfine or confectioners' sugar

1 tablespoon vanilla extract

1 large (about 10-ounce) yellow pound cake, cut into 1 1/2-inch cubes

1 large (about 10-ounce) chocolate pound cake, cut into 1 1/2-inch cubes

1 half-gallon chocolate chip ice cream, softened

1 half-gallon fudge ripple ice cream, softened

1 (32-ounce) package mini chocolate chip cookies

1 (10-ounce) bag mini marshmallows (colored, if possible)

1 (16-ounce) bag mini M&M's

16 ounces assorted roasted nuts (I like the salted kind)

2 (10-ounce) cans Hershey's chocolate syrup

Unsweetened natural cocoa powder, for dusting

In a large bowl, whip the cream, sugar, and vanilla with an electric mixer until soft peaks form. Set aside.

Place one third of the yellow and chocolate pound cake squares in the bottom of a very large serving bowl. Spread or scoop (if you haven't allowed the ice cream to soften enough) half of each of the ice creams over the cake. Sprinkle on a handful of the cookies, then toss on some of the marshmallows, M&M's, and nuts. Drizzle with some of the chocolate syrup, then repeat the order (or change it, if you wish) until you have run out of supplies—I mean ingredients. Mound on enough whipped cream to look as if it had snowed last night, and—to remind you that snow doesn't stay white for long around massive construction sites in the middle of a city—sift on a generous amount of cocoa powder.

Serve immediately. Hand out spoons, extra napkins (and bowls only if you must), and tell everyone to . . . dig in!

Chocolate Ice Cream Soda

Makes 1 serving

Americans have a love-hate relationship with diets. They hate going on them and they love going off. My hands-down favorite diet-breaker is an ice cream soda. It's easy to make, there's lots of it, it's easy to eat, and it's an in-your-face reminder that there's more to life than Ry-Krisp and cottage cheese.

Now, having said all that, it *is* possible to make a "low-cal" or "diet" chocolate ice cream soda that won't leave you awash in guilt. That recipe follows as well.

2 tablespoons chocolate syrup

Seltzer water, preferably from a chargeable seltzer bottle

1 large scoop chocolate ice cream

Whipped cream, for garnish (optional)

Place the chocolate syrup in the bottom of a tall (12- to 16-ounce) glass. Squirt or pour in the seltzer to within 2 inches of the top of the glass, stirring constantly with a long spoon. Add the ice cream to the glass; the traditional way is to "hang" the scoop on the rim of the glass with most of the scoop inside the glass, which creates the best foam. Top with a dollop of whipped cream, if desired, and serve immediately.

VARIATION
For a "diet" version, substitute low-calorie chocolate syrup and low-fat chocolate frozen yogurt. (Sorry, the diet version doesn't get whipped cream.)

7. Old World–New World

Blackout Cake

Chocolate Chip Mandelbrot

Chocolate Hamentaschen

Chocolate Walnut Rugelach

White Chocolate–Pistachio Biscotti

Chocolate–Pine Nut Meringues

Cranberry–Chocolate Chunk Scones

White and Dark Chocolate Cannoli

Chocolate Panini

White Chocolate–Banana Tiara Masseuse

Chocolate Linzer Torte

Chocolate Clouds

A Medley of Pound Cakes

IMMIGRANTS to America brought more than their hopes and dreams for a better life. They brought their recipes and ideas about how food should look and taste. Once here, they learned to adapt these to incorporate and make the best use of indigenous ingredients unheard of in the old country. Among their recipes were, of course, special chocolate desserts, which over time evolved into something uniquely American. The recipes remained true to their roots, but their tastes and textures were often transformed. For example, bread crumbs were substituted for hard-to-find ground almonds in a Sacher torte, and chocolate found its way into rugelach and mandelbrot. The European parents' preference for bittersweet chocolate was impacted by their children's affinity for milk chocolate.

In both their unaltered and modified states, these treasured recipes have been handed down from family to family. In each generation's kitchen, ingredients were substituted, steps were changed, and modern equipment eliminated a lot of the handwork.

Some recipes never changed, however; I know a baker who still makes his own marzipan for enrobing a chocolate cake before he smoothes on its milk chocolate frosting. My friends and I watch in awe as an elderly Austrian neighbor rolls out dough for strudel, knowing that when the time came for us to make it, we'd use frozen phyllo. I took a lot of flack when I served English visitors scones made with chocolate chips. At first they were aghast, but then as they nibbled away at the part that was familiar, they began to accept the part that was new. "Not too bad, after all," was the verdict, as they asked me to write out the recipe.

I like to think it's the universality of chocolate that made the evolution of these recipes easier to swallow for new Americans adapting to a new home and new ways.

Blackout Cake

Makes one 9-inch cake; 12 servings

If you are old enough to remember what happened on November 9, 1965, when there was a glitch in the power lines that ran from Niagara Falls to New York City, then this cake will have a special meaning for you. Of course, if you're not old enough to remember, the blackout of August 2003 will give you some idea ofthe chaos that resulted. Some said it was UFOs that caused the massive power failure that plunged all of New York, most of New England, and parts of Pennsylvania into complete darkness, in some areas for several days. Others, who spent the night in stalled elevators or candlelit apartments, were content to believe the official explanation of broken connectors mixed with poor allocation and massive overload. Whatever the cause, there were some pretty interesting results from the fact that creative people had time on their hands. There was an impressive spike in the birth rate the following August. My favorite result is the immediate craving my friends and I developed for a chocolate crumb–covered, chocolate custard–filled layer cake that was sold in Ebinger's Bakery in Brooklyn. Ebinger's was famous for using the very finest ingredients to make their signature cakes, pies, and cookies. One usually made a point of bringing the distinctive box to the table, so friends and family would know whence came their special dessert.

Since the Blackout Cake was developed in the fifties, Mr. (or Mrs.) Ebinger had a leg up when people like me came looking for something special to serve to celebrate the return of electricity. I've heard rumors that the Martians in the UFO made a pit stop in Brooklyn on their way out of town.

For the cake

Unsalted butter and flour for preparing the cake pans

3/4 cup (2.4 ounces) unsweetened Dutch-processed cocoa powder

1 teaspoon baking powder

1 teaspoon baking soda

1/2 teaspoon salt

1 stick (4 ounces) unsalted butter, at room temperature

1/4 cup (2 ounces) solid vegetable shortening

2 cups (16 ounces) sugar

3 extra-large eggs

2 teaspoons vanilla extract

2 1/4 cups (11.75 ounces) cake flour

1 cup (8 ounces) whole milk

For the filling and frosting

1 1/3 cups (10 ounces) sugar

1/4 cup (.75 ounce) cornstarch

1/2 teaspoon salt

3 cups (24 ounces) whole milk

6 ounces unsweetened chocolate, coarsely chopped

2 teaspoons vanilla extract

(CONTINUED ON NEXT PAGE)

Preheat the oven to 350°F. with the rack in the center position. Coat the interiors of two 9-inch round cake pans with butter. Dust with flour, knocking out the excess.

Sift the cocoa powder, baking powder, baking soda, and salt into a medium bowl. Place the butter, shortening, and sugar in a large mixing bowl. With an electric mixer on medium speed, beat the butter, shortening, and sugar until light and fluffy. Add the eggs, one at a time, mixing well after each addition. Beat in the vanilla. Reduce the mixer speed to low and add the cocoa mixture; mix until it is well incorporated. Scrape down the sides of the bowl often as you work. Mix in the flour alternately with the milk, beginning and ending with flour. Mix only until no traces of flour remain. Divide the batter between the two cake pans.

Bake for about 30 minutes, or until a cake tester inserted into the center of the layers comes out almost clean, with a few crumbs attached. Do not overbake these layers, as they will become dry. Cool the layers in their pans on a wire rack for 15 minutes, then invert them onto the rack to cool completely. Once the layers are cool, they can be wrapped well in plastic wrap and stored at room temperature for up to 24 hours before you assemble the cake.

To make the filling and frosting, place the sugar, cornstarch, and salt in a medium, heavy-bottomed saucepan and whisk well to combine. Slowly add the milk, whisking constantly. Place the saucepan over medium heat and whisk constantly until the mixture thickens and begins to bubble. Reduce the heat to low and cook for 2 minutes more, whisking constantly and taking care to scrape the bottom of the pan to prevent burning. Remove the saucepan from the heat and pour and scrape the custard into a medium metal bowl. Add the chocolate; stir until the chocolate has melted and the mixture is smooth. Stir in the vanilla. Press a piece of plastic wrap directly on the surface of the custard and let it sit, stirring occasionally, until it reaches room temperature. Refrigerate the custard, with the plastic on the surface, until it is cold, for at least 2 hours, or for as long as 24 hours.

To assemble the cake, use a long, sharp, serrated knife to cut each cake layer in half horizontally. Place 1 of the 4 half layers in the bowl of a food processor and pulse to make fine, uniform crumbs, or crumble the layer with your fingers. Place 1 of the remaining 3 layers cut-side up on a sturdy cardboard circle or the bottom of a springform pan. Spread about one-fourth of the chocolate custard on the cake layer, then top with a second layer. Spread a similar amount of custard on that layer. Top with the remaining layer, cut-side down. Use the remaining custard to frost the top and sides of the cake.

Line a large work surface with parchment paper, aluminum foil, or wax paper. Hold the cake on its base securely on the open palm of one hand. Working over the lined work area, sprinkle the reserved cake crumbs all over the top and sides of the frosted cake with your other hand. Pick up any fallen crumbs and apply them, too, pressing gently to cover the cake densely.

Cover the cake loosely with plastic wrap and refrigerate it for at least 1 hour before serving.

Chocolate Chip Mandelbrot

Makes 5 dozen cookies

Mandelbrot was enjoyed by German Jews long before Italian biscotti came on the scene. This heirloom treasure comes from my friend Susan Schwartz's grandmother, Lottie Koss. The addition of chocolate chips would surprise some old-world Europeans, but we think it adds yet another attraction to this lovely, homey cookie. Dipping them in coffee or tea is as traditional as the cookies themselves.

3½ cups (17.5 ounces) all-purpose flour

2 teaspoons baking powder

⅛ teaspoon salt

3 extra-large eggs

2 teaspoons vanilla extract

1 cup (8 ounces) sugar

½ cup (4 ounces) canola oil

4 tablespoons (2 ounces) unsalted butter, at room temperature

1 cup (4 ounces) almonds, finely chopped

1 cup semisweet mini chocolate chips

Preheat the oven to 350°F. with two racks as close to the center position as possible. Line 2 baking sheets with parchment paper or silicone pan liners.

Sift the flour, baking powder, and salt into a medium bowl. Break the eggs into a small bowl and stir them together with a fork, then add the vanilla. Place the sugar, oil, and butter in the bowl of an electric mixer. Beat on medium-high speed until light and very smooth, about 2 minutes. Reduce the mixer speed to low and add the flour mixture and the egg mixture alternately to the butter mixture, starting and ending with flour. Scrape the sides of the bowl with a rubber spatula as you work. Use a wooden spoon to stir in the nuts and chocolate chips. The dough will be quite stiff and it will appear oily.

Scrape the dough onto a work surface and form it into 4 logs that are 10½ inches long, 2 inches wide, and ½ inch high. Position the logs lengthwise on the prepared baking sheets, leaving 3 inches between them. Place both baking sheets in the oven and bake the logs for 25 minutes; reverse the baking sheets top to bottom after 12 minutes. Remove the baking sheets from the oven and reduce the oven temperature to 250°F. Let the logs cool on the baking sheets for 15 minutes. Carefully transfer each log to a cutting board and use a sharp, serrated knife to cut each log on a slight diagonal into ½- to ¾-inch-wide slices.

Return the cookies, cut-side up, to the baking sheets. Bake for an additional 25 to 30 minutes, or until the cookies are crisp and dry. Turn off the oven and let the cookies cool in the oven.

Store the cooled cookies in an airtight container at room temperature for up to 2 weeks.

Chocolate Hamentaschen

Makes about 3 dozen cookies

These three-cornered pillows of pastry filled with chocolate are traditional treats associated with Purim, which I like to think of as the Jewish feminist holiday, because it celebrates the bravery, cunning, and diplomatic skills of Queen Esther. Hamentaschen are traditionally filled with poppy seeds, prunes, or apricot lekvar (thick preserves); this recipe offers a new twist on an ancient theme.

There is a custom at Purim called Shaloch Manos, in which people pack goodies and take them as gifts to neighbors and friends. These would be well suited for that purpose—as long as you make enough for your own consumption.

This dough contains a lot of butter, so it's essential to chill the dough well before using it and to work in a cool place (away from the preheating oven), preferably on a cool work surface.

For the dough

3 sticks (12 ounces) unsalted butter, at room temperature

1 cup (8 ounces) sugar

2 extra-large eggs

1 teaspoon vanilla extract

4 cups (20 ounces) all-purpose flour

For the filling

6 ounces semisweet or bittersweet chocolate, coarsely chopped

1 tablespoon unsalted butter

1 extra-large egg

1 tablespoon milk

1 teaspoon vanilla extract

Place the butter and sugar in a large mixing bowl. With an electric mixer on high speed, beat the butter with the sugar until light and fluffy. Combine the eggs, 6 tablespoons of water, and the vanilla in a small bowl. With the mixer running, add the egg mixture to the butter mixture. Mix until it is well combined. Reduce the mixer speed to medium-low and gradually add the flour; mix until a soft ball of dough forms. Divide the dough into 4 portions. Scrape each portion onto a piece of plastic wrap, form it into a rough, flat disk, wrap well, and refrigerate for several hours or overnight.

To make the filling, melt the chocolate with the butter in a medium metal bowl set over, but not touching, a pan of simmering water, or in a microwave-safe bowl in a microwave oven. When the chocolate has melted, remove the bowl from over the water and let the chocolate cool for 5 minutes. Combine the egg, milk, and vanilla in a medium bowl; mix well. Scrape in the melted chocolate mixture and stir together thoroughly. Set aside.

When you are ready to make the hamentaschen, preheat the oven to 375°F. with the rack in the center position. Line 2 large baking sheets with parchment paper or silicone pan liners.

Place one disk of the chilled dough on a lightly floured work surface. Keep the rest of the dough chilled. Roll the portion of dough into a rough circle about ⅛ inch thick. Use a 2-inch round cookie cutter or the rim of a similar-size drinking glass dipped in flour to cut the dough into circles. Reroll the dough as necessary to make more circles. Place about 1 teaspoon of the filling in the center of each circle. Lift the edges and pinch them together to form a three-cornered triangle.

Place the formed cookies on a baking sheet, leaving 1½ inches between cookies. Repeat with additional disks of dough until the sheet is full. Bake the cookies one sheet at a time, for 15 minutes, or until the cookies are golden brown. Remove to a wire rack to cool. While they are baking, continue rolling and forming the remaining dough. Place the filled cookies on the second baking sheet; refrigerate the sheet until ready to bake.

The cookies can be stored in an airtight container at room temperature for up to 4 days. They may also be frozen in an airtight container for up to 3 months.

Chocolate Walnut Rugelach

Makes 32 cookies

While these can be somewhat time-consuming to make, they are not difficult to make and the result is worth the extra work. These cookies are fantastic when freshly baked, but they also freeze well. Freeze any extra cookies after the first day, so that they will retain their delectable flakiness.

For the pastry

8 ounces cream cheese, chilled, cut into small pieces

2 sticks (8 ounces) unsalted butter, chilled, cut into small pieces

2 cups (10 ounces) all-purpose flour

1/4 teaspoon salt

For the filling

1 cup (4 ounces) walnuts, finely chopped

3/4 cup (4 ounces) semisweet mini chocolate chips

1 teaspoon ground cinnamon (optional)

1/3 cup apricot jam

Place the cream cheese, butter, flour, and salt in the work bowl of a food processor fitted with the metal blade. Process until the mixture just forms a ball. (Alternatively, the dough can be made in a mixing bowl. Place the flour and salt in a large bowl. Use a pastry cutter or 2 kitchen knives to cut the cream cheese and butter into the flour and salt mixture. When the mixture resembles coarse meal, knead the dough into a ball with your fingers.) Divide the ball of dough into 4 equal parts; flatten each into a disk. Wrap each in plastic wrap and refrigerate for at least 3 hours, or overnight.

When you are ready to fill and bake the cookies, preheat the oven to 400°F. with two oven racks as close to the center as possible. Line 2 heavy-duty baking sheets with parchment paper or silicone pan liners. Set aside.

To make the filling, mix the walnuts, chocolate chips, and the cinnamon, if using, in a small bowl. Melt the jam in a small saucepan set over medium heat. When the jam is melted, set it aside but keep it warm.

Remove 1 portion of dough from the refrigerator and place it on a lightly floured work surface. With a heavy-duty rolling pin, roll it into a 9- to 10-inch circle. Use a pizza wheel or a small, sharp knife to cut the circle into 8 equal triangles. Brush each triangle with jam. Scatter about 1 teaspoon of filling over each triangle. Roll each triangle to enclose the filling, starting with the wide end. Place the rolled cookies on a baking sheet, 1 inch apart. Repeat with the remaining portions of dough, brushing, filling, and rolling the cookies in the same way.

Bake the rugelach for 15 to 20 minutes, or until golden. Reverse the baking sheets top to bottom and front to back after 10 minutes. Remove the rugelach from the oven and let them cool on the baking sheets.

The rugelach may be stored at room temperature in an airtight container for up to 2 weeks, or they may be frozen in an airtight container or heavy-duty resealable plastic bag for up to 3 months.

White Chocolate–Pistachio Biscotti

Makes about 36 biscotti

Made for dipping into a cup of espresso or a mug of tea, these lovely cookies are also the perfect accompaniment for a dish of gelato. Most likely it never occurred to your Italian grandparents to add anything as unlikely as coconut or pistachios to their biscotti dough, but these additions update a recipe to make it better than ever.

2 cups (10 ounces) all-purpose flour

3/4 teaspoon baking powder

1/4 teaspoon salt

2 extra-large eggs

2/3 cup (5 ounces) sugar

1/3 cup (3 ounces) vegetable oil

1 teaspoon almond extract

6 ounces white chocolate, coarsely chopped

1 cup (3.5 ounces) pistachios, toasted (see page 19)

1/2 cup (2 ounces) sweetened shredded coconut, toasted (see page 20)

1 egg white mixed with 1 tablespoon water

Preheat the oven to 350°F. with the rack in the center position. Line a baking sheet with parchment paper or a silicone pan liner.

Sift the flour, baking powder, and salt into a medium bowl. Place the eggs and sugar in the bowl of an electric mixer fitted with the flat paddle. Beat the eggs and sugar for 1 minute, or until the mixture is thicker and lighter in color. (Alternatively you may use a handheld electric mixer and a large bowl.) Add the oil and almond extract and beat for 30 seconds. Reduce the mixer speed to low and mix in the flour mixture. The dough will be quite stiff, but pliable. Mix in the chocolate, nuts, and coconut; mix until these are well incorporated.

Transfer the dough to a lightly floured work surface. Divide the dough in half and form each half into a 14-inch-long log. Transfer the logs to the prepared baking sheet and place them 3 inches apart. Flatten them so that they are 2 inches wide and 3/4 inch high. Brush the logs with the egg white and water mixture and bake for 30 minutes, or until they are golden brown and slightly cracked. Remove the logs from the oven and lower the temperature to 325°F. Use a long metal spatula (or 2) to transfer the logs to a cutting board. Use a sharp, serrated knife to cut the logs on a slight diagonal into 3/4-inch-wide slices. Return the slices, on their cut sides, to the baking pan and bake for 10 minutes more. Transfer the biscotti to a wire rack and let cool completely.

The biscotti can be stored in an airtight container at room temperature for up to 2 weeks.

Chocolate–Pine Nut Meringues

Makes 24 cookies

These light-as-a-cloud morsels are about as fat-free as you can get. To make them completely fat-free, you'd have to eliminate the nuts; an option is to reduce the measure of nuts. Bake these when the weather is dry, as humidity in the air will cause them to stay sticky instead of crisp.

2 ounces unsweetened chocolate

4 extra-large egg whites

1 cup (7 ounces) superfine or bar sugar (see page 16)

3/4 cup (3.5 ounces) pine nuts, lightly toasted

Preheat the oven to 300°F. with two racks as close to the center as possible. Line 2 heavy-duty baking sheets with parchment paper or silicone pan liners.

Melt the chocolate in a metal bowl set over, but not touching, a pan of simmering water, or in a microwave-safe bowl in a microwave oven. Remove the bowl from over the water and let the chocolate cool.

Place the egg whites in the bowl of a stand mixer. Use the whip attachment to beat the whites on high speed until they are foamy. (Alternatively, you may use a handheld electric mixer and a large mixing bowl.) Place the measuring cup with the sugar right at the lip of the bowl and, with the mixer still running, let the sugar drift slowly into the whites. Take about a minute to add all the sugar. Continue to beat until the meringue is thick and glossy. Reduce the speed to low and add the cooled melted chocolate, mixing only until the chocolate is incorporated. Remove the bowl from the mixer and use a large rubber spatula to fold in the pine nuts.

Use two soup spoons to scoop up 2½-tablespoon portions of the meringue and place them 1 inch apart on the prepared baking sheets. Bake the meringues for 20 minutes, then turn off the oven and let the cookies remain in the oven for another hour, with the door closed. Remove the baking sheets from the oven and allow the cookies to cool on the sheets to room temperature, then remove them from the sheets. Store the meringues in an airtight container at room temperature.

Cranberry–Chocolate Chunk Scones

Makes 8 to 10 scones

The Brits among us might raise an eyebrow at the addition of chocolate to this very traditional teatime treat, but one bite and even the most ardent purist will be converted.

2 cups (10 ounces) all-purpose flour

2 teaspoons baking powder

1/2 teaspoon salt

1/4 cup (2 ounces) granulated sugar

4 ounces semisweet chocolate, broken into 1/2-inch pieces

2/3 cup (2.4 ounces) dried cranberries

1 1/2 cups (12 ounces) heavy cream

2 tablespoons (1 ounce) unsalted butter, melted

2 tablespoons coarse or granulated sugar

Preheat the oven to 425°F. with the rack in the center position. Line a heavy-duty baking sheet with parchment paper, a silicone pan liner, or lightly buttered and floured aluminum foil.

Sift the flour, baking powder, salt, and the granulated sugar into a large mixing bowl. Mix in the chocolate and cranberries and toss together with a fork to coat the pieces with flour. Dribble in the cream while you stir with the fork until a crumbly mass begins to form. Transfer the dough to a lightly floured work surface and use your hands to knead gently 10 to 12 times until a sticky ball forms. Dust the ball lightly with flour and pat it into a 9-inch disk, about 1/2 inch thick. Use a 2-inch or 2 1/2-inch round cookie cutter or a glass with a similar-size opening dipped in flour to cut the dough into 8 or 9 circles. Place the circles 1 1/2 inches apart on the prepared baking sheet. Gently knead any dough scraps into extra scones. Brush the tops with the melted butter, then sprinkle with the coarse sugar.

Bake for 16 to 18 minutes, or until the tops are golden brown. Transfer the scones to a wire rack to cool for at least 15 minutes, to ensure that the insides have baked through.

Serve warm or at room temperature. Completely cooled scones can be stored in heavy-duty resealable plastic bags and frozen for up to 3 months.

White and Dark Chocolate Cannoli

Makes 12 cannoli

Now that you can buy cannoli shells in practically every Italian market and gourmet shop, and even in some supermarkets, there's no excuse not to make these at home. The biggest difference between these and the ones you can purchase already filled is that this filling isn't cloyingly sweet and the shell stays crisp, since you fill the cannoli just before serving. These are picture-perfect, with the chocolate-dipped ends announcing a creamy white chocolate, orange-scented interior. Melting chocolate chips and using them to dip the ends in results in a slightly thicker coating, better suited to covering the surface.

2^1/$_4$ cups (12 ounces) semisweet chocolate chips

12 purchased cannoli shells

1^1/$_2$ cups (.75 pound) whole-milk ricotta cheese

8 ounces cream cheese, at room temperature

^{1}/$_2$ cup (2 ounces) confectioners' sugar

3 ounces white chocolate, finely chopped

2 tablespoons grated orange zest

2 tablespoons Grand Marnier

Confectioners' sugar, for garnish

Melt the chocolate chips in a medium metal bowl set over, but not touching, a pan of simmering water, or in a microwave-safe bowl in a microwave oven. Stir the chocolate frequently as it melts. When the chocolate is melted and smooth, dip both ends of the cannoli shells in the chocolate so that about ^{1}/$_2$ inch on each end is covered. Set the shells on a baking sheet lined with wax paper or parchment paper. Let the chocolate harden at room temperature.

Place the ricotta and cream cheeses in a medium bowl. Cream them together with a wooden spoon until smooth. Stir in the confectioners' sugar, white chocolate, orange zest, and Grand Marnier. Refrigerate the filling for at least 4 hours.

Just before serving, transfer the filling to a pastry bag fitted with a large star tip. Pipe a generous portion of the filling into both ends of each cannoli shell. Sprinkle with confectioners' sugar and serve immediately.

Chocolate Panini

Makes 6 panini

Panini are Italian sandwiches, and in this country we've made it a fancy name for grilled sandwiches, the kind you can find in coffee "salons" and pizzerias. You won't have any trouble rounding up the troops when you make the dessert version: toasted, chocolate-filled sandwiches.

I thought about buying a panini maker until I realized my George Foreman grill operates on essentially the same principle, heating both sides of something at once. It works just dandy, and the results taste much better than any hamburger or chicken breast I've ever made. You can also make these on a griddle or in a skillet on the stovetop. Make the raspberry sauce before you begin to cook the panini.

8 ounces bittersweet chocolate, coarsely chopped

1 cup (8 ounces) mascarpone cheese

12 slices (1/2- to 3/4-inch thick) rich egg bread, such as challah, brioche, or Portuguese sweet bread

3 tablespoons (1.5 ounces) unsalted butter, melted

Unsalted butter for cooking the panini, if necessary

Raspberry Sauce (recipe follows)

Line a small (5½ × 3 × 2¼-inch) metal loaf pan (a disposable foil pan is great for this job) with plastic wrap, pressing it into the corners and letting plastic wrap extend beyond all sides of the pan. Set aside.

Melt the chocolate in a metal bowl set over, but not touching, a pan of simmering water, or in a microwave-safe bowl in a microwave oven. When the chocolate is melted and smooth, remove the bowl from over the heat and let cool slightly. Whisk the mascarpone into the chocolate and mix well. Scrape the chocolate mixture into the lined loaf pan. Pull the sides and ends up to form a roll approximately 6 inches long and 2½ inches thick. Pull the plastic wrap around the roll, tuck in the ends, and place the roll in the freezer for 2 hours or longer.

When you are ready to cook the panini, preheat the oven to 200°F. Have ready a baking sheet large enough to hold the cooked panini. Remove the filling from the freezer and transfer it from the loaf pan to a work surface; remove the plastic wrap. Brush one surface of each of 6 slices of bread with some of the melted butter and lay them, buttered-side down, on the work surface. Use a very sharp knife to cut the filling into generous 1/4-inch-thick slices. Place a slice on the exposed surface of each piece of bread, leaving about 1/2 an inch of bread around the filling. (You may have to cut the filling a bit to fit the bread, or add some pieces cut from the frozen filling.) Top each

(CONTINUED ON NEXT PAGE)

panini with a second slice of bread and brush the exposed bread surfaces with more of the melted butter.

Choose a panini grill, a George Foreman grill, a griddle, or a heavy-duty skillet. Grill the panini in the panini grill or the George Foreman grill according to the manufacturer's directions. If you are using a griddle or heavy-duty skillet, set it over medium heat and melt about 1 tablespoon of unsalted butter in either. Place as many panini as will fit in either utensil and place a flat pot lid or lids on top to press the panini down gently during grilling. Grill the panini on one side until the bottoms are light golden brown and the filling has softened. Flip the panini and cook until the bottoms are again golden brown. Keep the panini warm in the preheated oven as you cook the remaining panini.

Cut the panini on the diagonal and place 2 halves in the middle of each serving plate. Drizzle some raspberry sauce around the halves. Serve warm.

Raspberry Sauce

Makes 1 cup

1 (12-ounce) package frozen unsweetened raspberries, thawed

6 to 8 tablespoons sugar, to taste

Place the berries and their juice in the work bowl of a food processor or in a blender. Add 6 tablespoons of sugar and process or blend until smooth. Taste, and add more sugar if necessary. Pass the sauce through a fine-mesh sieve into a bowl. Cover and refrigerate for up to 2 weeks.

White Chocolate–Banana Tiara Masseuse

Makes 12 servings

No, it's not a typo—it's straight from the mouth of a waitress reciting the long list of desserts offered by her diner. Ticking them off as she pointed to the brightly lit four-tiered revolving glass case near the front door, she announced: "You got your chocolate pudding, your tapioca pudding, your rice pudding, your carrot cake, your cheesecake with and without fruit, and the special of the house, the White Chocolate Tiara Masseuse." I can't remember who said, "I'll have *that*—half on a plate and half on my neck and shoulders," but I do remember thinking, as I reached over for a bite, that bananas would make this already-good dessert even better. In this recipe the usual sponge fingers or savoiardi biscuits are replaced with crisp store-bought chocolate meringue cookies that measure about 2 inches in diameter and can be found in plastic containers in gourmet shops, supermarkets, and at places like Trader Joe's, Costco, and Sam's Club. (If chocolate meringue cookies are unavailable, plain are fine in this recipe.)

For the custard

8 ounces best-quality white chocolate

8 extra-large egg yolks

1/3 cup sugar

1/3 cup (3 ounces) whole milk

1/3 cup (3 ounces) bourbon

1 1/2 cups (12 ounces) mascarpone cheese, at room temperature

2 cups (16 ounces) heavy cream

To assemble the tiara masseuse

48 chocolate meringue cookies

1/2 cup (4 ounces) bourbon

3 bananas, ripe but not brown

For the topping

1 cup (8 ounces) heavy cream

1/4 cup sugar

1 teaspoon vanilla extract

1/4 cup unsweetened natural cocoa powder

Place the bowl of an electric mixer and the wire whip attachment in the freezer to chill. Set a sieve over a 2-quart metal bowl and set aside.

To make the custard, melt the white chocolate in a metal bowl set over, but not touching, a pan of simmering water, or in a microwave-safe bowl in a microwave oven. Stir the chocolate until smooth.

Place the egg yolks and sugar in a metal bowl; whisk to break up the yolks and mix in the sugar. Set the bowl over, but not touching, a pan of simmering water. Combine the milk and bourbon in a spouted measuring cup and slowly add it to the egg-yolk mixture, whisking constantly. Continue to whisk until the mixture is slightly thickened, about 5 minutes. As soon as the custard coats the back of a wooden spoon, strain it through the sieve. Whisk in the melted white chocolate and the mascarpone. Pour the cream into the chilled bowl and, with the chilled whisk attachment, whip the cream until it holds soft peaks. Use a rubber scraper to gently fold it into the white chocolate–mascarpone custard.

To assemble the tiara masseuse, place 3 to 4 cookies in the bottom of each of 12 parfait glasses, brandy snifters, large wineglasses, or small glass bowls. (The number of cookies you use will depend on the size of your serving dishes.) Sprinkle the cookies evenly with the bourbon. Peel the bananas and cut them into 1/2-inch slices. Divide the slices evenly over the bourbon-soaked meringues. Spoon a layer of custard over the bananas in each dish. Cover each dish with plastic wrap and refrigerate for at least 2 hours, or for as long as 8 hours.

When you are ready to serve, whip the cream for the topping with the sugar and the vanilla until stiff. Spoon the whipped cream on the custard, or use a piping bag and a large tip to pipe on the cream. Dust the whipped cream with a little cocoa powder.

Chocolate Linzer Torte

Makes 8 servings

A classic Linzer torte is an almost perfect dessert. It's beautiful to behold, it's made with all the right stuff (butter, sugar, eggs, ground almonds, raspberry preserves), its flavors enhance and complement each other, it's easy to cut and serve (a big issue when you have a lot of people to feed), and you can make it several days ahead. So what could make it better? A chocolate crust and a chocolate filling do the trick every time.

The crust for the torte is made with a chocolate sugar-cookie dough that is very easy to work with if you keep it chilled. If you've struggled with lattice toppings, you'll be happy to see the method I've devised that makes it a no-brainer.

For the crust

2 cups (10 ounces) all-purpose flour

½ cup (4 ounces) sugar

½ teaspoon salt

2 tablespoons unsweetened natural cocoa powder

⅓ cup (1.5 ounces) almonds, finely ground

14 tablespoons (7 ounces) unsalted butter, cut into tablespoon portions, chilled

2 extra-large egg yolks

Unsalted butter and flour for preparing the pan

For the filling and garnish

1 cup (8 ounces) heavy cream

6 ounces bittersweet chocolate, chopped

2 extra-large eggs

1½ cups (12 ounces) raspberry jam (with or without seeds, as you prefer)

Unsweetened whipped cream, for garnish

To make the crust, place the flour, sugar, salt, cocoa powder, and almonds in the bowl of a food processor fitted with the metal blade. Pulse to combine, then, with the motor running, drop in the butter, a piece at a time, through the feed tube. When the mixture resembles coarse meal, add the egg yolks and 2 tablespoons of cold water through the feed tube and pulse until the mixture forms a ball. Transfer the dough to a lightly floured work surface, divide it into two portions so that one portion equals two-thirds of the dough, the other one-third. Form each portion into a flat disk, wrap in plastic wrap, and refrigerate for 30 minutes.

On the lightly floured work surface, roll the smaller piece of chilled dough into an 8 × 10-inch rectangle. Use a knife or a fluted pastry cutter to cut the rectangle into eight 10 × 1-inch strips. On a lightly floured rimless cookie sheet, weave the strips into a lattice top. Use the bottom of a 10-inch springform pan as a guide to trim the ends of the lattice to form a lattice circle 10 inches in diameter. Cover the lattice with plastic wrap and place the cookie sheet with the lattice on it in the freezer until it is needed.

Butter the interior of a 10-inch springform pan that has 3-inch sides. Line the bottom of the pan with a round of parchment paper, then butter the parchment. Add some flour, shake to coat the pan with flour, then knock out the excess. Flour your

(CONTINUED ON NEXT PAGE)

hands, pull off walnut-size pieces of the second portion of dough, and press them into the bottom and two-thirds up the sides of the prepared pan. (I find using the palm of my hand works best.) Fit a square of foil in the pan, covering the dough. Place the pan in the freezer for 30 minutes.

Preheat the oven to 350°F. with the rack in the center position.

Bake the chilled crust for 15 minutes. Remove the foil and bake for another 5 to 7 minutes, or until the crust is dry.

While the crust is baking, prepare the filling. Heat the cream in a small pan set over medium heat until it is almost simmering and small bubbles start to form around the edges of the pan. Remove the cream from the heat and stir in the chocolate until it has melted and the mixture is smooth. Transfer the mixture to a metal mixing bowl and stir to help it cool. As soon as the mixture is no longer hot to the touch, whisk in the eggs.

When you take the crust out of the oven, maintain the oven temperature. Stir the raspberry jam to loosen it in the jar, then drop it by tablespoonfuls over the bottom of the crust. Use a rubber spatula or an offset spatula to spread it over the surface. Carefully ladle the chocolate mixture over the jam, and smooth the top. Remove the cookie sheet with the lattice top from the freezer. Use a wide metal spatula to guide the lattice from the cookie sheet onto the top of the torte. You may have to trim off bits of the ends of the lattice, so that it sits on top of the filling. It may sink a little into the filling, but this is fine.

Return the pan to the oven and bake for 35 to 40 minutes, or until the filling is set. Transfer the cake in its pan to a wire rack and let it cool completely before removing the sides of the pan. Run a wide metal spatula between the bottom of the torte and the parchment liner, then slide the torte onto a serving platter. (If you like, you can just set the cake on its pan base on the serving platter.)

Cut the torte into wedges and serve garnished with a dollop of unsweetened whipped cream.

The completed Linzer torte can be stored at room temperature, well covered with plastic wrap, for up to 3 days.

Chocolate Clouds

Makes 15 filled cookies

Less is most certainly more in the case of these elegant French meringue cookies I first saw in the windows of Parisian pastry boutiques. They came in a rainbow of pastels: rose pink, pistachio green, Easter lavender, and mocha, as well as, of course, chocolate. The wafer-thin crisp meringue shell opens into the ethereal cloud of sweet softness, then melts into flavored buttercream, and then the experience repeats itself as your mouth moves through the other side. I think you'll be delighted to see how easy it is to make something that looks like it belongs in a pastry shop.

The meringue is quite loose and needs to be spooned and scraped into a large pastry bag in one batch. The one I used was 14 inches long.

My version of the filling is made without eggs so that the meringues do not have to be refrigerated.

For the cookies

2 cups (8 ounces) confectioners' sugar, measured after sifting

1/2 cup (2 ounces) unsweetened cocoa powder, sifted to remove any lumps

4 extra-large egg whites, at room temperature

For the filling

1 cup (8 ounces) heavy cream

1 tablespoon instant espresso powder or granules

10 ounces bittersweet chocolate, chopped

1 tablespoon (.5 ounce) unsalted butter, cut into several pieces

To make the cookies, preheat the oven to 200°F. with the oven racks positioned as close to the center as possible. Line 2 heavy-duty baking sheets with parchment, silicone pan liners, or aluminum foil. Place a plain 1/2-inch piping tip inside a large pastry bag and set aside.

Sift 1 3/4 cups of the confectioners' sugar and 1/4 cup of the cocoa powder together into a medium mixing bowl. In the clean metal bowl of a heavy-duty electric mixer, with a very clean whisk attachment, whip the egg whites on high speed until they are opaque and they begin to hold soft peaks, about 3 minutes. Reduce the mixer speed to medium and start to add the sugar and cocoa mixture 1 heaping tablespoon at a time. When it has been added, increase the mixer speed to high and whip until the mixture is shiny and thick and resembles partially melted chocolate ice cream, 5 to 7 minutes. Scrape the mixture into the pastry bag and pipe thirty 2-inch disks onto the prepared baking sheets, 1 inch apart. Quickly use the back of a small spoon to smooth the tops. Place the remaining 1/4 cup of cocoa powder in a fine-mesh sieve and dust the tops of the cookies with cocoa. Place the remaining 1/4 cup of confectioners' sugar in the sieve and dust this over the cocoa.

(CONTINUED ON NEXT PAGE)

Bake the meringues for 2½ to 3 hours, or until the tops are dry and hard. Remove the meringues from the oven and cool them on the pan lining material; peel the cooled meringues off the lining material.

To make the chocolate cream filling, place a ¼-inch star piping tip inside another large pastry bag and set aside. Heat the cream and espresso powder or granules in a small saucepan over high heat. Whisk well, so the mixture does not boil up and overflow the pan. Remove the pan from the heat and add the chocolate. Whisk gently until it melts. Add the butter and whisk until it has melted. The chocolate cream filling must be cool, but not solidified, in order to whip properly. Scrape the cream into the metal bowl of a heavy-duty electric mixer, and place in the refrigerator. Stir the cream at 10-minute intervals. When the bottom of the bowl feels cold, whip the cream with the whip attachment of the mixer until it begins to turn light in color and holds firm peaks. It will look like chocolate whipped cream.

Immediately place the chocolate cream in the pastry bag and pipe a generous rosette of cream on the flat (shiny) side of 15 of the meringues. Start by piping a circle around the edge of the meringue, then spiral to fill in the center. When you have piped all 15 cookies, you may want to add more cream to them, depending on how much cream is left. Place a second meringue on top of the filling (flat, shiny side on the filling) and press very lightly with your fingers to seal the meringues to the filling.

The unfilled meringues can be stored in an airtight container at room temperature for up to 5 days. The filled cookies should be eaten within 24 hours.

A Medley of Pound Cakes

Being called the workhorse of the cake set isn't terribly glamorous, but where would we be without pound cake? Once upon a time it was indeed made with a pound each of butter, sugar, eggs, and flour. While today's versions are not nearly as dense and heavy, they are marvelous plain, cut in thick slices, and served with tea; they hold up under ice cream and fudge sauce; they can be cut up and served in trifle; or they can form the layers of an icebox cake, accompanied by fillings of your choice, soaked with liqueur, and topped with fresh fruit. They freeze beautifully, too.

This first (basic) recipe is perfection in itself. Adding "mix-ins" creates contrast in texture and flavor. A recipe for a simple glaze accompanies each cake variation, but you may omit it, especially if you are using the pound cake as the base of another dessert.

CHOCOLATE POUND CAKE

Makes one 9 1/2-inch cake; 12 servings

For the cake

Unsalted butter and flour for preparing the pan

1 1/2 cups (15 ounces) all-purpose flour

1/2 cup (1.6 ounces) unsweetened natural cocoa powder

1 teaspoon baking powder

1/2 teaspoon salt

1/4 teaspoon baking soda

2 sticks (8 ounces) unsalted butter, at room temperature

1 1/2 cups (12 ounces) sugar

2 extra-large eggs

1 cup (8 ounces) sour cream

1 1/2 teaspoons vanilla extract

For the glaze

1/2 cup (4 ounces) sugar

3 tablespoons Godiva chocolate liqueur, or Crème de Cacao

1 1/2 tablespoons unsweetened natural cocoa powder

Preheat the oven to 350°F. with the rack in the center position. Coat the interior of a 9 ¹/₂-inch Bundt pan with butter. Dust the bottom and sides with flour, knocking out the excess.

To make the cake, sift the flour, cocoa powder, baking powder, salt, and baking soda into a medium bowl. Place the butter and sugar in a large mixing bowl. Beat the butter with the sugar using an electric mixer on high speed until the mixture is light and fluffy, about 2 minutes. Reduce the mixer speed to low and add the eggs, one at a time, beating well after each addition. Scrape down the sides of the bowl with a rubber spatula as you work. Mix in half the flour mixture, then mix in the sour cream and vanilla. Mix in the remaining flour mixture.

Pour and scrape the batter into the prepared pan. Smooth the top with a rubber spatula. Bake for 50 to 55 minutes, until the cake has risen and has begun to pull away from the sides of the pan, the top has cracked, and a cake tester inserted into the center of the cake comes out clean. Remove the pan from the oven and let it cool on a wire rack for 15 minutes.

While the cake is cooling, prepare the glaze. Place the sugar, ¹/₄ cup (2 ounces) of water, the chocolate liqueur, and cocoa powder in a small saucepan. Whisk the mixture together and bring to a boil over medium heat. Lower the heat and let the mixture simmer for 30 seconds. Remove the glaze from the heat.

Use a small knife to loosen the cake from the sides of the pan. Invert the cake onto a serving platter. Use a metal or wooden skewer to make many 1¹/₂-inch-deep indentations all over the top and sides of the cake. Use a pastry brush to brush on the glaze, painting it as evenly as possible. Use all the glaze. Allow the cake to cool, then cut and serve.

The cake should be glazed right after it is baked. The cooled, glazed cake can be stored, covered, at room temperature for up to 1 week.

VARIATIONS

Chocolate Chip Pound Cake:
Make Chocolate Pound Cake as described, but after adding all the flour mixture, stir in 1¹/₂ cups semisweet mini chocolate chips. Bake as directed, and glaze or not, as desired.

Mocha Pound Cake:
Make Chocolate Pound Cake as described, but dissolve 2 tablespoons instant espresso powder or granules in 2 tablespoons of hot water, and add it with the sour cream. Bake as directed. For the glaze, substitute 1 tablespoon instant espresso powder or granules for the cocoa powder, and substitute Kahlúa for the Godiva liqueur.

White Chocolate–Orange Pound Cake:
For the cake, reduce the sugar to 1¹/₄ cups and omit the cocoa powder. With the sour cream add 6 ounces melted white chocolate and 2 tablespoons finely grated orange zest. Bake for 45 to 50 minutes. For the glaze, use ¹/₂ cup sugar, ¹/₄ cup orange juice, and 3 tablespoons Grand Marnier.

Cape Cod Chocolate Raspberry Squares

Zelda's Chocolate Demons

Chocolate-Filled Brioche

Orange Pistachio Milk Chocolate Chip Cookies

German's Chocolate Cake Squares

Mint Chocolate Brownies

8. I'd Like That to Go

Pistachio Brownies

Moon Rocks

Nuts About Chocolate Squares

Chocolate–Peanut Butter Shortbread Bars

Russell Crowe Bars

White Chocolate and Macadamia Nut Blondies

Toll House Cookies

White Chocolate–Cherry Cookies

I HAVE on my desk a framed cartoon that I cut out of the *New Yorker* magazine several years ago. A dozen people sit in a circle of chairs around a forlorn-looking chocolate Easter bunny, who sits on a stool in the center. The caption is, "Hi, I'm Bunny, and I'm a chocoholic." I can definitely relate to that—and I have lots of company. Raise your hands out there . . .

In restaurants my friends and I typically peruse the desserts on the menu before the main courses, negotiating with the waitstaff to put a "sold" sign on those last few pieces of anything made of chocolate that looks so good it might get sold out before we get to dessert. Not being able to choose between three or four different chocolate dessert recipes to serve for company, I give up and make them all. If a chocolate recipe can be doubled or tripled, I make the full complement, adding the extras to an already close-to-bursting dessert-filled freezer. I've been known to get up in the middle of the night to write down an idea for a new chocolate recipe that came to me in a dream. Sometimes this is a good thing, other times it results in a dessert that no one will ever see or taste.

The true chocolate nut's motto is, "I want it and I want it now!" So it follows that our most important survival tool is that portable piece, the take-along box of cookies, a plastic container or bag of Hershey's Kisses, a brownie or two, or, at the least, a bar of chocolate.

This urge to satisfy the need to eat chocolate impacts almost every aspect of our lives. We can drive, talk on the phone, fax the office, lip-synch along to the radio, *and* balance a White Chocolate and Macadamia Nut Blondie on one napkin-covered knee. Our friends and family know that, without fail, they can scrounge around in our freezer and come up with a plastic container full of Mint Chocolate Brownies with a delicious surprise center, or German's Chocolate Cake Squares, and that our pantry or desk drawer holds a stash of Nuts About Chocolate Squares or a dozen pieces of fudge.

If you agree that three meals of chocolate desserts every day would not begin to be enough to fulfill your desire for more; if sitting next to the bathtub soap dish is a plate with telltale chocolate cake crumbs on it; if you wouldn't dream of leaving the house without packing a chocolate fix, then welcome to the club—you've got lots of company.

Cape Cod Chocolate Raspberry Squares

Makes twenty 2-inch squares

My good friend, professional baker Rene Withstandley, lives in Brewster, Massachusetts, just west of Cape Cod's elbow. Her husband, Paul, was a marvelous gardener and his raspberry patch was his pride and joy. Early fall would find both of them out picking, carefully depositing the luscious, ripe berries into plastic containers. Next stop for the fruit was either jam or one of many confections Rene whips up at the drop of a hat. My hands-down favorite are these melt-in-your-mouth squares of buttery pastry that nestle a filling of raspberry jam and chocolate.

For the crust

1 cup (5 ounces) all-purpose flour

1/4 cup (2 ounces) sugar

Pinch of salt

1 stick (4 ounces) unsalted butter, cut into 4 to 5 pieces, at room temperature

1 extra-large egg yolk (save the white for the topping)

For the filling and top

1/2 cup (6 ounces) raspberry jam, with or without seeds

1 cup (5 ounces) semisweet chocolate chips

2 extra-large egg whites

1/4 cup (2 ounces) sugar

Preheat the oven to 375°F. with the rack in the center position. Have ready an ungreased 11 × 7 1/2-inch glass baking dish.

To make the crust, pulse the flour, sugar, and salt in a food processor to combine them. Scatter the butter pieces on the flour. Pulse until the dough starts to come together. Add the egg yolk and process until the dough forms a ball and the yolk is completely mixed in. Scrape the dough into the baking dish and press it onto the bottom and about 1/2 inch up the sides of the baking dish. Press it as evenly as possible. Bake the crust for 15 minutes, or until it is barely light golden brown and slightly dry on top. Remove the pan from the oven, but maintain the oven temperature.

Use a rubber spatula or an offset spatula to spread the jam evenly over the crust's surface. Sprinkle the chocolate chips on the raspberry layer. Place the egg whites in a very clean bowl. With an electric mixer with very clean beaters, beat the whites on medium-high speed until soft peaks form. Gradually beat in the sugar. Increase the mixer speed to high and beat until stiff, glossy peaks form. Carefully spread the meringue on the chocolate chip layer in the pan. Return the pan to the oven and bake for 10 to 12 minutes, or until the meringue is uniformly light golden brown.

While the crust and filling are still hot, loosen the edges with a small, sharp knife, and cut into 20 bars. Let the bars cool in the pan. The bars can be stored in their pan, covered, in a cool, dry place for up to 3 days. Don't refrigerate them, as the meringue will get sticky.

Zelda's Chocolate Demons

Makes 12 diamond-shaped cookies

While these diamonds aren't quite as big as the Ritz, they are tender as the night. Subtle as a perfectly turned phrase, and rich as Jay Gatsby, these melt-away morsels of butter and chocolate shortbread are the perfect gift for your literary friends (packaged together, perhaps, with a Fitzgerald novel). Serve them to your book group to munch on, no matter what the book of the month may be.

For the bars

Unsalted butter for preparing the baking dish

3 ounces unsweetened chocolate, coarsely chopped

1 cup plus 2 tablespoons (10.5 ounces) all-purpose flour

3 tablespoons unsweetened natural cocoa powder

1/4 teaspoon salt

1/2 cup (4 ounces) light brown sugar, packed

1/2 cup (4 ounces) granulated sugar

6 ounces (1 1/2 sticks) unsalted butter, at room temperature, cut into 4 pieces

For drizzling the bars

1/2 cup (2.5 ounces) white chocolate chips

1/2 cup (2.5 ounces) semisweet chocolate chips

Preheat the oven to 325°F. with the rack in the center position. Use a small amount of butter to coat the interior of a 9-inch square ovenproof baking dish.

To make the bars, melt the chocolate in a bowl set over, but not touching, a pan of gently simmering water, or in a microwave-safe bowl in a microwave oven. Remove from the heat and allow to cool slightly.

Place the flour, cocoa powder, salt, and both sugars in the bowl of a stand mixer or in a food processor fitted with the metal blade. Mix on low speed or pulse to combine. Add the butter and mix on medum speed or pulse until small crumbs form. Add the chocolate and 1/4 cup (2 ounces) water and mix on low speed or pulse until a soft ball forms. Scrape in the melted chocolate, and mix well. Press the dough into the prepared pan. Don't push the dough up the sides; you want the dough to be as flat as possible. Use the tip of a sharp knife to lightly score the dough on the diagonal into 12 diamonds. There will be an odd piece or two in each corner.

Bake for 35 minutes, or until the top is firm, slightly puffy, and dry to the touch. Remove the pan from the oven to a wire rack. Let the bars cool completely, then place a flat plate or cutting board over the top of the dish and invert it. Invert again onto a cutting board so the top side is up. Use a sharp knife to finish cutting the diamonds. Separate the bars by 1 1/2 inches on the work surface or cutting board.

To drizzle the baked and cooled bars, place the white chocolate chips in one small microwave-safe bowl or Pyrex measuring cup, and the semisweet chips in another. Microwave each separately as follows: microwave 30 seconds, stir, microwave 30 seconds, and stir again. The chips should be almost completely melted at that point. If not, continue to microwave at 5-second intervals.

Place a heavy-duty resealable sandwich-size plastic bag in each of 2 small drinking glasses; fold the open edge of each bag over the sides of the glass. Scrape one type of melted chocolate into each bag. Seal the bags, pressing out the air as you do. Cut a *very* small piece off one bottom corner of each bag; increase the cut as necessary to allow a slow but steady stream of chocolate to be released when you squeeze gently. Starting with the white chocolate, hold the bag over the shortbread and gently squeeze the chocolate onto the shortbread in a zigzag pattern. Repeat the process with the semisweet chocolate. Place the decorated shortbread in the refrigerator until the chocolate sets, about 20 minutes.

The bars can be stored in a tightly closed container at room temperature for up to 2 weeks.

Chocolate-Filled Brioche

Makes 8 medium brioche

You can turn your kitchen into a French bakery and dazzle hungry breakfast seekers with picture-perfect brioche. These buttery chocolate-filled pillows of rich yeasted dough can be made in stages, and the formed, filled, unbaked brioche can be either frozen or refrigerated overnight and popped into the oven for your morning enjoyment. Please note: This dough will be extremely sticky and is best made with either a stand mixer or bread machine. It will become slightly less sticky as the kneading progresses, but it won't form a discrete ball. Don't be tempted to add more flour; this is quite a loose dough. It will firm up as it chills. It is supposed to be wet during mixing.

For the brioche dough

3¹/₄ cups (16.25 ounces) all-purpose flour

3 tablespoons sugar

3 tablespoons Lora Brody's Dough Relaxer (See Sources, page 271), for a more tender crumb and lighter texture (optional)

1 tablespoon active dry yeast (*not* rapid rise)

1¹/₂ teaspoons salt

2 sticks (8 ounces) unsalted butter, melted and slightly cooled

3 extra-large eggs

For the filling and baking

2 to 3 tablespoons unsalted butter for preparing the pans

8 (1-ounce) chunks of bittersweet chocolate

1 extra-large egg yolk

¹/₄ cup (2 ounces) heavy cream

Coarse sugar

Stand mixer method

Place the flour, sugar, dough relaxer (if using), the yeast, salt, butter, and eggs in the bowl of a stand mixer fitted with the dough hook. Knead on low speed until the liquid is absorbed, then mix on medium speed for 5 to 7 minutes, adding ¹/₄ to ¹/₃ cup (2 to 3 ounces) of warm water, or until a very sticky dough forms. Cover the opening of the bowl loosely with a towel and let rest for 20 minutes, then knead for another 7 to 8 minutes or until the dough is soft and supple, but quite loose. Remove the dough hook, cover the bowl with plastic wrap or a towel, and let the dough rise in a warm place until doubled in bulk.

Bread machine method

Place the flour, sugar, dough relaxer (if using), the yeast, salt, butter, and eggs in the machine and program for dough or manual. Allow the dough to go through one knead and one rise, checking during the first knead cycle to make sure the dough is loose and fairly sticky. Add a little warm water if necessary.

After the dough, prepared by either method, has risen until doubled in bulk, place it in either an oiled bowl or a large, heavy-duty resealable plastic bag. Push out the air and refrigerate it for at least 24 hours, but not more than 36 hours. This dough must be chilled and firm in order to be worked successfully.

When you are ready to bake the brioche, generously coat the insides of 8 brioche tins (approximately 1³/₄ inches high and 3¹/₂ inches across the top) with butter. Choose a round cookie cutter or straight-sided glass that is slightly larger than the opening of one of the tins. Roll the chilled dough on a very lightly floured work surface into a circle roughly 16 inches in diameter. Cut 8 circles, dipping the cutter in flour, if necessary, to keep it from sticking. You may have to reroll the dough scraps to obtain 8 circles. Place a chunk of chocolate in the center of each circle of dough, then gather up the edges and pinch them together over the filling to make a ball. Place the balls of filled dough, seam-side down, in the prepared tins. In a small bowl, combine the egg yolk with the heavy cream. Brush the tops of the brioche with the egg wash, then sprinkle generously with coarse sugar. Place the filled tins on a heavy-duty baking sheet and place in a warm, draft-free space. Let the brioche rise until doubled in bulk.

Preheat the oven to 425°F. with the rack in the lower third, but not the lowest, position. Bake the brioche for 5 minutes, then lower the oven temperature to 375°F. and bake for 10 to 12 minutes more, or until the sides have begun to pull away from the tins and the tops are deep golden brown. If the tops turn very brown before the baking time is up, cover them loosely with a piece of aluminum foil.

Unmold the brioche and allow them to cool for 15 minutes on a wire rack and serve warm, or let them cool completely and serve at room temperature.

Orange Pistachio Milk Chocolate Chip Cookies

Makes about 4½ dozen cookies

If, like me, you enjoy sweet and salty flavors together, use salted natural pistachios (green, not dyed red) in their shells, and shell them yourself. Toss them in a fine-mesh sieve to remove just enough salt before adding to the batter.

2¼ cups (11.25 ounces) all-purpose flour

1 teaspoon baking soda

½ teaspoon salt

2 sticks (8 ounces) unsalted butter, at room temperature

¾ cup (6 ounces) granulated sugar

¾ cup (6 ounces) light brown sugar, packed

2 extra-large eggs

2 teaspoons almond extract

Grated zest of 2 large oranges or ¼ teaspoon orange oil

1½ cups (7.5 ounces) milk chocolate chips

1½ cups (6 ounces) shelled pistachios, salted or unsalted, left whole

NOTE
If you like flat, crisp, chewy cookies, slam the cookie sheets down on a work surface halfway through the baking time. If you like softer cookies, skip that step.

Preheat the oven to 375°F. with the rack in the center position. Line 2 baking sheets with silicone pan liners or parchment paper.

Sift the flour, baking soda, and salt into a medium bowl. Place the butter, granulated sugar, and brown sugar in a large mixing bowl. Using an electric mixer set on high speed, beat the mixture until it is light and fluffy, about 2 minutes. Reduce the mixer speed to low and add the eggs, one at a time, and mix well after each addition. Mix in the almond extract and orange zest and finally the flour mixture. When the flour mixture is totally incorporated, mix in the chocolate chips and nuts.

Drop the dough by rounded tablespoons on the prepared sheets, placing the portions 2 inches apart. Bake the cookies, one sheet at a time, until they just begin to brown around the edges, 10 to 12 minutes. The centers should remain pale. Let the cookies cool on the baking sheet for 2 minutes, then transfer them to a wire rack to cool. Bake the remaining cookies in the same way. (You do not have to replace the lining material for subsequent batches.)

Store in an airtight container at room temperature for up to 2 weeks.

These make great freeze-and-serve cookies: Form the dough into 2 logs 10 inches long and about 2 inches wide. Wrap the logs in plastic wrap and again in aluminum foil and freeze for up to 3 months. To bake: Use a sharp knife to cut the still frozen dough into ¾-inch slices. Place the slices 2 inches apart on prepared baking sheets and allow them to defrost for 15 minutes before baking them according to the directions above.

German's Chocolate Cake Squares

Makes 12 squares

Baker's German's Sweet Chocolate, named for its creator, Samuel German, has a fair amount of sugar added, along with milk solids and vanilla. This makes for mild, sweet eating, and a dessert that will win the heart of anyone with a sweet tooth. It is readily available in supermarkets. These cake squares contain all the ingredients of a classic American dessert: pecans, shredded sweetened coconut, evaporated milk, and, of course, German's chocolate. This is a gooey dessert that cries out for the accompaniment of a cup of coffee or tea, or a tall glass of cold milk.

Since this cake is frosted in the pan before it is cut, you might want to use an ovenproof glass pan to avoid scratching a metal one as you cut and serve the cake.

For the cake	For the frosting
Unsalted butter for preparing the pan	1 (12-ounce) can evaporated milk
6 ounces Baker's German's Sweet Chocolate, chopped	1½ cups (12 ounces) light brown sugar, packed
2¼ cups (6.25 ounces) all-purpose flour	1½ sticks (6 ounces) unsalted butter
2 teaspoons baking soda	4 extra-large egg yolks
2 teaspoons baking powder	1 teaspoon almond extract
¾ teaspoon salt	1¾ cups (7 ounces) sweetened shredded coconut
4 extra-large eggs, separated	
2 sticks (8 ounces) unsalted butter, at room temperature	1½ cups (6 ounces) pecans, toasted and coarsely chopped
1¾ cups (14 ounces) sugar	6 ounces Baker's German's Sweet Chocolate, chopped in ¼-inch pieces
1 tablespoon vanilla extract	
1 cup (8 ounces) sour cream	
1 cup (5 ounces) semisweet chocolate chips	

Preheat the oven to 350°F. with the rack in the center position. Butter a 9 × 13-inch baking pan (see headnote). If you use a metal pan, reduce the oven temperature to 325°F.

To make the cake, melt the chocolate in a metal bowl placed over, but not touching, a pan of simmering water, or in a microwave-safe bowl in a microwave oven. Stir the chocolate with a wooden spoon as it melts. When the chocolate is melted and smooth, remove the bowl from over the water.

Sift the flour, baking soda, baking powder, and salt into a medium bowl. In a very clean bowl with very clean beaters, beat the egg whites with an electric mixer until stiff, but not dry, peaks form. Set aside.

Place the butter and sugar in a large mixing bowl. With the beaters you used for the egg whites, beat the mixture together on medium speed until it is well combined. Add the egg yolks, one at a time, beating about 1 minute after each addition. Beat in the melted chocolate and the vanilla and mix until the batter is smooth. Scrape down the sides of the bowl with a rubber spatula as you work. Add the flour mixture alternately with the sour cream, beginning and ending with the flour mixture. Use a large rubber spatula to fold the beaten egg whites into the batter. Pour and scrape the batter into the prepared pan. Sprinkle the chocolate chips over the batter. Bake for about 45 minutes, or until a cake tester inserted into the center of the cake comes out clean. Remove the cake from the oven and cool it in the pan on a wire rack.

To make the frosting, place the evaporated milk, brown sugar, butter, egg yolks, and almond extract in a heavy, large saucepan. Place the pan over medium-high heat and whisk until the mixture simmers. Adjust the heat so that the mixture continues to simmer. Cook for about 18 minutes, whisking occasionally, until the mixture leaves a path on the back of the spoon when you draw your finger across it. Remove the frosting from the heat and stir in the coconut and pecans. Spread the warm frosting on the cake. Sprinkle the top with the chopped chocolate. Let the cake stand until the frosting is set, about 2 hours, before cutting into 12 squares.

Store the cake at room temperature, well covered, for up to 3 days.

Mint Chocolate Brownies

Makes 16 brownies

I grew up on Junior Mints, and I never lost my love of the flavor combination of chocolate and peppermint. My idea of a good time (still) is sitting in a movie theater clutching a bag of popcorn in one hand and a box of Junior Mints in the other.

These brownies are the fudgiest I've ever eaten. They are lit from within by a sparkle of mint from both the extract and a surprise ingredient. I tried making them with Junior Mints but the results weren't all I'd hoped for. After Eight mints offer the perfect solution, but if you're like me you should buy extra—I ate one for every three I laid in the pan. If you can't find After Eight mints you can use York Peppermint Patties; they are thicker but do a fine job.

If you really want to go the distance in the taste department, then use the brownie as a base for a Mint Brownie Sundae (recipe follows).

Unsalted butter for preparing the pan

4 ounces unsweetened chocolate, chopped

1 stick (4 ounces) unsalted butter

³/₄ cup (3.75 ounces) all-purpose flour

¹/₄ teaspoon salt

1¹/₄ cups (10 ounces) sugar

3 extra-large eggs

³/₄ teaspoon vanilla extract

¹/₂ teaspoon peppermint extract

20 to 25 After Eight mints or 8 York Peppermint Patties, unwrapped

Preheat the oven to 325°F. with the rack in the center position. Line an 8-inch square baking pan with aluminum foil, allowing it to overlap 2 opposite sides by 2 inches. Butter the foil.

Melt the chocolate and butter in a metal bowl placed over, but not touching, a pan of simmering water, or in a microwave-safe bowl in a microwave oven. Stir until the mixture is melted and smooth. Remove the bowl from over the water and let the mixture cool slightly.

Sift the flour and salt into a small bowl. Set aside. Place the sugar and eggs in a medium bowl. With an electric mixer on medium speed, beat the sugar and eggs until light yellow and fluffy, about 2 minutes. Reduce the mixer speed to low and add the vanilla and peppermint extracts. Add the melted chocolate mixture and mix well. Add the flour mixture and mix just until blended. Scrape half the batter into the prepared pan. Layer the mints evenly over the top surface of the batter. Scrape the remaining batter over the mint layer, being careful not to dislodge the mints. Use an offset spatula or a butter knife to gently smooth the batter; make sure all the mints are covered.

Bake the brownies for 35 to 40 minutes, or until the top is shiny and a cake tester inserted in the center comes out with a few moist crumbs attached. The batter may puff irregularly,

(CONTINUED ON NEXT PAGE)

which is fine. It is better to underbake than to overbake these brownies. Transfer the pan to a wire rack and let the brownies cool completely in the pan.

Use the foil to lift the entire cake of brownies from the pan to a work surface. Peel away the foil and cut the brownies into 16 equal squares. Wrap the brownies individually in plastic wrap and store them at room temperature in an airtight container for up to 2 weeks.

Mint Brownie Sundae

Makes 1 sundae

1 Mint Chocolate Brownie
1 generous scoop of mint chip or peppermint stick ice cream
1/2 cup (4 ounces) Mint Hot Fudge Sauce (recipe follows)
Whipped cream

To assemble the sundae, place a brownie in a shallow bowl. Top with a scoop of ice cream, then pour on the sauce. Place a generous dollop of whipped cream on the sauce.

Mint Hot Fudge Sauce

Makes 3 1/2 cups

2 cups (16 ounces) heavy cream
1/2 cup (4 ounces) dark brown sugar, packed
8 ounces bittersweet chocolate, coarsely chopped
2 ounces unsweetened chocolate, coarsely chopped
3 tablespoons (1.5 ounces) unsalted butter, cut into pieces
1/2 teaspoon peppermint extract, or more to taste

Place the cream in a large saucepan set over medium heat. Bring the cream to a simmer and allow it to cook slowly until it is reduced by about half. (This will take 15 to 20 minutes.) Add the brown sugar and stir until it dissolves. Remove the pan from the heat and stir in the bittersweet and unsweetened chocolates and the butter. Stir until the mixture is smooth. Cool the sauce for 10 minutes, then add the extract. Serve warm.

The sauce can be refrigerated in a tightly sealed plastic container for up to 1 month, or it can be frozen for up to 3 months.

Pistachio Brownies

Makes 9 brownies

If you are looking for something slightly—but not jarringly—new and different, consider these pistachio-studded brownies with a subtle but discernible almond essence. They fill all my essential brownie requirements in that they are fudgy (especially if you take care not to over-bake them), they deliver a big chocolate impact, and they offer some contrasting texture. You can enjoy them as is, or use them as the base of a brownie sundae by placing a scoop of either vanilla or pistachio ice cream on top and adding a healthy serving of your favorite hot fudge sauce. If you really want to go the distance, add some whipped cream and a sprinkling of coarsely chopped salted pistachios on top.

This is another recipe in which it's your call about using salted or unsalted nuts. I've only seen salted pistachios in the shell, so you might want to use the undyed variety if you are going to "crack your own."

Unsalted butter for preparing the pan

6 tablespoons (3 ounces) unsalted butter

3 ounces bittersweet chocolate, chopped

1/2 cup (2.5 ounces) all-purpose flour

1/2 cup (1.6 ounces) unsweetened natural cocoa powder

1/4 teaspoon baking powder

1/4 teaspoon salt

1/2 cup (4 ounces) granulated sugar

1/2 cup (4 ounces) light brown sugar, packed

2 extra-large eggs

1 1/2 teaspoons almond extract

3/4 cup (3 ounces) shelled pistachios, salted or unsalted, very coarsely chopped

Preheat the oven to 350°F. with the rack in the center position. Lightly butter the interior of an 8-inch square baking pan. Set aside.

Melt the butter and chocolate together in a metal bowl set over, but not touching, a pan of simmering water, or in a microwave-safe bowl in a microwave oven. Stir to combine well. Set aside. Sift the flour, cocoa, baking powder, and salt into a small bowl. Set aside. Place the granulated sugar, brown sugar, and eggs in a large mixing bowl. With an electric mixer on high speed beat the mixture until it is pale and thick, about 2 minutes. With the mixer on low speed, beat in the chocolate mixture and almond extract. Remove the bowl from the mixer, scrape down the sides with a rubber spatula, then use the spatula to fold the flour mixture into the chocolate batter. Fold in the nuts. Scrape the batter into the prepared pan. Bake for 30 to 35 minutes, or until the top is shiny and a cake tester inserted into the center of the brownies has very moist crumbs. Cool in the pan before cutting into 9 equal portions.

The brownies can be stored in an airtight container at room temperature for up to 4 days.

Moon Rocks

Makes 24 mini-muffins

These taste just like baked, glazed donuts—without the holes. Sort of a cross between a mini-cake and a muffin, they are completely irresistible. They get dipped in a sugary white glaze as soon as they are cool enough to handle, and they will be eaten as soon as they are discovered.

For the moon rocks

Unsalted butter for preparing the muffin tin

4 ounces unsweetened chocolate, chopped

1½ sticks (6 ounces) unsalted butter

2½ cups (12.5 ounces) all-purpose flour

¼ cup (.75 ounce) unsweetened natural cocoa powder

2 teaspoons baking powder

2 teaspoons baking soda

½ teaspoon salt

2 extra-large eggs

1 cup (8 ounces) sugar

¾ cup (6 ounces) sour cream

For the glaze

1⅓ cups (5.5 ounces) confectioners' sugar, sifted

6 tablespoons (3 ounces) unsalted butter, melted and cooled

Preheat the oven to 350°F. with the rack in the center position. Generously butter the cups of a 24-cup mini-muffin tin.

Melt the chocolate and butter together in a metal bowl set over, but not touching, a pan of simmering water, or in a microwave-safe bowl in a microwave oven. Stir until smooth, then remove from the heat and allow to cool to room temperature. Sift the flour, cocoa, baking powder, baking soda, and salt into a medium bowl. Place the eggs and sugar in the bowl of an electric mixer and beat on high speed until thick and light yellow in color, about 5 minutes for a stand mixer and 10 minutes for a hand mixer. With the mixer on low speed, add the melted chocolate mixture. When it is completely incorporated, add the flour mixture. When just a few flecks of flour remain, add the sour cream. Mix thoroughly and scrape down the sides of the bowl with a rubber spatula. The batter will be thick and slightly fizzy; the baking soda is beginning to work, and you must get the batter into the oven quickly. Use two soup spoons or a small scoop to divide the batter among the muffin cups.

Bake the moon rocks for 15 to 17 minutes, or until the tops are shiny and cracked and a tester inserted in the center comes out clean.

While the moon rocks are baking, prepare the glaze. Place the confectioners' sugar, butter, and 2 tablespoons of hot water in a small bowl. Whisk until smooth. Cover with plastic wrap or a plate to keep the top of the glaze from developing a crust.

When you remove the muffin tins from the oven, immediately tip each moon rock on its side while still in the muffin tin, to allow the bottom and sides to cool for 5 minutes. As soon as the moon rocks are cool enough to handle, but while the tops are still hot, dip the top of each in the glaze, coating with enough glaze to allow some excess to run down the top and sides when the moon rock is placed upright. Set them on a wire rack or baking sheet to cool.

Store the moon rocks in a covered container at room temperature for up to 3 days.

Nuts About Chocolate Squares

Makes thirty-five 2-inch squares

When I ran my catering business I had a loyal customer who ordered a batch of these squares once a week. She told me she served them to her bridge group, but I know she kept them in a plastic container in the freezer and ate a couple every day—without defrosting them. These are rich, rich, rich, so cut them into small bars.

For the crust

Unsalted butter for preparing the pan

3 cups (15 ounces) all-purpose flour

$1/2$ cup (4 ounces) sugar

Finely grated zest of 2 large oranges or $1/4$ teaspoon orange oil

$1/4$ teaspoon salt

2 sticks (8 ounces) unsalted butter, cut into 1-tablespoon pieces, at room temperature

1 extra-large egg

For the chocolate nut topping

2 sticks (8 ounces) unsalted butter, cut into pieces

$1/2$ cup (4 ounces) honey

$1/4$ cup (2 ounces) granulated sugar

1 cup (8 ounces) dark brown sugar, packed

4 ounces unsweetened chocolate, finely chopped

$1/4$ cup (2 ounces) heavy cream

$13/4$ cups (7 ounces) pecan halves or large pieces

$13/4$ cups (7 ounces) walnut pieces

$13/4$ cups (7 ounces) blanched almonds, coarsely chopped

Butter the interior sides and bottom of a $151/2 \times 10$ $1/2$-inch jelly-roll pan. Place the pan in the freezer or refrigerator to chill, as it is easiest to spread the dough for the crust in a cold pan.

To make the crust, preheat the oven to 375°F. with the rack in the lower third position. Place the flour, sugar, orange zest, and salt in the work bowl of a food processor fitted with the metal blade. Pulse to combine. Scatter the butter pieces over the flour mixture and pulse until the dough resembles coarse meal. Add the egg and pulse until the dough holds together. (Alternatively, the crust can be made with an electric mixer. Place the butter and sugar in a large mixing bowl and beat them together on medium speed to combine. Add the orange zest, salt, and egg, and beat until combined. Gradually add the flour and beat only until the dough holds together.)

Place large spoonfuls of dough all over the bottom of the prepared pan. Flour your fingertips and use them to press the dough firmly and evenly onto the bottom and up the sides of the prepared pan. There must not be any holes or thin spots in the bottom portion of the pastry. Prick the bottom surface of the crust with a fork at $1/2$-inch intervals, then place the pan in the refrigerator or freezer for 10 minutes. Bake the crust for 15 to 20 minutes, until it is slightly firm and lightly browned around the edges. If the dough puffs while baking, prick it gently with a fork in a few places. Remove the crust from the oven but maintain the oven temperature while you make the topping.

To make the topping, place the butter and honey in a heavy 3-quart saucepan. Place over medium heat and cook until the butter has melted. Stir in the granulated sugar and brown sugar, and stir until the sugar has dissolved. Increase the heat to high and bring the mixture to a boil without stirring. Boil for exactly 2 minutes. Immediately remove the pan from the heat and stir in the chocolate, heavy cream, and all the nuts. Quickly pour and scrape the mixture into the partially baked crust, and use a rubber spatula or the back of a wooden spoon to spread it as evenly as possible.

Bake for 20 to 25 minutes, or until the chocolate mixture is bubbling and the crust is golden brown. Remove the pan from the oven and place it on a rack to cool completely. When cool, cut around the sides of the bars with a small, sharp knife. Unless you don't mind cutting these squares in your baking pan, first cover the pan with a cookie sheet, then invert the bars onto the cookie sheet. If some of the filling has penetrated the crust and has caused it to stick to the pan, bang the inverted pan sharply on the cookie sheet. Remove the baking pan. Cover the exposed crust surface with another cookie sheet or a wire rack and re-invert the bars. Carefully slide the block off onto a cutting board and use a long, heavy knife to cut it into small squares. Wipe the blade frequently with a damp cloth as you cut.

The squares can be kept, covered, at room temperature for up to 1 week or can be frozen in a tightly sealed container for up to 3 months. My family loves them straight from the freezer.

Chocolate–Peanut Butter Shortbread Bars

Makes 16 bars

Peanut butter holds a place of honor in the comfort-food department. Straight from the jar, spread on a Ritz cracker, or melting on hot toast, one taste means that no matter how lousy life is, things are going to get better. The idea of putting peanut butter in cookies must have come right after someone thought of putting it between two slices of soft white bread and adding either a cloak of grape jelly, a layer of bananas, or a glob of Fluff.

Peanut butter gives a deep, but not cloying sweetness, and the fat keeps the texture tender and melting in your mouth. While the people of Scotland might wince at what we out-of-control Americans are doing to their national cookie, I say peanut butter only makes this shortbread even better.

For the shortbread

Unsalted butter and flour for preparing the pan

2 cups (10 ounces) all-purpose flour

1/2 cup (2 ounces) confectioners' sugar

2 sticks (8 ounces) unsalted butter, chilled and cut into small pieces

1 1/2 cups (12 ounces) chunky peanut butter

1/2 cup (2.5 ounces) semisweet mini chocolate chips

For the chocolate frosting

3 ounces bittersweet chocolate, coarsely chopped

3 tablespoons unsalted butter, at room temperature

1/3 cup (3 ounces) sour cream

1/2 cup (2 ounces) confectioners' sugar

Preheat the oven to 350°F. with the rack in the center position. Coat the bottom and sides of either an 11 × 7-inch or a 9-inch square ovenproof glass baking pan with butter. (You can use a metal pan, but using glass completely eliminates the damage a knife might do when you cut the bars.) Dust with flour, knocking out the excess.

To make the shortbread, sift the flour and confectioners' sugar into the work bowl of a food processor. Pulse to combine, then add the butter and 1/2 cup of the peanut butter. Process until the dough forms a ball. Scrape the dough onto a work surface and knead in the chocolate chips. Press the dough into the bottom of the prepared pan. Do not force the dough up the sides of the pan; it should form a solid, flat layer in the pan. Bake the shortbread for 30 minutes, or until it is fairly firm to the touch and barely golden. Transfer the pan to a wire rack and let stand for 10 minutes. Meanwhile, place the remaining 1 cup of peanut butter in a small saucepan over low heat. Stir continuously with a wooden spoon or heat-proof rubber spatula just until melted. While the shortbread is still warm, pour the melted peanut butter over the surface and use an offset spatula or a butter knife to spread the peanut butter evenly over the shortbread. Place the pan in the refrigerator for about 30 minutes to cool the shortbread.

To make the frosting, melt the chopped chocolate in a medium metal bowl set over, but not touching, a pan of gently simmering water, or in a microwave-safe bowl in a microwave oven. Remove the chocolate from the heat. Place the butter and sour cream in a medium bowl. With an electric mixer on medium speed, beat the butter mixture until well combined. Scrape in the chocolate and mix until combined. Add the confectioners' sugar and mix on low speed for 30 seconds, then beat on high speed for 1 minute, until the mixture is light and fluffy.

Use an offset spatula or a butter knife to spread the frosting over the peanut-butter layer on the shortbread. To serve, cut the shortbread into 16 bars and remove them from the baking dish with an offset spatula.

The shortbread can be stored in an airtight container at room temperature for 1 week.

Russell Crowe Bars

Makes 9 bars

My sons are always amazed (and, I must admit, a trifle embarrassed) by my unabashed adoration of certain movie stars. They guffawed when I swooned over John Travolta in *Saturday Night Fever* (although they did finally see my point when *Pulp Fiction* and *Get Shorty* came out). The same thing happened with the early Russell Crowe movies: I spotted him right off the bat in a little-seen low-budget Australian cowboy flick called *Hammers over the Anvil.* The opening scene of him riding bareback and bare-assed reveals all (as far as I'm concerned). My very favorite movie of his was *Mystery, Alaska* because it combines three things I love: sports (hockey, to be exact), romance, and off-beat humor. During my second or third screening of this movie I decided a guy as delicious as R.C. needs a dessert of his own. So I went shopping for good things Australian, combined them with chocolate, and the rest, as they say, is history.

For the crust

1³/4 cups (7 ounces) macadamia nuts, toasted

1¹/2 cups (7.5 ounces) all-purpose flour

1/3 cup (1.5 ounces) confectioners' sugar

2 teaspoons grated orange zest

1 extra-large egg yolk

1/4 teaspoon salt

1 stick (4 ounces) unsalted butter, chilled, cut into 8 pieces

For the filling

1/3 cup (1.3 ounces) crystallized ginger pieces, packed

1/3 cup (1.6 ounces) dried apricot halves, packed

1/3 cup (1.6 ounces) dried mango pieces, packed (see Note)

1 cup (8 ounces) heavy cream

1/4 cup (2 ounces) sugar

1/2 teaspoon vanilla extract

2 extra-large eggs

6 ounces bittersweet chocolate, coarsely chopped

Preheat the oven to 350°F. with the rack in the center position. Have ready an ungreased 9-inch square baking pan. (A glass baking pan works well here, as it may scratch a metal pan to cut the bars in the pan.)

To make the crust, place 1 cup of the nuts in the bowl of a food processor. Set the remaining nuts aside to use with the filling. Process until the nuts are finely ground. Add the flour, confectioners' sugar, zest, egg yolk, and salt; process, pulsing, until the ingredients are well mixed. Scatter the butter pieces on the dough and continue to pulse until the dough clumps together. Scrape the dough into the baking pan. Press it evenly into the bottom and $1/2$ inch up the sides of the pan. Bake the crust for 15 minutes, until the crust is light brown and somewhat firm to the touch. Remove the pan from the oven. Let it cool on a wire rack while you prepare the filling. Maintain the oven temperature.

Use a pair of kitchen scissors to cut the ginger into $1/4$-inch-wide strips, then use the scissors to cut the strips into $1/4$-inch dice. Use a sharp, heavy knife to cut the apricots and mangos into thin strips, then cut the strips crosswise into small dice. Set aside. Coarsely chop the remaining $3/4$ cup macadamia nuts, and set them aside. Place the heavy cream, sugar, and vanilla in a medium bowl. Whisk together, then add the eggs. Whisk until thoroughly combined, then stir in the ginger, apricots, and mango. Pour the custard mixture into the prepared crust. Sprinkle on the chopped nuts and chocolate.

Bake for 25 to 30 minutes, until a knife inserted into the center of the custard comes out clean. Transfer the pan to a rack to cool to room temperature before cutting into squares.

The bars can be stored, covered, at room temperature for up to 3 days.

NOTE
If dried mango is unavailable,
use an additional $1/3$ cup apricot
halves as a substitute.

White Chocolate and Macadamia Nut Blondies

Makes nine 2½-inch squares

Loaded with goodies, this unconventional take on brownies is rich, moist, and packed with flavor. While the recipe calls for cutting them into nine squares, you might want to cut them smaller, as a little goes a long way.

Unsalted butter and flour for preparing the pan

8 ounces white chocolate

1 cup (5 ounces) all-purpose flour

½ teaspoon salt

1 stick (4 ounces) unsalted butter, at room temperature

¾ cup (6 ounces) light brown sugar, packed

2 teaspoons instant espresso powder or granules

1 teaspoon vanilla extract

2 extra-large eggs

1 cup (4 ounces) macadamia nuts, chopped (if the nuts are salted, toss them in a sieve to remove excess salt before chopping)

Preheat the oven to 350°F. with the rack in the center position. Butter the interior of an 8-inch square baking pan. Line the pan with aluminum foil so that the foil extends beyond two opposite edges of the pan by about 2 inches. (This will help you remove the baked blondies from the pan for cutting later.) Butter the foil. Dust with flour, knocking out the excess.

Coarsely chop 4 ounces of the chocolate. Melt it in a medium metal bowl set over, but not touching, a pan of simmering water, or in a microwave-safe bowl in a microwave oven. Chop the remaining 4 ounces of chocolate in uniform pieces, no larger than ½ inch square. Set aside.

Sift the flour and salt into a small bowl. Set aside. Place the butter, brown sugar, espresso powder, and vanilla in a large bowl. Beat the mixture with an electric mixer on high speed until it is light and fluffy, about 1 minute. Beat in the eggs, one at a time, beating well after each addition. Reduce the mixer speed to low and scrape in the melted chocolate; mix until it is well combined. With the mixer still on low, mix in the flour mixture. Use a rubber spatula to fold in the chopped chocolate and the nuts. Pour and scrape the batter into the prepared pan.

Bake for 35 minutes, or until the top is lightly browned, the blondies have begun to pull away from the sides of the pan, and a cake tester inserted into the center comes out clean. Remove the pan from the oven and let the blondies cool in the pan for 20 minutes. Use the foil to help you lift the blondies from the pan to a cutting board. Cut the blondies into 9 bars. When they are completely cool, wrap them individually in plastic wrap and store at room temperature for up to 3 days.

Toll House Cookies

Makes about 5 dozen cookies

I imagine innkeeper Ruth Wakefield didn't have a clue that day in 1937 that the outcome of adding pieces of chopped chocolate to her butter cookies at her Whitman, Massachusetts, inn, the Toll House, would have such a long-lasting and far-reaching impact on cookie lovers all over the world.

2¼ cups (11.25 ounces) all-purpose flour

1 teaspoon baking soda

1 teaspoon salt

2 sticks (8 ounces) unsalted butter, at room temperature

¾ cup (6 ounces) granulated sugar

¾ cup (6 ounces) dark brown sugar, packed

1 teaspoon vanilla extract

2 extra-large eggs

2 cups (10 ounces) semisweet chocolate chips

1 cup (4 ounces) toasted walnuts, very coarsely chopped

Preheat the oven to 375°F. with a rack in the upper third and a rack in the lower third of the oven. Line 2 heavy-duty baking sheets with parchment paper or silicone pan liners; it is not necessary to butter the lining material.

Place the flour, baking soda, and salt in a small bowl and whisk with a fork or wire whisk until well combined. Place the butter, granulated and brown sugars, and vanilla in the bowl of an electric mixer. (If you are mixing by hand, place the ingredients in a medium mixing bowl.) Beat the butter mixture on medium-high speed or beat with a wooden spoon until the mixture is smooth and creamy. Add the eggs, one at a time, mixing or stirring well after each addition. Mix or stir in the chocolate chips and nuts.

Drop the batter by rounded tablespoons onto the prepared baking sheets. Bake for 9 to 11 minutes, or until the cookies are golden brown and the edges look crisp. Transfer the baking sheets to wire racks to cool for 10 minutes, then use a spatula to lift the cookies from the baking sheets to the racks. (If your oven heats unevenly, rotate the baking sheets front to back and top to bottom halfway through the baking tme. For chewier cookies, slam the baking sheets on the counter once or twice before placing them on the wire racks to cool.)

When cool, the cookies can be stored in an airtight container at room temperature for up to 2 weeks. They may be frozen in heavy-duty resealable plastic bags for up to 3 months. The mixed, raw dough can be frozen in a covered plastic container for up to 3 months. Defrost the dough in the refrigerator before forming and baking the cookies.

White Chocolate–Cherry Cookies

Makes about 30 cookies

While no one in his or her right mind would ever get sick of good old chocolate chip cookies, every once in a while a change from tradition can do us all a bit of good. These gems with bright nuggets of dried cherries have a bounce that will wake up your mouth and make everyone around you wonder what you're smiling at.

1 cup plus 2 tablespoons (6 ounces) all-purpose flour

1/2 teaspoon baking powder

1/4 teaspoon baking soda

1/4 teaspoon salt

1 stick (4 ounces) unsalted butter, at room temperature

1/3 cup (3 ounces) light brown sugar, packed

1/4 cup (2 ounces) granulated sugar

1 extra-large egg

3/4 teaspoon almond extract

3/4 cup (4 ounces) dried cherries

1/2 cup (2 ounces) slivered almonds, toasted

5 ounces white chocolate, coarsely chopped

Preheat the oven to 375°F. with the rack in the center position. Line 2 baking sheets with parchment paper or silicone pan liners.

Sift the flour, baking powder, baking soda, and salt into a medium bowl. Place the butter, brown sugar, and granulated sugar in a large mixing bowl. With an electric mixer on medium-high speed, beat the mixture until it is light and fluffy, about 1 minute. Add the egg and almond extract and mix well. Reduce the mixer speed to low and add the flour mixture. Stir in the cherries, almonds, and chopped white chocolate.

Use a 1-tablespoon measure or scoop to place rounded tablespoons of dough 2 inches apart on the prepared baking sheets. Bake the cookies one sheet at a time for 10 minutes, or until the cookies are golden around the edges but still somewhat soft in the centers. Transfer the cookies to a wire rack to cool completely.

The cookies can be stored at room temperature in a tightly closed container for 2 weeks.

9. Kids in the Kitchen

IT TAKES a special kind of adult to cook with children. You have to have a high mess tolerance, almost unlimited patience, no hang-ups about turning out picture-perfect food, and you have to come armed with a recipe that lets the kids actually do some of the cooking without the danger of incineration, electrocution, or other bodily harm.

Any recipe that declares itself to be kid-friendly must be made with foods that kids like to eat; no matter how much chocolate you pile on that prune or those glacéed fruits, you're going to have a hell of a sales job when it comes to finding school-age volunteers to chow it down. The recipe must include at least one step in which everyone gets to put their hands in the bowl to toss, stir, knead, or shape the contents. Time is important; very few children are interested in waiting three hours for something to harden, mellow, chill, or rise. In order for the adult to stay interested in the project it helps if the finished dessert is something that a grown-up might eat.

The following recipes have all been kid-tested as well as adult-tested, and everyone agrees they pass both tests with flying colors. In this testing, particularly of the recipes involving dipping things in melted chocolate, I have to admit we got a little carried away. I can't remember whose idea it was to make chocolate handprints, but I do remember how much fun it was. Months later I find a stray chocolate fingerprint under the table or in the back of the refrigerator, and I have to smile at the memory of my hand slipping into a shallow pan of slightly-warmer-than-body–temperature melted milk chocolate, how good it felt to move my fingers around in the silky smoothness, and what a satisfying feeling it was to plop my hand flat down on the brown paper bag someone had left on the counter, making my mark in my favorite medium. If this is what it means to be a kid again, then bring on the chocolate: I'm ready.

Chocolate-Covered Graham Crackers and Pretzels

Makes 32 to 36 graham crackers or 38 to 40 pretzels

If you are faced with a houseful of kids on a rainy day or need a project for Cub Scouts, Brownies, or the school cooking class, consider this recipe. Fair warning: it will be messy and kids will not stay clean, but oh, will they be happy. When my kids were little I let them finger-paint in the bathtub or outside on a picnic table within easy access of the garden hose—two places you might want to consider for undertaking this project.

Nonstick vegetable cooking spray

1 pound (16 ounces) bittersweet chocolate, coarsely chopped

8 to 9 whole graham crackers, each cracker broken into 4 pieces, following the scoring on the crackers; or 38 to 40 2-inch pretzels or 5-inch-long pretzel rods

Coat a wire rack with nonstick spray and place it on a baking sheet. Temper the chocolate according to the directions on page 11.

Place 2 graham crackers or pretzels in the chocolate. Use a spatula or wooden spoon (or your fingers) to gently move them around in the chocolate. Try to discourage the licking of fingers until all the crackers or pretzels have been coated. When they are evenly coated, remove them from the bowl with a fork or table knife (or your fingers) and place them on the prepared wire rack. Repeat with the remaining crackers or pretzels. If the chocolate becomes too cool to cover the crackers or pretzels, place the chocolate bowl back over simmering water and stir as it softens.

(You may have chocolate left over. You can warm it just a bit and drizzle it over the surface for decoration. The easiest way to do this is to dip the tines of a fork in the chocolate and gently swing it over the pretzels or crackers.) Place the baking sheet with the rack in the refrigerator until the chocolate has set, about 20 minutes.

Store the graham crackers or pretzels in an airtight container at room temperature for up to 1 week.

Chocolate Cereal Treats

Makes 12 to 16 treats

This is our very own version of the classic Rice Krispies treats, which once were considered kids-only food, but now, at least in my house, qualify as a popular snack for all ages. A camp lunch box wasn't complete without a wax paper–wrapped cube or two. Funny how things change: when I saw a cover story about both lunch boxes and Rice Krispies treats in *Martha Stewart Living* I wondered whether if I had kept the kids' Scooby-Doo or Speed Racer lunch boxes around, they might be worth a fortune.

4 tablespoons (2 ounces) unsalted butter, plus additional for preparing pan

10 ounces (5 cups) mini or regular marshmallows (if using regular marshmallows, use scissors to cut each in several pieces to make melting easier)

²/₃ cup (2 ounces) unsweetened Dutch-processed cocoa powder

4 cups (about 5 ounces) Rice Krispies

2 cups (about 2 ounces) Cheerios

¹/₂ cup (2.5 ounces) dried sweet or tart cherries (optional)

Butter a 13 × 9 × 2-inch pan.

Place the 4 tablespoons of butter and the marshmallows in a 2-quart saucepan. Stir them together over low heat. When the marshmallows are almost completely melted, stir in the cocoa powder. Continue to stir over low heat until the mixture is smooth and evenly colored. Stir in the Rice Krispies and the Cheerios. Scrape the mixture into the prepared pan and use a piece of wax paper or plastic wrap to smooth the mixture in the pan. Sprinkle the dried cherries over the cereal, if you are using them. Use the wax paper or plastic wrap to press them in gently.

Place the pan in the refrigerator until the mixture is cold. Turn the contents of the pan out onto a cutting board, turn it right side up, and cut into 12 or 16 servings using a heavy, sharp knife.

Store the cereal treats in an airtight container at room temperature for up to 1 week.

Soft Chocolate Toffee Bit Cookies

Makes 24 cookies

Kids love cookies and, until they are a certain age, they like them without nuts. In addition, most kids don't like to chew (thus the clamor for soft white bread when the obvious choice should be crusty artisan loaves full of seeds and mysterious dark grains). These soft cookies will delight any child longing for something good (and easy) to eat. They are so good you might even get him or her to agree to a green vegetable first.

8 ounces bittersweet chocolate, coarsely chopped

2 tablespoons (1 ounce) unsalted butter

¼ cup (1.25 ounces) all-purpose flour

½ teaspoon baking powder

⅛ teaspoon salt

¾ cup (6 ounces) light brown sugar, packed

2 extra-large eggs

2 teaspoons vanilla extract

¾ cup (3.5 ounces) toffee bits (found in the baking aisle of the supermarket)

1 cup (5 ounces) semisweet chocolate chips

Preheat the oven to 350°F. with the rack in the center position. Line 2 heavy-duty baking sheets with parchment paper, silicone pan liners, or buttered aluminum foil. Set aside.

Melt the chocolate and butter in a metal bowl set over, but not touching, a pan of simmering water, or in a microwave-safe bowl in a microwave oven. When they have melted, remove the bowl from over the water and set aside to cool to lukewarm.

Sift the flour, baking powder, and salt into a small bowl. Place the light brown sugar and eggs in a medium mixing bowl. With an electric mixer on medium-high speed, beat the mixture until the eggs are thick and light-colored. Beat in the melted chocolate mixture and vanilla. Reduce the mixer speed to low and mix in the flour mixture. Scrape the sides of the bowl with a rubber spatula as you work. Use a wooden spoon to stir in the toffee bits and chocolate chips. Use a 1-tablespoon measure or scoop to drop portions of batter onto the prepared sheets, about 2½ inches apart.

Bake the cookies, one sheet at a time, for about 12 minutes, or until the tops are cracked and dry but the cookies are still soft to the touch. Do not overbake; the cookies will firm up as they cool. Remove the cookies from the oven and allow them to cool, on their baking sheets, on wire racks.

Store the cookies in an airtight container at room temperature for up to 1 week.

Chocolate-Covered Cape Cod Potato Chips

Makes 50 to 75 chips, depending on the size of the chips

Here's another child-centered activity that presents a great opportunity to introduce the concept of salt and sweet to impressionable minds and mouths.

Cape Cod brand russet or thick-cut potato chips are the perfect chips to use when making these, as they are sturdier and less apt to break during the dipping process than other brands, and I think the taste is first-class.

Whatever you do, don't be tempted to refrigerate the dipped chips to expedite the hardening process—unless you like soggy chips.

9 ounces bittersweet or semisweet chocolate, chopped, or 9 ounces (scant 2 cups) semisweet chocolate chips

1 (5.5-ounce) bag of Cape Cod potato chips, russet or thick-cut

Line 2 baking sheets with parchment paper, silicone pan liners, or aluminum foil. Set aside.

Temper the chocolate according to the directions on page 11.

Grasp a potato chip between your thumb and forefinger and gently drag it through the chocolate, covering about three-fourths of the chip on both sides. Allow any excess chocolate to drip back into the bowl. Use a teaspoon or a small rubber spatula to smear more chocolate on places that you might have missed. (Some people prefer to coat only one side of the chip—it's up to you.) As each chip is coated, place it on a prepared baking sheet until the chocolate sets. Repeat with the remaining chips.

These probably won't last long enough to pack up to save for later, but if you do have some left over, place them in an airtight container. Stored in a cool, dry place, they will keep for several days.

Chocolate Sugar Cookies

Makes 24 to 48 cookies, depending on the size of your cookie cutters

This dough resembles soft Tootsie Roll–type modeling clay, which makes it easy to work with as long as you remember to chill it before rolling. The cookies are tender and tasty, yet durable enough for a cookie jar or for packing and shipping to your favorite college student or grandchild.

Get out your cookie cutters and have a ball. Sprinkle the tops with sugar before baking, or allow the cookies to cool and go to town with Royal Icing (recipe follows).

2³/₄ cups (13.75 ounces) all-purpose flour

1 teaspoon baking powder

1 teaspoon baking soda

1 teaspoon salt

¹/₄ cup (.75 ounce) unsweetened Dutch-processed cocoa powder

1¹/₂ sticks (6 ounces) unsalted butter, at room temperature

³/₄ cup (6 ounces) granulated sugar

2 extra-large eggs

2 teaspoons vanilla extract

Coarse sugar or Royal Icing (recipe follows), optional

Preheat the oven to 350°F. with 2 racks as close to the center position as possible. Line 2 cookie sheets with parchment paper or silicone pan liners.

Sift the flour, baking powder, baking soda, salt, and cocoa powder into a medium mixing bowl.

Place the butter and sugar in the bowl of a stand mixer or in a large mixing bowl. With either the stand mixer or a handheld electric mixer on high speed, beat the butter and sugar together until light and fluffy. Reduce the mixer speed to low and add the eggs, one at a time, mixing well after each addition. Mix in the vanilla. Add the flour mixture, ¹/₂ cup at a time, mixing only until a stiff dough forms. (Alternatively, the dough can be mixed by hand with a wooden spoon.) Divide the dough in half and flatten each half into a rough disk. Dust with flour if sticky, then cover with plastic wrap and refrigerate for at least 1 hour, or overnight.

Place 1 chilled disk of dough between 2 pieces of plastic or deli wrap, or on a lightly floured work surface. Roll it into a ¹/₄-inch-thick circle. Try to avoid getting flour on the top surface of the dough, because it will cause white spots on the finished cookies. If necessary, use a pastry brush to remove any flour on the dough surface. Cut the dough into shapes with cookie cutters or the rim of a glass that has been dipped in flour or lightly buttered. Sprinkle each cookie with coarse sugar, or leave the surfaces plain if you plan to decorate them later. Place the

(CONTINUED ON NEXT PAGE)

cookies ½ inch apart on the prepared baking sheets. Bake for 9 to 12 minutes, or until they are puffy and the bottoms are dry. Transfer the cookies to a rack to cool.

Royal Icing

Makes about 2½ cups

The great thing about royal icing is that it hardens, so you can stack the decorated cookies without smudging the frosting.

3 extra-large egg whites

½ teaspoon cream of tartar

4 cups (1 pound) confectioners' sugar, sifted

1 teaspoon vanilla extract or other extract or flavoring of your choice

Food coloring (optional)

Use a very clean bowl and beaters of an electric mixer to beat the egg whites and cream of tartar on high speed until foamy. On medium speed, add the sugar, ¼ cup at a time. When all the sugar has been added, scrape down the sides of the bowl, then set the mixer on high speed. Beat for 5 to 7 minutes, until the mixture is stiff and shiny. Beat in the vanilla and food coloring, if desired. The more you beat, the stiffer it will become. If it becomes too stiff to be pushed through a piping tip, add warm water 1 teaspoon at a time until the frosting has been thinned to the right consistency. The icing dries very quickly, so be sure to keep a damp cloth over the bowl when you have finished beating the icing. Scoop the icing into a piping bag fitted with a small piping tip and decorate the cookies.

The sugared or decorated cookies may be stored in an airtight container at room temperature for up to 2 weeks.

NOTE
I love to use meringue powder (see Sources, page 271) instead of raw egg whites for royal icing —it's easy and makes, I think, a superior icing. A recipe comes on the side of the container. Meringue powder is not the same as the powdered egg whites you find in the health-food store.

Peanut Butter Cups

Makes 36 candies

I was such a mean mother. Every Halloween I made my kids hand over all the Reese's Peanut Butter Cups they had collected. I realize I could have gone out and bought a bag of my own and let the kids scarf down theirs in peace, but somehow it just wasn't the same as pawing through all the other stuff to get to pay dirt. I had forgotten just how good the combination of chocolate and peanut butter can be until Susan Schwartz reminded me with the following recipe for homemade peanut butter cups.

With supervision, kids can make these—just make sure they save some for the grown-ups.

2¹/₂ cups (12 ounces) semisweet chocolate chips

¹/₄ cup (2 ounces) confectioners' sugar

2 tablespoons sour cream

1 tablespoon heavy cream

¹/₄ teaspoon vanilla extract

1 tablespoon (.5 ounce) unsalted butter, at room temperature

³/₄ cup (6 ounces) peanut butter, chunky or smooth

³/₄ cup (3 ounces) roasted, salted peanuts, chopped (optional)

Place 36 foil mini-muffin cups (they are about 1 inch across) on 2 cookie sheets or in mini-muffin tins.

Melt 1¹/₄ cups (6 ounces) of the chocolate chips in a metal bowl set over, but not touching, a pan of simmering water, or in a microwave-safe bowl in a microwave oven. Stir until melted and smooth. Remove the bowl from over the water. Place about 1 teaspoon of melted chocolate in each foil cup. Rotate each cup as you fill it, and use a small, flat knife or spatula to spread the chocolate about ³/₄ inch up the inside of the cup. Refrigerate until the chocolate is set, about 20 minutes.

In a medium bowl, place the confectioners' sugar, sour cream, cream, vanilla, and butter. Mix the ingredients together well, then add the peanut butter. Stir well to combine. Set aside at room temperature until the chocolate cups are set.

Use a small spoon to drop a rounded teaspoon of the peanut butter mixture into each chocolate-lined cup. Flatten the peanut butter mixture with the spoon. Melt the remaining 1¹/₄ cups (6 ounces) of chocolate chips. Spoon enough of the melted chocolate into each cup to cover the filling completely. If you are using the chopped peanuts, sprinkle some over each peanut butter cup. Dip a fork into the remaining melted chocolate and carefully wave the fork from side to side over the tops of the peanut butter cups to form a decorative pattern. Refrigerate until the chocolate is set, about 20 minutes. To store, cover with plastic wrap, or place them in an airtight container in the refrigerator.

Chocolate Caramel Popcorn

Makes 4 cups

An appreciation of the combination of salty and sweet isn't an acquired taste; it's something you are hardwired with. Of course, while this recipe calls for the kind of salty popcorn you find in the snack aisle of the supermarket, you can certainly pop your own and skip the salt. This recipe was perfected and contributed by Lesley Abrams-Schwartz, who has a uniquely refined sense of what goes well with chocolate. The chocolate in this recipe must be tempered. Directions for tempering are on page 11.

1 cup sugar

4 cups salted, store-bought popcorn, or homemade popcorn, salted to taste

8 ounces bittersweet chocolate, coarsely chopped

Line a baking sheet with parchment paper or a silicone pan liner. It is not necessary to butter or oil the lining material.

Place the sugar and $3/4$ cup (6 ounces) of water in a large saucepan. Attach a candy thermometer to the side of the pan. Make sure the end does not touch the bottom of the pan. Heat the mixture over medium-low heat and stir with a whisk until the sugar dissolves. Increase the heat to high and bring to a rapid boil without stirring. Reduce the heat to medium-high. Use a wet pastry brush or dampened paper towel to brush down the sides of the pan to prevent sugar crystals from forming. Cook until the thermometer registers 320°F. Add the popcorn to the saucepan and stir quickly with a wooden spoon to coat the popcorn completely. Pour and scrape the mixture onto the prepared baking sheet. When the popcorn is cool enough to touch, use your fingers to break any clumps of popcorn into smaller pieces.

Temper the chocolate, using a large metal bowl for the process. Pour all the caramel-coated popcorn into the bowl with the melted chocolate and stir with a wooden spoon to coat each piece completely. Pour and scrape the coated popcorn onto the baking sheet you used earlier, and scrape any remaining chocolate onto the popcorn. Use a large rubber spatula to gently spread the popcorn and chocolate on the baking sheet, separating the pieces of popcorn as much as possible. Some pieces will stick together to form little clusters, while others will remain separate. Set aside to cool. The popcorn can be stored in an airtight container at room temperature for 2 weeks.

Candy-Filled Peanut Butter Cookies

Makes about 36 cookies

One day I was stuck in traffic for a very long time behind two delivery trucks that had collided and spilled their contents across the roadway. One of the trucks was owned by a grocery home-delivery service and had disgorged several shopping carts' worth of dry goods. As we crawled by the site I saw a squashed box of peanut butter cookies sitting on top of a box of Snickers candy bars. Since I had little else to do, I began to think about how yummy a bite of Snickers would taste inside a warm peanut butter cookie. . . .

$1^{1}/_{2}$ cups (7.5 ounces) all-purpose flour

$1/_2$ teaspoon baking powder

$1/_2$ teaspoon salt

1 stick (4 ounces) unsalted butter, at room temperature

$1/_2$ cup (4 ounces) chunky peanut butter

1 teaspoon vanilla extract

$1/_2$ cup (4 ounces) granulated sugar

$1/_2$ cup (4 ounces) light brown sugar, packed

1 extra-large egg

3 (2.07-ounce) Snickers bars, cut into $1/_4$-inch pieces

Preheat the oven to 350°F. with the rack in the center position. Line 2 baking sheets with silicone pan liners or parchment paper. It is not necessary to butter or oil the lining material.

Sift the flour, baking powder, and salt into a medium mixing bowl. Place the butter, peanut butter, and vanilla in a large mixing bowl. Beat the mixture with an electric mixer on medium speed until well blended, about 1 minute. Add the granulated and brown sugars and beat until they are well blended, scraping down the sides of the bowl with a rubber spatula as needed. Add half the flour mixture and beat well. Add the egg and beat well to combine. Beat in the remaining flour mixture until no traces of flour remain.

To form the cookies, use your fingers to roll 1 tablespoon of dough into a $1^{1}/_{4}$-inch-diameter ball. Flatten the ball slightly against the palm of one hand and press one piece of candy onto the dough. Wrap the dough around the candy to enclose it. Continue with the remaining dough and candy. Place the cookies 2 inches apart on the prepared pans. Mark the top of each cookie by pressing it very lightly with the tines of a fork, in a crisscross pattern. Bake the cookies, one sheet at a time, for 12 to 14 minutes, or until the cookies are dry on top, lightly browned around the edges, and golden brown on the bottoms. For chewier cookies, bang the baking sheet once on the counter after removing it from the oven. Cool the cookies on the baking sheet for 5 minutes, then use a metal spatula to transfer them to a wire rack to cool completely.

The cooled cookies can be stored in an airtight container at room temperature for up to 3 days.

Denver Chocolate Pudding Cake

Makes 8 servings

This cake might not win any beauty contests, but it will win a place in your heart for its ease of preparation and its magical metamorphosis in the oven. The very last step, in which you pour boiling water over a layered batter, creates a cake with its own sauce. While a variety of names, from "Chocolate Pudding Cake" to "Chocolate Surprise Cake," have been attached to this unique dessert, I've always known it as Denver Chocolate Pudding Cake and my guess (completely unsubstantiated) is that it got this name because it's the perfect dessert to make when you live at a high altitude. It doesn't rise at all and it's not completely solid when it's done cooking—the two earmarks of a high-altitude baking disaster. In this case, however, the results are magnificent.

Unsalted butter for preparing the pan

4 ounces unsweetened chocolate, coarsely chopped

1 cup (5 ounces) all-purpose flour

1 1/2 teaspoons baking powder

1/2 teaspoon salt

1 stick (4 ounces) unsalted butter, at room temperature

1 1/3 cups (11 ounces) granulated sugar

1/2 cup (4 ounces) whole milk

2 teaspoons vanilla extract

2 teaspoons Crème de Cacao, or other chocolate liqueur (optional)

1/2 cup (4 ounces) dark brown sugar, packed

1/4 cup (.75 ounce) unsweetened natural cocoa powder

1 1/2 cups (12 ounces) boiling water

1 tablespoon instant espresso powder or granules

1 cup (8 ounces) heavy cream (optional)

Preheat the oven to 350°F. with the rack in the center position. Coat an 8-inch square baking pan with butter.

Melt the chocolate in a medium metal bowl set over, but not touching, a pan of simmering water, or in a microwave-safe bowl in a microwave oven.

(CONTINUED ON NEXT PAGE)

Place a mesh sieve over a small bowl and put the flour, baking powder, and salt in the sieve. Set aside. Place the butter and 2/3 cup of the granulated sugar in a large mixing bowl. Beat the mixture with an electric mixer on high speed until it is light and fluffy, about 2 minutes. Stop the mixer and position the sieve with the flour mixture over the butter mixture. Sift in the flour mixture and add any that remains in the small bowl. Pour in the milk. Mix on low speed until the ingredients are just combined; do not overbeat. Use a rubber spatula to fold in the melted chocolate, 1 teaspoon of the vanilla, and the Crème de Cacao (if using). Pour and scrape the mixture into the prepared pan. Spread the batter evenly in the pan.

In the same bowl (no need to wash it) combine the remaining 2/3 cup granulated sugar, the brown sugar, and the cocoa powder. Sprinkle this mixture evenly over the batter in the pan. Add the remaining teaspoon of vanilla to the boiling water and stir in the espresso powder. Pour the boiling liquid over the batter, being careful not to disturb the bottom layer. The water will cause the brown-sugar mixture to float, but that is all right.

Bake the cake for 35 minutes, or until the top is firm and browned and the cake bubbles around the edges. Cool the cake in its pan on a wire rack for about 15 minutes, then cut it into squares, spooning the sauce from the bottom over the servings. This cake is best served warm from the oven, drizzled with heavy cream, if desired.

Quick and Easy Rocky Road Fudge

Makes 1¼ pounds; 24 generous pieces

I appreciate that there are some people who like having more than just nuts in their fudge. So for you lovers of fudge-to-the max, this one's for you.

Unsalted butter for preparing the pan

1²/₃ cups (13 ounces) sugar

²/₃ cup evaporated milk

2 ounces unsweetened chocolate, chopped

1½ cups (3 ounces) miniature marshmallows

³/₄ cup (3 ounces) toasted nuts of your choice, coarsely chopped

6 ounces semisweet chocolate chips

Generously butter an 8-inch square baking pan. Line the pan with enough aluminum foil to overlap two opposite sides of the pan by 2 inches. Butter all the foil that touches the bottom and sides of the pan.

Place the sugar and evaporated milk in a 2-quart saucepan and set it over medium heat. Stir constantly until the sugar dissolves and the mixture starts to simmer. Allow the mixture to come to a slow boil, and cook it for 5 minutes, stirring constantly. Stir well around the bottom of the pan so that the mixture doesn't burn.

Remove the saucepan from the heat and add the unsweetened chocolate. Stir until the chocolate melts. Add the marshmallows and nuts and stir until the fudge begins to cool and thicken. Stir in the chocolate chips and pour and scrape the mixture into the prepared pan. Press the mixture into the pan and allow it to cool until firm.

Unmold the fudge onto a cutting board. Peel off the foil and use a long, sharp knife dipped in hot water and dried to cut the fudge into portions.

The fudge can be stored in an airtight container at room temperature for several weeks.

Chocolate Marshmallow Fluff or Marshmallows

Makes about 6 cups

Making homemade marshmallow fluff is like concocting a mini-miracle. Looking at the assembled ingredients you'd never think that such a simple cast of characters could produce such a magnificent result. The chocolate taste isn't huge—what you mostly get is a light brown effect with a mild chocolate taste. If you want a bigger impact you can double the amount of unsweetened chocolate.

You'll need a heavy-duty mixer with a whip attachment for this recipe, and if you want to make it ahead of time, you'll need a microwave oven to return it to its proper consistency. And here's another mini-miricle: Stir in $1/3$ cup each cornstarch and sugar, pour into a greased 9-inch pan, and when it sets—marshmallows.

3 tablespoons unflavored gelatin

2 cups (16 ounces) sugar

$3/4$-cup (6 ounces) light corn syrup

2 ounces unsweetened chocolate, melted and cooled to room temperature

Place $1/2$ cup (4 ounces) of cold water in the large bowl of a heavy-duty mixer fitted with the wire whip attachment. Sprinkle the gelatin over the surface of the water and set aside.

Place the sugar, corn syrup, and $1/2$ cup (4 ounces) of cold water in a heavy-bottomed $1^1/2$ quart saucepan set over moderate heat. Stir with a whisk until the sugar dissolves and the mixture comes to a simmer. Use a pastry brush or a dampened paper towel to wipe any sugar crystals from the sides of the pan. Raise the heat to high, insert a candy thermometer, and let the syrup boil, without stirring, until the temperature reaches 240°F. Remove the pan from the heat and set aside.

With the mixer on medium speed, add the sugar syrup slowly to the gelatin mixture. When all the syrup has been added, drape a clean dish towel over the top of the mixer to protect yourself from hot splatters, then increase the mixer speed to high and beat for 15 minutes, or until the mixture has cooled to lukewarm and is extremely thick. With the mixer on low speed, add the melted chocolate and mix until it is combined

Use the marshmallow fluff immediately, or pour and scrape it into a microwave-safe container with an airtight lid. Just before using the fluff, microwave it on high for 30-second intervals, stirring between each, until it is soft and slightly flowing.

10. Some Like It Hot

Chile Cha-Cha Brownies

Bittersweet Chocolate Soufflé

Bocca Negra

Candy Manor Peppermint Hot Chocolate

Classic Hot Chocolate

Chocolate Chile Cake

Chocolate Croissant Bread Pudding

Molten Chocolate Cakes

Milk Chocolate Fondue

White Chocolate Soufflés with Strawberry Centers

FIRE AND SPICE are the two delivery systems that put heat into food. The Aztecs took their chocolate cold in temperature and hot from chile peppers and ground spices such as cinnamon and cloves. The fact that the cacao beans were fermented gave the brew, which was reserved for royalty and sipped from golden goblets, a third kind of "heat" as well. When cacao crossed the Atlantic from Mexico to Spain, devotees substituted sugar for the spices and warmed the brew in copper pots. The first hot chocolate was an instant hit and for the longest time people were content with the liquid form until the solid confectionery bar came along.

Heat intensifies flavor and, in the case of chocolate, boosts the taste as well as perfumes your entire house with the promise of something very good to eat. The other thing heat does to chocolate is change it from a solid to a semi-liquid state. The sight of the warm gooey center oozing from the core of a Molten Chocolate Cake is indeed something to behold, and the taste experience is almost beyond description. I can't think of a more luxurious experience than that of spooning the creamy interior of a hot chocolate soufflé into my mouth. The warm, melting smoothness juxtaposed with the crisp crackle of crust brings a smile of pleasure to my lips and a general feeling of well-being to my soul.

Many grown-ups think of hot chocolate as "kid stuff," and turn up their noses when it is offered. Drinking even a small amount of those powdered, cloyingly sweet hot-chocolate mixes would turn anyone off. Try the Classic Hot Chocolate on page 233 and you may change your mind.

In this chapter I've included two recipes in which the heat comes from chiles. This concept may be a leap of faith for you—I know it was for me—but the subtle, deep, velvet warmth this ingredient adds feels like a lover's embrace, and makes me believe the Aztecs weren't far off the mark when they added spices to cacao to make their magical drink.

Chile Cha-Cha Brownies

Makes one 9 × 13-inch pan of brownies

Food writer Mary Lou Heiss and her husband, Bob, own *the* place to shop for gourmet food and equipment in Northampton, Massachusetts. When I visit Culinary Specialties/Coffee Gallery I feel like a kid in the proverbial candy store, wanting everything I set my eyes on. Mary Lou visited a produce market in Tijuana and was inspired by the local coffee, seasoned with brown sugar, cinnamon, and chocolate. The chile powder here lends a warm mellowness to these moist, deeply dark chocolate brownies.

Unsalted butter and flour for preparing the pan

8 ounces best-quality bittersweet chocolate, coarsely chopped

1½ sticks (6 ounces) unsalted butter

1¼ cups (6.25 ounces) all-purpose flour

½ cup (1.6 ounces) unsweetened Dutch-processed cocoa powder

4 teaspoons ground cinnamon

1 teaspoon pure chile powder, such as New Mexico sandia, ancho, or chimayo

½ teaspoon salt

4 extra-large eggs

1½ cups (12 ounces) sugar

2 teaspoons vanilla extract

¼ teaspoon orange oil

1¼ cups (5 ounces) toasted pecans, coarsely chopped

Preheat the oven to 350°F. with the rack in the center position. Coat the interior of a 9 × 13-inch baking pan with butter. Dust the pan with flour, knocking out the excess.

Melt the chocolate with the butter in a medium metal bowl set over, but not touching, a pan of simmering water, or in a microwave-safe bowl in a microwave oven. When the mixture is melted and smooth, let it cool.

Sift the flour, cocoa powder, cinnamon, chile powder, and salt into a medium bowl. Set aside. Place the eggs and sugar in a large mixing bowl. With an electric mixer, beat the mixture on high speed for 5 minutes until it is light-colored and doubled in volume. Stir the vanilla and orange oil into the cooled chocolate mixture, then scrape the chocolate mixture into the egg mixture. Beat on medium speed until no light streaks remain. Reduce the mixer speed to low and mix in the flour mixture in three additions, mixing well after each addition. Mix in the nuts. The batter will be quite stiff.

Scrape the batter into the prepared pan and smooth well with a rubber spatula. Bake for 30 to 35 minutes, or until the top is shiny, the brownies start to pull away from the sides of the pan, and a cake tester inserted into the middle of the brownies comes out clean. Transfer the pan to a wire rack and let the brownies cool completely. Invert them onto a wire rack, then invert them again onto a cutting board. Cut them into bars or squares.

The brownies can be kept in a covered container at room temperature for up to 2 weeks.

Bittersweet Chocolate Soufflé

Makes 6 servings

You say you have a fear of heights—or, more accurately, a fear of not attaining heights? Well, here is your golden opportunity to triumph over that soufflé avoidance complex! Picture a crisp crust cradling a lava flow of deep, dark chocolate. Picture a dessert you can put together and whip into the oven in time for a finale people will remember with a sigh and a smile. Here it is— and you *can* do it, trust me.

Unsalted butter and sugar for preparing the soufflé dish

1 cup (8 ounces) granulated sugar

½ cup (4 ounces) whole milk

2 teaspoons instant espresso powder or granules

1 tablespoon instant or quick-mixing flour, such as Wondra

4 ounces bittersweet chocolate, cut into small pieces

4 ounces unsweetened chocolate, cut into small pieces

1 tablespoon (.5 ounce) unsalted butter

4 extra-large eggs, at room temperature, separated

3 to 4 tablespoons confectioners' sugar, for garnish

NOTE
Leftover soufflé can be refrigerated and served cold. It makes a really nice mousse with a very interesting texture because of the crusty top.

Preheat the oven to 400°F. with the rack in the upper, but not top, position. Butter the interior of a 6-cup soufflé dish. Sprinkle the inside with sugar, knocking out the excess.

Place the sugar, milk, and espresso powder in a medium, heavy saucepan and stir them together. Set the pan over high heat and bring the mixture to a rolling boil. Whisk in the flour and cook for 1 minute more. Remove the pan from the heat and stir in the bittersweet chocolate and the unsweetened chocolate. Stir until the chocolate has melted. Add the butter, and stir until it has melted. Add the egg yolks, one at a time, stirring the mixture well after each addition.

In a very clean large bowl with very clean beaters, whip the egg whites until they are stiff but not dry. Scoop a large spoonful of whites into the chocolate mixture to lighten it. Pour the chocolate mixture over the whites and fold it in gently but thoroughly. Pour the mixture into the prepared dish.

Bake for 20 minutes. While the soufflé is baking, place the confectioners' sugar in a fine-mesh sieve set over a small bowl; set aside. When the soufflé has baked for 20 minutes, reduce the oven temperature to 350°F. and bake for 5 to 10 minutes more. This soufflé will not rise dramatically, but the top should be very crusty and the soufflé should be firm (not too wiggly when the pan is shaken). If the top is browning too fast, gently lay a piece of foil over it. Remove the soufflé from the oven, dust with confectioners' sugar, and serve it immediately by using two soup spoons to scoop up some of the crusty top and the molten filling onto dessert plates.

Bocca Negra

Makes one 9-inch cake; 12 servings

I made my reputation on a flourless chocolate cake called Bête Noire. The consistency resembled a hot truffle and it brought me many new friends, several marriage proposals, and the challenge of coming up with something like it to offer in this book. I think its sister cake, Bocca Negra, fits the bill. It has a little booze—which makes it even more grown-up than the original—but then, the original wasn't for kids, either. You can eat this hot out of the oven or at room temperature. It loses a lot of its unique personality after refrigeration, so try to avoid that if possible. Baked correctly, it's more like pudding than cake.

I serve it with unsweetened whipped cream or some crème fraîche. If you can't find the latter in the dairy case at your supermarket, a recipe follows for making your own.

Unsalted butter for preparing the cake pan

12 ounces bittersweet chocolate, broken into small pieces

5 extra-large eggs, at room temperature

1 1/3 cups (10 ounces) superfine or bar sugar (see page 16)

1/2 cup (4 ounces) bourbon

2 sticks (8 ounces) unsalted butter, at room temperature, cut into 10 chunks

2 level tablespoons instant flour, such as Wondra

Unsweetened whipped cream or crème fraîche (recipe follows) for garnish (optional)

Preheat the oven to 350°F. with the rack in the center position. Coat the interior of a 9-inch round cake pan with butter, and line the bottom with a 9-inch circle of parchment. Lightly butter the parchment. Set the prepared cake pan in a jelly-roll pan or a roasting pan. Bring a large pot of water to a boil and keep it warm.

Place the chocolate in the work bowl of a food processor. Crack the eggs into a spouted cup. Combine the sugar and the bourbon in a saucepan. Cook, stirring occasionally, over medium-high heat until the sugar dissolves and the mixture comes to a vigorous boil. With the processor turned off, pour the boiling syrup into the food-processor bowl. Put the cover in place and process for about 12 seconds, or until the chocolate is completely melted and the mixture is smooth. With the machine running, add the butter through the feed tube, one chunk at a time, then the eggs, one at a time through the tube, and then the flour. Process for an additional 15 seconds.

Pour and scrape the batter into the prepared pan and level the top with a rubber spatula. Place the cake pan in its larger pan on the oven shelf; pour about an inch of hot water into the larger pan. Bake the cake for exactly 40 minutes. When it is done the cake will have a thin, dry crust on top, but the interior will be very moist. Carefully remove the cake pan from the larger pan (leave the water bath in the turned-off oven to cool before removing). Let the cake rest in the pan for 15 minutes, then carefully invert the cake onto a flat serving plate. Peel off the parchment liner. The hot cake will be fragile and wet, so use a sharp knife and a long, narrow spatula to cut wedges, then transfer them to individual dessert plates.

Serve hot or at room temperature. Top each serving with a generous dab of whipped cream or crème fraîche, if you like.

Crème Fraîche

Makes 1 cup

$\frac{1}{4}$ cup (2 ounces) full-fat unflavored (plain) yogurt

1 cup (8 ounces) heavy cream (not ultra-pasteurized; this can be found in health-food stores and some supermarkets)

Whisk the yogurt with the heavy cream in a small bowl. Cover the mixture with plastic wrap and leave at room temperature overnight, or until it has thickened. Once it has thickened, it may be stored, covered, in the refrigerator for up to 2 weeks.

Candy Manor Peppermint Hot Chocolate

Makes 4 to 6 servings

If you ever have the good fortune to be on Cape Cod during the Christmas season, head on over to Chatham to the Chatham Candy Manor. The long line you'll see coming out the door will be folks who wait all year long to indulge themselves with a cup of the famous Peppermint Hot Chocolate. If you can't get to the Cape, here's the recipe so you can make it at home.

All peppermint extracts are not alike. One stands head and shoulders above the rest. It's made by a wonderful Massachusetts company called Boyajian. The whole line of flavorings and essences is available in gourmet shops and many grocery stores (see Sources, page 271).

For the whipped cream

1 cup (8 ounces) heavy cream, chilled

2 tablespoons confectioners' sugar

$1/4$ teaspoon peppermint extract

2 tablespoons crushed peppermint candy

For the hot chocolate

3 ounces unsweetened chocolate, grated

1 quart (32 ounces) whole milk

$1/3$ cup (3 ounces) sugar

$1/3$ cup (3 ounces) boiling water

1 teaspoon vanilla extract

1 teaspoon peppermint extract

Candy canes, for garnish

Thirty minutes before you make the hot chocolate, place in the freezer a $1^1/2$-quart metal bowl plus the beaters from your mixer.

To make the whipped cream, place the cream, confectioners' sugar, and peppermint extract in the chilled bowl and beat on high speed until soft peaks form. Use a rubber spatula to fold in the crushed candy. Refrigerate the whipped cream.

To make the hot chocolate, place the chocolate in a $2^1/2$-quart metal mixing bowl. Place the bowl over, but not touching, a pan of simmering water. (The bowl will seem large at this point, but you will need this large a bowl to mix in the milk.) Stir the chocolate occasionally with a rubber spatula. While it melts, pour the milk into a heavy-bottomed, 2-quart saucepan. Whisk in the sugar and cook over medium heat, stirring occasionally, until the milk begins to simmer and small bubbles form around the edge. Turn off the heat.

When the chocolate has melted, reduce the heat under its pan so that the water barely simmers. Pour the $1/3$ cup of boiling water into the melted chocolate and whisk or beat with an electric mixer until smooth. Dribble in the hot milk mixture while you continue to whisk or beat. When the ingredients are well incorporated, remove the bowl from the water bath and stir in the vanilla and peppermint extracts.

To serve, ladle the hot chocolate into mugs and top with a generous dollop of the whipped cream. Garnish with a candy cane.

Classic Hot Chocolate

Makes four 12-ounce servings

Our house sits on a narrow peninsula on the Charles River about twelve miles from downtown Boston. There are several shallow coves practically outside our door that freeze up long before the rest of the river. We keep our ice skates on a hook by the door and use them as long as the ice holds. A big thermos full of steaming hot chocolate is the fuel that keeps us warm in even the bitterest cold.

Hot chocolate needs to be more than just big in flavor; it needs to be thick enough to coat your tongue with creamy, deep, dark velvet chocolate warmth. This version does it best.

1 cup (8 ounces) heavy cream

8 ounces semisweet chocolate, coarsely chopped

3 cups (24 ounces) milk

Unsweetened whipped cream, for garnish

Heat the heavy cream in a medium saucepan set over moderate heat until tiny bubbles form around the edges of the pan. Remove the pan from the heat and add the chocolate. Stir until the chocolate melts. Divide this mixture among 4 large (12-ounce) mugs. Heat the milk in the same saucepan until small bubbles appear around the edges but before a skin starts to form on top. Divide the milk among the mugs. Stir the hot chocolate and serve immediately with a generous dollop of whipped cream.

Chocolate Chile Cake

Makes one 9-inch cake; 10 servings

Years ago I was a judge in a chocolate bake-off in Albany, New York. We were so full of choco-late desserts that we hardly had the room or the energy to consume yet another, and this recipe was something so off-the-wall that we judges laughed and in fact put off tasting it until the end. Which makes the reaction to this very plain-looking cake all the more extraordinary. It won first prize. This amazing confection, a deep, rich, flourless chocolate cake, is studded with just enough chile flavor to light your interest, but not inflame your palate. The figs add body and sweetness. While Montezuma and his legions didn't feast on this dessert, chiles, chocolate, cinnamon, and dried figs were indeed part of the Aztecs' diet.

I was given a copy of the recipe by the organizers of the bake-off. Unfortunately, they neg-lected to add the name of the person who submitted the recipe. So, as much as I would love to credit the incredibly creative mind who came up with this, I am unable to do so. If you're out there and reading this please e-mail me—especially if you have other recipes as good as this you are willing to share.

Unsalted butter and flour for preparing the pan

2 medium dried ancho chiles

20 dried black mission figs, stems removed

⅓ cup (3 ounces) light brown sugar, packed

2 tablespoons vanilla extract

16 ounces bittersweet chocolate, chopped

2 sticks (8 ounces) unsalted butter

3 teaspoons ground cinnamon

6 extra-large eggs

1 tablespoon granulated sugar

Unsweetened whipped cream, for garnish

Preheat the oven to 425°F. with the rack in the center position. Generously coat a 9-inch springform pan with butter. Line the bottom with a circle of parchment paper and butter the paper. Dust with flour, knocking out the excess. Wrap the exterior of the pan securely with a double layer of aluminum foil to pre-vent leaks. Have ready a kettle of hot water and a roasting pan whose sides are lower than the springform pan's but that is large enough to contain the springform pan.

Place the chiles on a small baking sheet and put them in the preheated oven for about 3 minutes, or until they are just soft-ened. If they stay in too long they will become crisp and unus-able. Remove them from the oven and remove the stems and seeds. Maintain the oven temperature.

Place the chiles, figs, brown sugar, and 1 tablespoon of the vanilla in a medium saucepan and add enough water to cover by one inch. Bring the mixture to a simmer over medium heat, and cook until the figs are soft. Purée the mixture (including the liquid) in a blender or food processor until smooth. A blender will yield a smoother mixture. (You may strain the puréed mixture to remove some of the fig seeds if you wish. I like the slightly crunchy texture they give, so I leave them in.) Set aside to cool. Do not chill.

Place the chocolate and butter in a metal bowl set over, but not touching, a pan of simmering water. As soon as they have almost completely melted, remove the bowl from the heat and stir the mixture until smooth. Add the remaining tablespoon of vanilla and 2 teaspoons of the cinnamon. When the mixture has cooled to room temperature (do not chill), stir in $^3/_4$ cup of the fig mixture. (If there is more than $^3/_4$ cup, discard it.) The chocolate-fig mixture will now be rather lumpy. Set aside.

Place the eggs in a medium metal mixing bowl or the bowl of a stand mixer, set over a pan of very hot water. Stir the eggs over the hot water until they are just warm to the touch. Use a hand mixer or a stand mixer to beat the eggs on medium-high speed until they have tripled in volume. (If you use a hand mixer, leave the bowl over the hot water to maximize volume.) Use a rubber spatula to fold one-fourth of the eggs into the chocolate-fig mixture. When the eggs are just incorporated, add the rest of the eggs and fold until no light steaks are visible. Pour the batter into the prepared pan. Place the empty roasting pan in the oven, place the springform pan inside it, and carefully fill the roasting pan with very hot water. Bake the cake, uncovered, for 15 minutes, then cover loosely with buttered foil and bake for another 10 minutes. At this point the cake will appear quite loose. Remove the cake from the water bath, remove the buttered foil, and place the cake pan on a wire rack to cool completely. When the cake is cool, remove the foil pan wrapping, cover the pan tightly with plastic wrap, and refrigerate for at least 3 hours.

To unmold the cake, wipe the outside of the springform pan with a hot towel. This should soften the cake enough to remove it from the pan. Remove the sides, invert the cake onto a plate, and remove the pan base and the parchment paper. (It is not necessary to invert the cake again.) Mix the remaining teaspoon of cinnamon with the tablespoon of sugar and sift over the top of the cake. Use your fingers to rub it smoothly over the top of the cake. Serve the cake at room temperature, garnished with unsweetened whipped cream.

Store the cake, wrapped in foil, in the refrigerator for up to 1 week.

Chocolate Croissant Bread Pudding

Makes 12 servings

A friend once said of this dish, "Next to kissing Paul Newman, it's the best thing a girl could do for her mouth." Wildly indulgent, rich as all get-out, laced with chocolate, butter, and cream—how could it be anything but fabulous?

Bread pudding is really a way of making French toast casserole-style. It's a perfect dish for brunch or even for a dessert after a light meal. The combination of this rich egg bread, the bits of chocolate, and the rum caramel topping make for a truly unforgettable eating experience. When I make this, I buy a package of two dozen chocolate croissants at my local warehouse club and stick half of them in the freezer for the next time.

For the pudding

Unsalted butter for preparing the baking dish

12 day-old chocolate croissants (see headnote)

1 stick (4 ounces) unsalted butter, at room temperature

1 cup (8 ounces) sugar

5 extra-large eggs

2 cups (16 ounces) heavy cream

1/2 cup (4 ounces) dark rum

2 teaspoons vanilla extract

1/2 teaspoon ground cinnamon

For the topping

1 cup (8 ounces) light brown sugar, packed

1/2 cup (4 ounces) orange juice

1/3 cup (3 ounces) dark rum

1/4 cup (2 ounces) molasses

4 tablespoons (2 ounces) unsalted butter

Butter the inside of a 2 1/2-quart round or oval glass or ceramic baking dish with 3- to 4-inch-high sides. Cut each croissant vertically on a slight diagonal into 1-inch slices.

Place the butter and sugar in a large mixing bowl. Use either an electric mixer or a wire whisk to beat them until light and fluffy, then beat in the eggs, one at a time, mixing well after each addition. Stir in the cream, rum, vanilla, and cinnamon. Ladle one third of the cream mixture into the prepared baking dish. Place an overlapping layer of croissant pieces over the cream, then ladle on half of the remaining cream mixture. Layer on the remaining croissant pieces, then pour on the remaining cream mixture. (Depending on the size and shape of your pan, you may make more layers; just make sure that all the croissant pieces are well coated with the cream mixture.) Press down lightly on the croissants with a wide metal spatula to make sure all the bread is moistened. Cover the pudding with foil and allow it to rest at room temperature while you preheat the oven to 350°F. with the rack in the center position. Bake the pudding, covered with aluminum foil, for 45 minutes, or until the top has browned lightly and the egg mixture is just set; the pudding should be soft, not firm. Remove it from the oven and let it sit, covered with the foil, while you prepare the topping; maintain the oven temperature.

To make the topping, combine the brown sugar, orange juice, rum, molasses, and butter in a small saucepan. Cook the topping over medium heat, stirring constantly, for 5 minutes, or until it is smooth and comes to a simmer. Remove and discard the foil from the pudding and pour the brown sugar mixture over. Bake the pudding for 15 minutes more. Serve hot, warm, or at room temperature.

NOTE
You may use 12 baked and cooled Instant Chocolate Croissants (page 59), or simply split 12 store-bought plain croissants horizontally and brush each bottom half with 1 ounce melted semisweet or bittersweet chocolate; replace the tops and chill the croissants to allow the chocolate to set up before proceeding with the recipe.

Molten Chocolate Cakes

Makes 6 cakes

We had a lot of fun making these little chocolate gems (the new favorite dessert of trendy restaurants and TV chefs), and just as much fun eating them. Tucking a frozen chocolate truffle into the batter just before baking creates a creamy, almost liquid center that provides a lovely contrast to the slightly more solid soufflé–like cake that cradles it. If you wish to make these ahead, store the unbaked cakes in the freezer and pop them in the oven to bake while you have dinner. They will not have the clearly defined liquid center that you get when you bake the cakes immediately, but the centers will still be significantly moister than the surrounding cake. Both versions are delicious.

Unsalted butter and sugar for preparing the ramekins

1 cup (8 ounces) granulated sugar

1/2 cup (4 ounces) milk

2 teaspoons instant espresso powder or granules

1 tablespoon all-purpose flour

4 ounces bittersweet chocolate, coarsely chopped

4 ounces unsweetened chocolate, coarsely chopped

1 tablespoon (.5 ounce) unsalted butter

4 extra-large eggs, at room temperature, separated

6 Chocolate Truffles (page 32), formed into 1-inch balls and uncoated, frozen solid

Confectioners' sugar, for garnish (optional)

Generously butter six 4-ounce ramekins. Line the bottoms with parchment-paper circles and butter the liners. Sprinkle the insides with sugar, knocking out the excess. Place the ramekins on a rimmed baking sheet and set aside. If you are going to bake the cakes right after mixing, preheat the oven to 425°F. with the rack in the upper third of the oven.

Place the granulated sugar, milk, and espresso powder in a medium saucepan. Bring the mixture to a rolling boil and whisk in the flour. Reduce the heat and simmer the mixture vigorously for 1 minute. Remove the pan from the heat and stir in the bittersweet and unsweetened chocolates until melted. Stir in the butter. Add the egg yolks, one at a time, and whisk or stir well after each addition. Set aside.

In a very clean medium bowl with very clean beaters, beat the egg whites on medium-high speed until they are stiff but not dry. Scoop a large spoonful of whites into the chocolate mixture and stir it in to lighten the mixture. Pour the chocolate mixture over the rest of the beaten whites and fold together gently until thoroughly combined. Pour the batter into the prepared ramekins, but reserve about 1 cup of the batter. Insert a frozen truffle into the center of each portion of batter and push down gently. Top off each ramekin with some of the reserved batter so that the truffles are completely covered.

Bake the cakes in the upper third of the oven for 10 to 12 minutes, or until the tops are puffed and dry around the edges. It's better to underbake these cakes. Remove the tray of ramekins from the oven and immediately run a small knife around the sides of the ramekins to loosen the cakes. Invert the ramekins onto serving plates, lift off the ramekins, and discard the parchment liners. Sift confectioners' sugar over the cakes, if desired, and serve immediately.

NOTE

The cakes may be prepared without the truffles. Simply divide the batter among the ramekins and bake as described. The unbaked cakes, filled or unfilled, may be prepared and refrigerated up to 1 day ahead, or they can be frozen for up to 1 week. Cover the ramekins with plastic wrap and refrigerate or freeze. Preheat the oven as instructed above, remove the cakes from the refrigerator or freezer, discard the plastic wrap, and bake until puffed, but the cake tester must show some moist batter. Those taken from the refrigerator will take 16 to 8 minutes to bake; the frozen ones will take 24 to 26 minutes.

VARIATION

Molten Chocolate Sundaes:

Prepare the cake batter as instructed in the recipe for Molten Chocolate Cakes, but use 6- or 8-ounce ramekins, so that the baking dishes are substantially higher than the finished cakes. Do not use parchment liners in the ramekins. These cakes may be made with or without a truffle center. Bake as for the molten cakes. As soon as the cakes are out of the oven, place a scoop of premium vanilla ice cream in the ramekins. Drizzle on some chocolate sauce of your choice, then a dab of whipped cream. Serve immediately.

Milk Chocolate Fondue

Makes 4 servings

In the early 1960s, when I got married, fondue pots were the gift of choice, and I got more than my share. I used them with great enthusiasm for about a year and then gave them up for more pressing things like diapers and formula. The craze passed and fondue became as passé as I hope stiletto heels will one day. Now fondue has come roaring back with a vengeance that can only be ascribed to the news that melted cheese and heavy cream won't kill us after all. Well, I knew that all along. While you don't need an official fondue set to make this recipe (you can heat the mixture in a saucepan and return it to the stove for reheating as necessary), it's much more fun to use one. Another option is to use a small slow-cooker on the lowest heat setting.

Chocolate fondue is one of life's great pleasures. It's a dessert that bridges any age gap, fits almost any occasion, and makes everyone look at dipable foods in a whole new way. Next year, when my grandson turns eight, I'm going to give him a chocolate fondue birthday party, with the longest fork going to the birthday boy.

½ cup (4 ounces) heavy cream

10 ounces milk chocolate, coarsely chopped

3 to 4 tablespoons of the liqueur or spirits of your choice, such as Kirsch, Grand Marnier, rum, or Cognac (optional)

Sliced fruit, such as apples, bananas, mangos, peaches, or pears

Whole or sections of fruit such as grapes, oranges, strawberries, or tangerines

Dried apricots or prunes

Small or broken macaroons or pieces of ladyfingers, angel food cake, or pound cake

Place the cream in a small, heavy saucepan. Set the pan over medium-high heat and bring the cream almost to a boil. Remove the pan from the heat and stir in the chocolate until the mixture is melted and smooth. Stir in the liqueur or spirits, if using.

Pour the fondue into a fondue pot, or set the saucepan on a hot plate or warming tray. Use long wooden picks or fondue forks to dip a piece of fruit or cookie or cake into the fondue.

White Chocolate Soufflés with Strawberry Centers

Makes 8 servings

If you've ever suffered from soufflé phobia (what if it doesn't rise, what if it falls before I get it to the table, what if . . . ?) this recipe will catapult you into the category of Soufflé Expert. These are virtually foolproof and they can even be made the night before and stored in the refrigerator until you pop them into the oven to cook. Serving up a hot soufflé, especially one with a surprise center, looks like an act of derring-do, but in fact it's hardly any challenge at all.

8 small fresh strawberries, rinsed, stemmed, and dried thoroughly

Butter and granulated sugar for preparing the ramekins

³/₄ cup (6 ounces) granulated sugar

¹/₂ cup (4 ounces) whole milk

1 teaspoon vanilla extract

2 tablespoons all-purpose flour

6 ounces white chocolate, coarsely chopped

1 tablespoon (.5 ounce) unsalted butter

4 extra-large eggs, separated

Confectioners' sugar, for garnish (optional)

At least 2 hours before you plan to make the soufflés, place the strawberries on a small plate in the freezer. Leave the strawberries in the freezer until you are ready to bake the soufflés.

If you are going to bake the soufflés right after preparing them, preheat the oven to 400°F. with the rack in the upper third of the oven. Lightly butter eight 4-ounce ramekins. Sprinkle the insides with sugar, knocking out the excess. Place the ramekins on a rimmed baking sheet or in a roasting pan.

Place the granulated sugar, milk, and vanilla in a medium saucepan. Set the pan over high heat and bring to a rolling boil, stirring constantly. Whisk in the flour, reduce the heat to medium-low, and cook, stirring, for 1 minute more. Remove the pan from the heat and stir in the chopped chocolate. Stir until it has melted, then stir in the butter. Stir in the egg yolks, one at a time, stirring well after each addition. Set aside.

Beat the egg whites in a medium mixing bowl at high speed until they are stiff but not dry. Stir a large spoonful of beaten whites into the chocolate mixture to lighten it. Pour the chocolate mixture over the remaining egg whites and fold together gently until the two mixtures are thoroughly combined. Divide the soufflé mixture among the ramekins. Place one frozen strawberry in each ramekin, and push it down so that it is completely submerged. Smooth some of the surrounding soufflé mixture over any berries that show through.

Bake for 12 to 14 minutes, or until the tops are puffed and dry and the soufflés wiggle only slightly when the ramekins are moved. Remove the soufflés from the oven, sift a fine layer of confectioners' sugar on top, if desired, and serve right away.

The unbaked soufflés may be prepared up to 24 hours ahead. Cover the ramekins with plastic wrap and refrigerate. Allow the uncooked soufflés to come to room temperature before baking. Place a frozen strawberry in each just before you put the soufflés in the oven.

11. Isn't It Romantic?

White Chocolate Cœurs à la Crème

Chambord Coffee with Chocolate Whipped Cream

Black Bottom Pie

Oreo-Crusted White Chocolate Mousse Torte

Mary Frankel's Chocolate Cheesecake

Chocolate Polenta Cake with Kirsch Crème Anglaise (Cinderella Cake)

Narsai David's Chocolate Decadence

Optimism Tart

White Chocolate Eggnog

Sweet Cherry Cobbler with Chocolate Truffle Crust

Double Chocolate Espresso Meringue Cake

Chocolate Raspberry Torte

I HAVE A FRIEND who wooed his wife with chocolate cakes. He started by making a Chocolate Decadence (page 258), which he had delivered to her office. He hadn't meant for it to be an anonymous gift, but she couldn't decipher his attempt to write his phone number on the top of the cake in chocolate icing. Knowing that she loved white chocolate, his next project was an Oreo-Crusted White Chocolate Mousse Torte (page 253) around which he tied a red velvet ribbon. That was delivered with a dozen roses and a card on which someone with good penmanship had written his phone number. That got her attention. Several months later when he tucked a diamond ring inside a truffle-filled heart-shaped chocolate box, there was no doubt in her mind that she had found Mr. Right.

If you are looking to wow your sweetie and win his or her heart for good, then allow me to suggest whipping up the White Chocolate Cœurs à la Crème, opposite. Both individual and large heart-shaped molds (with holes in the bottom to drain out the liquid that accumulates while the dessert is chilling) are available in practically every cookware and gourmet shop. Don't wait for Valentine's Day; a gift from the heart that says "I love you" is welcome any day of the week, any month of the year.

White Chocolate Cœurs à la Crème

Makes 6 servings

This simple dessert speaks volumes when words don't quite do the trick. It's an edible valentine guaranteed to win the heart of any recipient. Made with but four ingredients, it hovers in your mouth like a dream and then melts into a modestly sweet cream as it glides down to touch your heart. The accompanying raspberry sauce adds beautiful color and sparkle.

While these cœurs à la crème can be made successfully in round ramekins, they are beautiful when heart-shaped. Traditional heart-shaped molds are available in most gourmet food shops or online from www.cooking.com. You may also choose to make this in one large 4- to 5-cup mold. For individual molds you will need six 6 × 6-inch squares of cheesecloth, dampened. For the larger version you'll need a piece about 18 × 18 inches.

4 ounces white chocolate, coarsely chopped

1 cup (8 ounces) heavy cream

8 ounces cream cheese, at room temperature

Finely grated zest of 1 lime, or ⅛ teaspoon lime oil

Raspberry Sauce, for serving (recipe follows)

Place six 4-ounce cœur à la crème molds or ramekins on a rimmed baking sheet or tray. Line each ramekin or mold with a square of dampened cheesecloth, letting the excess hang over the edges.

Melt the white chocolate in a large metal bowl set over, but not touching, a pan of simmering water, or in a microwave-safe bowl in a microwave oven. Stir the chocolate with a wooden spoon as it melts. When the chocolate is melted and smooth, remove the pan from over the water and set aside to cool slightly.

Pour the heavy cream into a medium mixing bowl. Beat the cream with an electric mixer on medium speed until soft peaks form. Set aside. Place the cream cheese in the bowl with the melted chocolate. Beat the cream cheese and chocolate with an electric mixer (no need to wash the beaters) on medium speed until well combined. Beat in the lime zest or oil. Use a large rubber spatula to thoroughly fold the whipped cream into the chocolate mixture.

Divide the white chocolate mixture among the lined ramekins or molds. Fold the overlapping cheesecloth over the filling in each. Cover the entire baking pan with plastic wrap and refrigerate for at least 12 hours.

(CONTINUED ON NEXT PAGE)

To serve, spoon some raspberry sauce on each serving plate and spread it to cover the entire surface. Remove the plastic wrap from over the ramekins or molds. Pull the cheesecloth away from the tops, unmold the cœurs à la crème onto a baking sheet, and discard the cheesecloth. Use a spatula to gently transfer the cœurs à la crème to the serving plates.

Raspberry Sauce

Makes about 1 cup

10 ounces frozen unsweetened raspberries, thawed but not drained

$^2/_3$ cup (6 ounces) sugar

2 tablespoons lime juice

Place the raspberries, sugar, and lime juice in the work bowl of a food processor or in a blender. Process or blend until smooth. Use as is, or strain through a fine-mesh sieve to remove the seeds.

Chambord Coffee with Chocolate Whipped Cream

Makes 4 servings

The combination of coffee and chocolate is the culinary equivalent of the moon being in the seventh house and Jupiter aligning with Mars (if you are too young to understand this reference, go borrow your parents' LP of *Hair*). Adding a splash of raspberry liqueur elevates the experience to an even higher celestial plane.

The makers of Chambord promise that their liqueur is unique because it's formulated from oak-mellowed cognac infused with special tiny black raspberries. While you can certainly use another brand of raspberry liqueur, the bottle with the tiara will look particularly smashing on your pantry shelf.

2 ounces bittersweet chocolate

½ cup (4 ounces) heavy cream

5½ teaspoons sugar

4 cups (32 ounces) brewed coffee

½ cup (4 ounces) Chambord or other raspberry-flavored liqueur

4 teaspoons vanilla extract

Use a fine grater to shave 1 ounce of the bittersweet chocolate onto a plate or a piece of wax paper. Set aside. Coarsely chop the remaining 1 ounce of chocolate and melt it in a metal bowl set over, but not touching, a pan of simmering water, or in a microwave-safe bowl in a microwave oven. When the chocolate is melted and smooth, remove the bowl from over the water and set aside.

Place a small metal bowl and the beaters of an electric mixer in the freezer to chill for 5 minutes, then remove. Place the cream and 1½ teaspoons of the sugar in the chilled bowl. With the electric mixer on high speed, beat the cream until it begins to thicken. Scrape in the melted chocolate and continue to beat on high speed until soft peaks form. Set aside.

Place the coffee, the remaining 4 teaspoons of sugar, the Chambord, and vanilla in a medium saucepan. Place the saucepan over medium-high heat and stir the mixture until it is very hot. Pour the hot coffee mixture into 4 mugs. Top each with a large dollop of the chocolate whipped cream. Sprinkle some of the shaved chocolate over each dollop, and serve the coffee immediately.

Black Bottom Pie

Makes one 9-inch pie; 8 servings

My version of this classic Southern pie with its chocolate custard bottom layer and a vanilla meringue top layer uses a chocolate crumb crust and milk chocolate in place of the traditional dark chocolate in the filling. My friend Sam Arnold, who owns the Fort restaurant in Morrison, Colorado, introduced me to an Austrian rum called Stroh which is (hang on to your hats) 180 proof. It can be a challenge to find, but a good liquor store can order it for you. Get a small bottle, because a little goes all the way from here to eternity. While other rums will do the job, Stroh will make you a legend in your own time.

For the crust

4½ ounces (about 20 cookies) chocolate wafers, crumbled

4 tablespoons (2 ounces) unsalted butter, melted

¼ cup (2 ounces) sugar

For the filling and topping

3 extra-large eggs, separated

1 cup (8 ounces) sugar

1 tablespoon cornstarch

1¼ cups (10 ounces) whole milk

1 teaspoon vanilla extract

9 ounces milk chocolate, chopped into small pieces

1½ teaspoons unflavored gelatin

⅓ to ½ cup (3 to 4 ounces) dark rum (Stroh, if possible)

Chocolate wafer crumbs, for garnish

To make the crust, preheat the oven to 350°F. with the rack in the center position. Place the crumbled wafers in the work bowl of a food processor fitted with the metal blade. Pulse until the wafer pieces are reduced to small crumbs, then add the melted butter and the sugar. Pulse until the butter is evenly dispersed among the crumbs. Press the crust mixture into the bottom and up the sides of a 9-inch pie plate. Bake the crust for 18 to 20 minutes, or until it is fragrant, has darkened a little, and is slightly firm to the touch. Remove the plate to a wire rack to cool. Turn off the oven.

To make the filling, place the egg yolks in a heavy, 2-quart saucepan, and place the whites in a very clean, medium metal mixing bowl. Add ⅔ cup of the sugar, the cornstarch, and milk to the saucepan with the yolks and whisk the ingredients just to combine. Place the saucepan over medium heat and cook, stirring constantly, until the mixture boils and thickens. Remove the pan from the heat and add the vanilla. Pour half the custard into a mixing bowl, and stir in the milk chocolate. Stir until the chocolate is melted and smooth, then pour and scrape the chocolate custard into the prepared pastry shell. Chill thoroughly.

To make the topping, place 3 tablespoons of cold water in a small bowl and sprinkle the gelatin over the top. Stir until the gelatin dissolves. Stir the softened gelatin into the remaining warm custard in the saucepan. Stir in the rum. Transfer the custard to a mixing bowl and refrigerate until it is cooled and has begun to thicken (about 30 minutes). With an electric mixer with clean beaters, beat the egg whites on medium-high speed until they form soft peaks. Gradually add the remaining $1/3$ cup of sugar, and continue beating on medium-high until stiff peaks form. Fold the beaten whites into the partially set rum and gelatin mixture. Chill for 20 to 30 minutes, until the mixture holds its shape, then spoon it over the chocolate layer in the pie plate and chill overnight. You may be tempted to cover the pie, but chances are you'll ruin the top, so leave it uncovered, but far away, if possible, from other foods that give off strong smells.

Before serving, sprinkle the top of the pie with chocolate wafer crumbs.

Oreo-Crusted White Chocolate Mousse Torte

Makes one 9-inch cake; 12 servings

If you spent a childhood dipping Oreo cookies in milk, or gently prying the two chocolate cookies apart so you could scrape the filling off with your teeth, then you'll appreciate the idea of a cake that looks just like a giant Oreo cookie. The best news is that it tastes even better than any Oreo possibly could.

This refrigerator cake is a no-bake recipe, so if you are seeking something elegant that will serve a crowd and you don't want to turn on your oven, this is perfect. It's a great make-ahead crowd pleaser that will have your guests looking at those cream-filled sandwich cookies with a whole new respect.

For the crust and garnish

Unsalted butter for preparing the pan

24 Oreo cookies, roughly broken in thirds

6 ounces bittersweet chocolate, finely chopped

1/2 cup (4 ounces) heavy cream

For the filling

10 ounces white chocolate, coarsely chopped

2 cups (16 ounces) heavy cream

1 teaspoon vanilla extract

2 teaspoons unflavored gelatin

Coat the interior or a 9-inch springform pan with butter. Place a circle of parchment in the bottom and butter it as well.

Place the bowl of an electric mixer and wire whip attachment or the beaters in the freezer to chill.

To make the crust, place the broken cookies in the work bowl of a food processor fitted with the metal blade. Pulse until medium-size crumbs are formed. They won't be uniform. Don't process long enough to make mush—just to grind the cookies into uneven crumbs. Leave the crumbs in the food processor. Place the bittersweet chocolate in a medium metal bowl. Pour the 1/2 cup heavy cream into a small saucepan; set over medium heat and bring the cream to a very gentle simmer. Pour it over the chocolate and stir until the mixture is smooth. Add two-thirds of the cookie crumbs; reserve the remaining crumbs. Stir the crumbs to coat them with the chocolate. Spoon and scrape the mixture into the bottom of the prepared pan. Press the chocolate-coated crumbs evenly over the bottom all the way to the edge of the pan, but not up the sides. Set aside.

To prepare the filling, place the white chocolate and 2/3 cup of the heavy cream in a metal bowl placed over, but not touching, a pan of simmering water. Stir occasionally as the chocolate melts. When the mixture is smooth, remove it from over the water and set aside to cool.

(CONTINUED ON NEXT PAGE)

In a chilled bowl using the chilled beaters, whip the remaining 1⅓ cups of heavy cream and the vanilla until soft peaks form.

Pour 3 tablespoons of water into a small saucepan and sprinkle the gelatin over it. When the gelatin has softened, place the saucepan over very low heat and stir the mixture just until the gelatin has dissolved and liquefied. Immediately scrape the gelatin mixture into the white chocolate mixture, and fold gently until well combined. Fold the white chocolate–gelatin mixture into the whipped cream until the mixture is uniform. Scrape the filling into the prepared crust.

Refrigerate the torte until the gelatin has set, at least 4 hours or overnight. To serve, loosen the edges of the torte from the sides of the pan with a small knife. Remove the sides of the pan and run a wide metal spatula between the bottom of the torte and the parchment liner, then lift the torte onto a flat serving plate. Just before serving, sprinkle the torte with the reserved cookie crumbs. (If the crumbs are sprinkled on ahead of time, they will soften. They will still be delicious.)

The torte can be refrigerated, covered, for up to 4 days.

VARIATION
For a torte that looks and tastes like peanut butter–filled or chocolate and peanut butter–filled Oreos, use peanut butter–filled or peanut butter and chocolate–filled Oreo cookies in place of the plain Oreos. Stir ⅔ cup creamy peanut butter into the white chocolate and cream mixture after the chocolate has melted. Prepare, serve, and store the torte as directed.

Mary Frankel's Chocolate Cheesecake

Makes one 9½-inch cheesecake

My dear friend Mary Frankel is the queen of cheesecakes. This one is particularly spectacular in its role as a chocolate delivery system. It's almost closer to fudge than it is to cheesecake. Mary accomplishes all she does in life with beauty and grace, but in my eyes, her finest accomplishment is her daughter Joanna, who married my middle son, Max. Yes, the moms fixed them up— and I got to make a chocolate wedding cake!

For the crust

9 ounces (about 40 cookies) chocolate wafers, crumbled

5 tablespoons (2.5 ounces) unsalted butter, at room temperature

2 tablespoons sugar

For the filling

12 ounces semisweet chocolate, coarsely chopped

3 extra-large eggs, at room temperature

1 cup (8 ounces) sugar

24 ounces (1.5 pounds) cream cheese, at room temperature

1 cup (8 ounces) sour cream

1 teaspoon vanilla extract

⅛ teaspoon salt

Preheat the oven to 350°F. with the rack in the center position.

To make the crust, place the crumbled cookies in the work bowl of a food processor fitted with the metal blade. Pulse until the cookie pieces are reduced to small crumbs, then add the butter and sugar. Pulse until the butter is evenly dispersed among the crumbs. Press the crumb mixture onto the bottom and ½ inch up the sides of a 9½-inch springform pan. Set aside at room temperature.

To make the filling, melt the chocolate in a medium metal bowl set over, but not touching, a pan of simmering water or in a microwave-safe bowl in a microwave oven. Set aside. Place the eggs and sugar in a large mixing bowl. With an electric mixer on high speed, beat them together until light and foamy, about 1 minute. Add the cream cheese and continue to beat at high speed until very smooth, 3 to 4 minutes. Add the melted chocolate, sour cream, vanilla, and salt. Beat on high speed until the mixture is completely blended and smooth.

Pour and scrape the filling into the prepared crust and bake for 1 hour, or until the cake has a dry top crust and the filling moves as a whole when the cake is shaken gently. (Cracks may develop around the edges as the cake bakes, but these will be less visible as the cake cools and sinks slightly.) Transfer the cake pan to a wire rack and let the cake cool completely. Do not try to remove the sides of the pan until the cake is completely cool.

When the cake has cooled, cover with plastic wrap and refrigerate for up to 1 week. For optimum flavor, bring the cake to room temperature before serving.

Chocolate Polenta Cake with Kirsch Crème Anglaise (Cinderella Cake)

Makes one 9½-inch cake; 10 servings

This cake got its name from the magic that can come from combining chocolate with simple, homey, everyday ingredients. The result is something a prince would most certainly want to serve at the ball. Based on a traditional Italian cake, it's rich and moist, but not cloyingly sweet. Served up in a pool of delicate Kirsch-flavored crème anglaise, it makes a dramatic dessert with great eye appeal.

For the polenta cake

Unsalted butter for preparing the pan

4 ounces unsweetened chocolate, coarsely chopped

4 ounces bittersweet chocolate, coarsely chopped

½ cup (2.5 ounces) all-purpose flour

3 tablespoons unsweetened natural cocoa powder

1 teaspoon baking powder

1 teaspoon baking soda

1 teaspoon salt

¾ cup (4 ounces) finely ground cornmeal

2 sticks (8 ounces) unsalted butter, at room temperature

1 cup (8 ounces) sugar

4 extra-large eggs

1 cup (8 ounces) buttermilk

For the crème anglaise

2 cups (16 ounces) whole milk

4 extra-large egg yolks

⅓ cup (3 ounces) sugar

3 tablespoons Kirsch

Pinch of salt

Fresh sweet cherries, or defrosted frozen sweet cherries, for garnish

Preheat the oven to 350°F. with a rack in the center position. Coat the interior sides and bottom of a 9½-inch springform pan with butter. Line the bottom with a circle of parchment paper, then butter the parchment.

To make the cake, melt the unsweetened and bittersweet chocolates together in a metal bowl set over, but not touching, a pan of gently simmering water, or in a microwave-safe bowl in a microwave oven. Sift the flour, cocoa powder, baking powder, baking soda, and salt together into a medium mixing bowl. Whisk in the cornmeal. Place the butter and sugar in a large

(CONTINUED ON PAGE 258)

mixing bowl. With an electric mixer on high speed, mix the butter and sugar until they are light and fluffy, about 5 minutes. Reduce the mixer speed to medium and add the eggs, one at a time, beating well after each addition. Scrape down the sides of the bowl with a rubber spatula as you mix. Beat in the buttermilk; the mixture will appear very curdled at this point. Scrape in the melted chocolate and mix well on low speed. Gradually add the flour mixture and mix on low speed just until no signs of flour remain. Pour and scrape the batter into the prepared pan.

Bake for about 40 minutes, or until the cake starts to pull away from the sides of the pan and the top of the cake is firm around the edges but just slightly soft at the center. Transfer the pan to a wire rack and let cool for 10 minutes. Remove the springform and let the cake cool completely on the rack on the pan base. When the cake is cool, invert it onto a cookie sheet or another wire rack and remove the pan base and the parchment. Re-invert the cake onto a serving platter.

To make the crème anglaise, scald the milk in a small, heavy saucepan set over moderate heat. In a medium metal bowl, whisk the egg yolks with the sugar until thick and creamy. Gradually whisk the hot milk into the egg yolks and sugar, then scrape the mixture back into the saucepan. Stir the mixture constantly with a heat-proof rubber spatula or wooden spoon over medium-low heat, scraping the bottom and corners of the saucepan thoroughly. The sauce will begin to thicken gradually as you stir. You can use a candy thermometer to check the temperature; the sauce will be almost ready when it reaches 160°F. Remove the pan from the heat and test the sauce from time to time; when it is perfectly cooked the sauce will coat your spatula or spoon and when you draw your fingertip through the coating it will leave a distinct trail. When the sauce is thick and smooth, remove it from the heat and strain it into a bowl. Stir in the Kirsch and the salt.

Serve the cake warm or at room temperature, surrounded by Kirsch-flavored crème anglaise and garnished with sweet cherries.

Narsai David's Chocolate Decadence

Makes 12 servings

This cake is known by many names, including "Death by Chocolate." Each person who comes upon the recipe tweaks it a bit and makes it his or her own. While I have no problem with this, I want the world (or that percentage of the world reading this book) to know that the original recipe was created by Narsai David. Narsai, who lives in San Francisco, has worn many hats, from restaurateur and caterer to radio and television personality. He's a marvelous teacher, a treasured friend, and a true chocolate genius.

This cake requires either a handheld or stand mixer.

Unsalted butter for preparing the pan

1 pound (16 ounces) bittersweet chocolate, finely chopped

1 stick plus 2 tablespoons (5 ounces) unsalted butter

4 extra-large eggs, at room temperature

1 tablespoon sugar

1 tablespoon all-purpose flour

1 teaspoon vanilla extract

Fresh raspberries and unsweetened whipped cream, for garnish

Preheat the oven to 425°F. with the rack in the center position. Coat the bottom and sides of a 9-inch round cake pan with butter. Line the pan bottom with a circle of parchment paper and butter the parchment.

Melt the chocolate and butter together in a metal bowl set over, but not touching, a pan of gently simmering water. or in a microwave-safe bowl in a microwave oven. Stir occasionally with a wooden spoon or wire whisk until the mixture is smooth. The mixture may harden at first, but will smooth out as you stir. Remove the bowl from over the water and set aside to cool slightly.

Place the eggs and sugar in a large mixing bowl or the bowl of a stand mixer. Fit the mixer with the wire whip attachment if you have one; if not, use the regular beaters. Beat the eggs with the sugar on high speed for 10 to 15 minutes, or until the mixture has thickened, has tripled in volume, and is very light in color. Reduce the mixer speed to low and mix in the flour and vanilla. With the mixer still on low, add the melted chocolate mixture and mix until the two are combined. The eggs will deflate somewhat, but this is fine. Make sure that there are no visible traces of egg remaining in the bowl.

Pour and scrape the mixture into the prepared pan. Bake for 15 minutes. Remove the pan from the oven and place it on a wire rack to cool completely. Place the cake, in its pan, in the freezer and allow it to freeze solid; this will take about 2 hours.

To unmold the cake, spin the bottom of the pan briefly over a gas or electric burner for a few seconds, just enough to slightly melt and loosen the bottom surface of the cake from the pan. Place a cake plate on top of the pan and invert the cake onto it. You may have to bang the pan down a couple of times on the work surface to get it moving. Allow the cake to come to room temperature before serving. To cut the cake easily, run a long, sharp knife under very hot water, dry it, and then cut. Repeat the warming process for each cut.

Serve the cake with fresh raspberries and a dab of unsweetened whipped cream.

Optimism Tart

Makes 12 servings

The name for this tart, with its crisp sugar-cookie crust and smooth-as-silk chocolate filling punctuated with tiny bits of roasted, shelled cocoa beans, was inspired by my daughter-in-law, Joanna Frankel, who tries to look on the bright side of everything and finds it especially easy to feel hopeful when a chocolate dessert is coming her way.

For the crust

1¼ sticks (5 ounces) unsalted butter, at room temperature

¾ cup (3 ounces) confectioners' sugar

⅓ cup (1.5 ounces) finely ground almonds

¼ teaspoon salt

2 teaspoons vanilla extract

1 extra-large egg, lightly beaten

1¾ cups (8.75 ounces) all-purpose flour

2 tablespoons Lora Brody's Dough Relaxer (optional; see Sources, page 271), for a flakier crust that is easy to roll

For the filling

1¼ cups (10 ounces) heavy cream

12 ounces bittersweet chocolate, finely chopped

¼ cup (2 ounces) dark rum

1 heaping tablespoon Scharffen Berger Cacao Nibs (available in gourmet stores and by mail order; see Sources, page 271)

For the caramel sauce

2 cups (16 ounces) sugar

1 tablespoon lemon juice

4 tablespoons (2 ounces) unsalted butter, cut in several pieces

½ cup (4 ounces) heavy cream

⅓ cup (3 ounces) dark rum (optional)

1 tablespoon vanilla extract

Unsweetened whipped cream for garnish (optional)

To make the crust, place the butter and confectioners' sugar in the work bowl of a food processor fitted with the metal blade. Process until smooth and light, then add the almonds, salt, vanilla, and egg. Pulse to combine. Add the flour and the dough relaxer (if using), and process just until a ball of dough forms. Take care not to overmix the dough.

(CONTINUED ON NEXT PAGE)

Form the dough into a flat disk; dust it with flour if it is sticky. Wrap the disk tightly in plastic wrap and refrigerate for 1 hour. On a lightly floured work surface, roll the chilled dough into a 15-inch circle, then fit it into a 12-inch tart pan with a removable bottom. Take care not to stretch the dough, as this will make the crust shrink as it bakes. Prick the surface of the dough all over with a fork. Line the pastry with aluminum foil that has been lightly oiled or sprayed with nonstick vegetable cooking spray. Cover the bottom and sides of the pastry, pressing the oiled surface of the foil lightly against the dough. Chill the crust for 30 minutes.

While it is chilling, preheat the oven to 350°F. with the rack in the center position. Bake the crust for 15 minutes. Remove the foil and bake for another 10 minutes, or until the crust is golden brown. Cool to room temperature before assembling the tart.

To make the filling, bring the heavy cream to a simmer in a heavy-bottomed 1-quart saucepan over high heat. When the cream is hot, remove the pan from the heat and add the chocolate. Stir until smooth. Stir in the rum and cacao nibs, and cool to room temperature without refrigerating, until the filling flows sluggishly when the bowl is tilted. Pour and scrape the filling into the cooled tart shell. Let the tart sit at room temperature until it sets up, which will take about an hour, depending on the temperature of the room.

To make the caramel sauce, place the sugar, 1 cup (8 ounces) of water, and the lemon juice in a heavy-bottomed 2-quart saucepan. Place over high heat and stir just until the sugar dissolves and the mixture is clear. Bring the syrup to a rapid boil, then cook without stirring until the syrup turns a deep amber color, 12 to 15 minutes. Do not let the syrup burn. Remove it from the heat and stir in the butter, bit by bit, then add the cream, rum (if using), and vanilla. Cool the sauce to room temperature; it may be refrigerated to cool it faster.

To assemble and serve the tart, cut it into 12 wedges with a long, sharp knife. For each serving, spoon some of the caramel sauce onto a rimmed dessert plate and tilt the plate so that the sauce covers the bottom of the plate. Place a slice of the tart on top of the sauce and garnish, if desired, with a dollop of unsweetened whipped cream just before serving.

White Chocolate Eggnog

Makes 2 quarts

If you're looking for a new twist on a classic holiday drink, then you've come to the right place. While some may say that eggnog is fine just the way it is, those of us who think there's never enough chocolate in our lives would argue that point with this recipe in hand. As with all recipes in this book, when white chocolate is called for it's essential that it be real white chocolate; be sure to read the ingredient label to find cocoa butter—not palm kernel or coconut oil.

6 extra-large eggs, separated

¼ cup (2 ounces) sugar

⅓ cup (3 ounces) bourbon

⅓ cup (3 ounces) brandy

6 ounces white chocolate, finely chopped

1 cup (8 ounces) heavy cream

1½ cups (12 ounces) whole milk

Grated nutmeg or unsweetened natural cocoa powder, for garnish

Place the egg yolks and sugar in a large metal bowl. Whisk them together until slightly thickened, then dribble in the bourbon and brandy, whisking constantly. Cover the mixture and refrigerate for 20 minutes, or for up to 24 hours.

When you are ready to mix the eggnog, melt the white chocolate in a medium metal bowl set over, but not touching, a pan of simmering water, or in a microwave-safe bowl in a microwave oven. When the chocolate is melted and smooth, remove from over the water and whisk in the heavy cream. Set aside.

Place the egg whites in a very clean metal bowl and beat them on high speed with an electric mixer until they hold firm peaks. Set aside.

With the same beaters (no need to clean them), beat the white chocolate mixture until it has thickened and looks like whipped butter. Whisk the milk into the egg-yolk mixture, then whisk in the white chocolate mixture until the eggnog is smooth. Stir in the egg whites; some clumps of whites should remain visible in the eggnog. The eggnog can be refrigerated, covered, for up to 12 hours. Stir well before serving.

Ladle the eggnog into wineglasses or punch cups. Sprinkle each serving with nutmeg or cocoa powder.

Sweet Cherry Cobbler with Chocolate Truffle Crust

Makes 12 servings

My good friend Diane Phillips is a culinary genius when it comes to dreaming up fantastic recipes that taste as good as they look. I think of her as the Joyce Carol Oates of the cookbook set. From potpies to homemade mixes, she's cornered the market on easy-to-make dishes that win raves at the table. This particular dessert is a hands-down winner in the chocolate department. A tender chocolate crust covers a lovely filling of sweet cherries spiked with Grand Marnier. Diane suggests eating it while it's warm, and I suggest adding a scoop of good vanilla ice cream to the plate.

Unsalted butter for preparing the pan

For the filling

48 ounces frozen unsweetened pitted sweet cherries, defrosted

1 cup (8 ounces) sugar

1/4 cup (1 ounce) cornstarch

2 tablespoons (1 ounce) Grand Marnier, or other orange-flavored liqueur

For the crust

8 ounces semisweet chocolate, coarsely chopped

1 stick (4 ounces) unsalted butter

4 extra-large eggs

1 extra-large egg yolk

1/2 cup (4 ounces) sugar

1 teaspoon vanilla extract

1/4 cup (1.25 ounces) all-purpose flour

2 pints vanilla ice cream, for serving

If you are going to bake the pie immediately after preparing it, preheat the oven to 375°F. with the rack in the center position. Have ready a buttered 9 × 13-inch glass baking dish.

Drain the cherries over a large mixing bowl. Reserve 1/2 cup of the cherry juice; discard the rest. Place the cherries in the bowl. In another, smaller bowl, stir together the reserved 1/2 cup cherry juice, the cup of sugar, cornstarch, and Grand Marnier. Pour the sugar mixture over the cherries and mix well. Transfer the cherry mixture to the baking dish. (The cherries can be prepared up to 1 day ahead and refrigerated. Remove the baking dish from the refrigerator and preheat the oven when you start to prepare the crust.)

To make the crust, melt the chocolate with the butter in a medium metal bowl set over, but not touching, a pan of simmering water, or in a microwave-safe bowl in a microwave oven. When the mixture is smooth, remove the bowl from over the water to cool.

Place the eggs and yolk, sugar, and vanilla in a large mixing bowl. With an electric mixer on high speed, beat the mixture for 5 to 7 minutes, until it is very pale and has tripled in volume. Reduce the mixer speed to medium, sprinkle the flour over the egg mixture, and beat until the flour is incorporated. Use a large rubber spatula to thoroughly fold in the melted chocolate mixture. (The crust batter can be made and refrigerated in the bowl for up to 8 hours; bring to room temperature, then pour it over the cherries and bake as directed.) Stir the cherry mixture in the baking dish, then spread the chocolate batter over it. Bake for 30 to 35 minutes, until the surface of the crust appears dry, a skewer inserted into the crust has moist crumbs attached, and the fruit is bubbling. The cobbler is wonderful served warm; allow it to cool for 15 to 20 minutes, then serve with vanilla ice cream.

Double Chocolate Espresso Meringue Cake

Makes 10 servings

Chocolate meringue with a thin, crisp crust and a soft interior floats above a slightly gooey (if you don't overcook it) chocolate espresso-infused brownie cake. This was one of the recipes I had trouble restraining myself from eating in its entirety. Pretty as a picture and seductive as all get out, this is a cake to think of when you want a dessert that will satisfy the craving of the most ardent chocophile.

For the cake

Unsalted butter and flour for preparing the pan

1 cup (5 ounces) all-purpose flour

1/3 cup (1 ounce) unsweetened natural cocoa powder

1 teaspon baking soda

1/2 teaspoon salt

1 1/2 sticks (6 ounces) unsalted butter, at room temperature

1 cup (8 ounces) light brown sugar, packed

3 extra-large eggs

1 tablespoon instant espresso powder or granules, dissolved in 1/4 cup boiling water

2 teaspoons vanilla extract

1 cup regular or espresso-flavored chocolate chips (available in the supermarket and in specialty food stores)

For the chocolate meringue topping

3 extra-large egg whites, at room temperature

1 cup (7 ounces) superfine or bar sugar (see page 16)

1/3 cup (1 ounce) unsweetened natural cocoa powder

1/2 cup Scharffen Berger Cacao Nibs (available in specialty food stores and by mail order; see Sources, page 271)

Preheat the oven to 350°F. with the rack in the center position. Butter the bottom and sides of a 9 × 3-inch springform pan, line the bottom with parchment paper, and butter the paper. Dust the pan with flour, knocking out the excess.

To make the cake, sift the flour, cocoa powder, baking soda, and salt into a small bowl. In a large bowl, beat the butter and brown sugar together, either by hand or with an electric mixer, until light and fluffy. Add the eggs, one at a time, beating well after each addition. The mixture will appear slightly lumpy; this is fine. Add the espresso and vanilla, then gently mix in the flour mixture, scraping down the sides and bottom of the bowl to incorporate all the ingredients. Stir in the chocolate chips. Scrape the batter into the prepared pan, leveling the top with a rubber spatula. Bake the cake for 35 minutes, or until the top is dry and a cake tester comes out with a few moist crumbs. It's better to underbake the cake at this stage than to overbake it. Remove the cake from the oven; maintain the oven temperature.

To make the topping, in the clean bowl of an electric mixer, beat the egg whites on high speed until foamy. Slowly add the superfine sugar and beat on high speed until the mixture is glossy and quite stiff. Use a rubber spatula to fold in the cocoa powder and then the cacao nibs. Try not to deflate the meringue too much while you mix. Spread the meringue over the top of the warm cake and return it to the oven. Bake for an additional 25 minutes, or until the meringue has formed a crisp crust.

Cool the cake in the pan for 15 minutes, then run a knife around the edge, releasing both the meringue and the cake below it. Remove the sides of the pan and transfer the cake to a cake plate. (If you wish, you can carefully slide a wide offset spatula under the cake and remove it from the springform base.) Tear a length of plastic wrap long enough to encircle the cake and fold it several times, lengthwise, to form a long strip. Wrap the strip around just the brownie part of the cake; this will keep it from drying out as it cools and is stored.

The cake can be stored at room temperature for up to 2 days with the plastic wrap around it. Do not refrigerate.

Chocolate Raspberry Torte

Makes one 5 × 5-inch cake; 12 servings

Love and marriage, springtime and robins, Paul Newman and Joanne Woodward, the Red Sox and aggravation—all things that go together naturally. I rank chocolate and raspberries right up there in the matches-made-in-heaven category. It's not just the way they complement each other—rubies sitting on the backdrop of luxurious brown velvet—or the sublime sparkles of energy the raspberries send through the sweet smoothness of the chocolate. It's the delicate finesse of the fruit tempering the heft of the chocolate. Whatever your reason for liking the combination, this very lovely raspberry-scented chocolate torte with its mirrorlike glaze will have you celebrating this classic marriage of ingredients.

For the torte

Unsalted butter for preparing the pan

6 ounces unsweetened chocolate, finely chopped

1½ sticks (6 ounces) unsalted butter

½ cup (4 ounces) seedless raspberry jam

1 cup (5 ounces) all-purpose flour

¼ teaspoon salt

4 extra-large eggs

2 cups (16 ounces) sugar

2 teaspoons vanilla extract

For the frosting and topping

7 ounces bittersweet chocolate, finely chopped

1 ounce unsweetened chocolate, finely chopped

½ cup (4 ounces) heavy cream

⅓ cup (3 ounces) seedless raspberry jam

1 tablespoon (.5 ounce) unsalted butter

1 pint fresh raspberries

Confectioners' sugar (optional)

Preheat the oven to 350°F. with the rack in the center position. Coat the interior of an 11 × 17-inch half-sheet pan with butter. Line the bottom with parchment paper and butter the parchment.

To make the cake, place the unsweetened chocolate, butter, and jam in a metal bowl set over, but not touching, a pan of simmering water, or in a microwave-safe bowl in a microwave oven. Melt the mixture together, stirring occasionally, until it is smooth and well blended. Remove the bowl from the heat to cool. Sift the flour and salt into a small bowl.

Place the eggs in a large mixing bowl. Beat the eggs with an electric mixer on medium speed until well mixed, about 30 seconds. With the mixer still on medium speed, add the sugar gradually. When all the sugar has been added, beat on high speed until the mixture is light and has doubled in volume. Scrape down the sides of the bowl with a rubber spatula as you work. Reduce the mixer speed to low and beat in the vanilla and then the flour mixture. Beat in the melted chocolate mixture until the batter is completely combined.

Spread the batter in the prepared pan, smoothing it into the corners. Bake for 12 to 14 minutes, or until a cake tester inserted near the middle comes out with some moist crumbs attached. Do not overbake. Transfer the cake pan to a wire rack to cool for 20 minutes, then invert the cake onto the wire rack. (If your rack just fits inside the cake pan, this will be easy to do. If you have to invert the cake onto two racks, it will be trickier.) Remove the pan and the parchment and let the cake cool completely.

Carefully slide the cake onto a cutting board. Trim off about 1 inch around the cake, as the edges may be a little dry and uneven. With a long edge of the cake in front of you, measure and cut the cake vertically into three equal pieces; each will be about 10 inches long and 5 inches wide. Cut those in half, too, to make six 5-inch square layers. Stack the layers on a flat plate with a piece of plastic wrap or deli wrap between them. If you are not planning to fill and frost the cake right away, cover the layers securely with plastic wrap. The covered layers can be kept at room temperature, well covered, for up to 2 days.

When you are ready to make the frosting, place the chopped bittersweet and unsweetened chocolate in a medium metal bowl. Place the cream, jam, and butter in a small saucepan and bring to a simmer over medium heat. Stir until the jam has melted and the mixture is very hot. Immediately pour the cream mixture over the chocolate. Stir until the mixture is melted and smooth. Let stand until the frosting is thick enough to spread; refrigerate it, if necessary.

To fill the torte, carefully lift off the top layer and place it on a work surface. Use an offset spatula to spread a thin, even layer of chocolate–raspberry frosting on the layer. Stack and frost the next 4 layers, then place the sixth layer on the exposed frosted layer. Use a serrated knife to trim the sides of the cake so that they are even all the way down. Cover the top and sides with the frosting. Use two wide spatulas to carefully transfer the torte to a serving plate. Refrigerate the torte until the frosting sets, then place a layer of plastic wrap loosely over the top and place the torte in a resealable plastic bag or container large enough to accommodate the serving plate. The filled and frosted torte will keep, refrigerated, for up to 4 days.

Thirty minutes before you plan to serve the torte, remove it from the refrigerator to soften the frosting a little. Cover the top of the cake with 36 fresh raspberries, placed in a 6 × 6 grid pattern. Dust the torte with confectioners' sugar, if desired. Cut the torte into pieces so that each serving contains 3 raspberries in a row. Once the cake is covered with fresh berries, it can be refrigerated, covered, for up to 1 day.

Sources

Boyajian Inc.
144 Will Drive
Canton, MA 02021
(800) 419-4677
www.boyajianinc.com

Infused oils and flavorings

Cooking.com
(800) 663-8810
www.cooking.com

Specialty bakeware, Scharffen Berger
Cacao Nibs, Lora Brody's Dough Relaxer

Dairy Fresh Candy Company
57 Salem Street
Boston, MA 02113
(617) 742-2639
www.dairyfreshcandies.com

Chocolate, marzipan, nuts (ground
and whole)

Fante's Gourmet & Kitchen Wares Shop
1006 S. Ninth Street
Philadelphia, PA 19147-4798
(800) 44-Fantes
www.fantes.com

Specialty bakeware (hard to find pans),
Silpat, molds, unusual chocolate tools,
real chocolate jimmies (sprinkles), cake
decorating supplies, equipment, Lora
Brody's Dough Relaxer

**The King Arthur Flour Company's
Baker's Catalogue**
Norwich, VT 05055
(800) 827-6836
www.kingarthurflour.com

Specialty bakeware, cake decorating
supplies and equipment, Silpat, flavored
baking chips, specialty flour, many different kinds of chocolates, specialty
sugars, oils and essences, ground nuts,
marzipan, Lora Brody's Dough Relaxer

lorabrody.com

To reach me with baking questions, send
comments and suggestions, and find
information about my teaching schedule

Williams-Sonoma
Call (800) 541-1262
for store locations
www.williams-sonoma.com

Specialty bakeware, cake decorating
supplies, and serving dishes

Wilton Industries
2240 W. 75th Street
Woodridge, IL 60517
(630) 963-1818
www.wilton.com

Specialty cake pans, parchment, cake
decorating supplies and equipment

Index

Note: *Italicized* page references indicate photographs.

Conversion Chart

EQUIVALENT IMPERIAL AND METRIC MEASUREMENTS

American cooks use standard containers, the 8-ounce cup and a tablespoon that takes exactly 16 level fillings to fill that cup level. Measuring by cup makes it very difficult to give weight equivalents, as a cup of densely packed butter will weigh considerably more than a cup of flour. The easiest way therefore to deal with cup measurements in recipes is to take the amount by volume rather than by weight. Thus the equation reads:

1 cup = 240 ml = 8 fl. oz.   1/2 cup = 120 ml = 4 fl. oz.

It is possible to buy a set of American cup measures in major stores around the world.

In the States, butter is often measured in sticks. One stick is the equivalent of 8 tablespoons. One tablespoon of butter is therefore the equivalent to 1/2 ounce/15 grams.

LIQUID MEASURES

Fluid Ounces	U.S.	Imperial	Milliliters
	1 teaspoon	1 teaspoon	5
1/4	2 teaspoons	1 dessertspoon	10
1/2	1 tablespoon	1 tablespoon	14
1	2 tablespoons	2 tablespoons	28
2	1/4 cup	4 tablespoons	56
4	1/2 cup		110
5		1/4 pint or 1 gill	140
6	3/4 cup		170
8	1 cup		225
9			250, 1/4 liter
10	1 1/4 cups	1/2 pint	280
12	1 1/2 cups		340
15		3/4 pint	420
16	2 cups		450
18	2 1/4 cups		500, 1/2 liter
20	2 1/2 cups	1 pint	560
24	3 cups		675
25		1 1/4 pints	700
27	3 1/2 cups		750
30	3 3/4 cups	1 1/2 pints	840
32	4 cups or 1 quart		900
35		1 3/4 pints	980
36	4 1/2 cups		1000, 1 liter
40	5 cups	2 pints or 1 quart	1120

SOLID MEASURES

U.S. and Imperial Measures		Metric Measures	
Ounces	Pounds	Grams	Kilos
1		28	
2		56	
3 1/2		100	
4	1/4	112	
5		140	
6		168	
8	1/2	225	
9		250	1/4
12	3/4	340	
16	1	450	
18		500	1/2
20	1 1/4	560	
24	1 1/2	675	
27		750	3/4
28	1 3/4	780	
32	2	900	
36	2 1/4	1000	1
40	2 1/2	1100	
48	3	1350	
54		1500	1 1/2

OVEN TEMPERATURE EQUIVALENTS

Fahrenheit	Celsius	Gas Mark	Description
225	110	1/4	Cool
250	130	1/2	
275	140	1	Very Slow
300	150	2	
325	170	3	Slow
350	180	4	Moderate
375	190	5	
400	200	6	Moderately Hot
425	220	7	Fairly Hot
450	230	8	Hot
475	240	9	Very Hot
500	250	10	Extremely Hot

Any broiling recipes can be used with the grill of the oven, but beware of high-temperature grills.

EQUIVALENTS FOR INGREDIENTS

all-purpose flour—plain flour
coarse salt—kitchen salt
cornstarch—cornflour
eggplant—aubergine

half and half—12% fat milk
heavy cream—double cream
light cream—single cream
lima beans—broad beans

scallion—spring onion
unbleached flour—strong, white flour
zest—rind
zucchini—courgettes or marrow